T0381515

THE HISTORY OF THE GAELIC ATHLETIC

ASSOCIATION IN CANADA

ABOUT THE AUTHOR

John O'Flynn's father, Thomas O'Flynn (Kilmeedy, County Limerick), first came to Toronto in 1953, and his late mother, Elizabeth (nee O'Keeffe) (Duagh, County Kerry), arrived together as a married couple in 1962 to British Columbia. John was the first born in 1964 and attended St. Patrick's Elementary in Vancouver, Vancouver College and graduated from the Seminary of Christ the King in Mission.

John's parents introduced him and his brothers Thomas, James and sister Mary to Ireland's national games of Gaelic Football and Hurling with the members of the Vancouver Irish Sporting and Social Club who would gather at John Hendry Park.

John had the opportunity to represent Vancouver and play Gaelic Football in two North American County Board Championships: 1984 Boston and 1985 Chicago. He has also played in a number of tournaments in both American and Canadian cities including San Diego, San Francisco, Portland, Tacoma, Seattle, Victoria, Vancouver, Calgary, Edmonton and Ottawa.

John attended the founding meeting in Toronto of the Canadian County Board of the Gaelic Athletic Association in 1987 and currently serves as secretary. He has presented workshops on Gaelic Football to teachers and summer camps that introduce the Gaelic games to youth. John has served as a referee in both minor and adult football games in the States and Canada.

John resides in the District of North Vancouver, B.C. with his wife, Kathleen, and is father to Matthias, Kristiann, Kelleigh, Emily and Michael. A graduate of Simon Fraser University, John has taught in both denominational and non-denominational schools in Richmond (St. Paul's K-7), Powell River (Assumption K-9), Vancouver (Vancouver College K-12) and West Vancouver (Mulgrave K-12) where he is presently a grade 6 teacher.

John serves as a Commissioner on the North Vancouver Museum and Archives Commission.

THE HISTORY OF THE GAELIC ATHLETIC

ASSOCIATION IN CANADA

———

BY

JOHN O'FLYNN

&

AINSLEY BALDWIN

 www.trafford.com

North America & international
toll-free: 1 888 232 4444 (USA & Canada)
fax: 812 355 4082

*For my parents and club who shared their love
of Ireland's sporting gifts to Canada.*

*To my wife Kathleen and children Matthias, Kristiann, Kelleigh, Emily and Michael—
thank you for your patience with me on the phone and on the computer.*

*To all those who supported Gaelic games in Canada—
take your "pints" when you can!*

CONTENTS

PREFACE

Since the days of Ras Tailteann and Feiseanna, at Tara in Ireland, Irish games have tended to symbolize the irrepressible nature of Ireland's spirit. The Tailteann games were an ancient sporting event held in honour of Queen Tailte. They ran from 1829 BC to AD 1180 when they died out after the Norman invasion. A sporting festival bearing the same name was held by the Gaelic Athletic Association (GAA) in 1924, 1928 and 1932; all people of Irish birth or ancestry participated. The 800 m champion in 1928 was Canada's Phillip Edwards.

The history of Gaelic games in Canada, before the founding of the GAA in Ireland in 1884 and in the years since, proves a determination by Irish immigrants who have arrived on these shores of Canada. Through their dedication the flag of Irish sports has flown strong, and will continue to fly in the years to come.

Our elders came from the "Auld Country" of Ireland—rich in heritage and culture—to this "Great White North" of Canada. They brought the skills, crafts and trades to help build railroads and skyscrapers, construct highways, mine, fish and log. In addition to the introduction of their cuisine, arts and culture, they played their games in the Canadian mosaic.

The sporting traditions include the oldest European field game of hurling—a masterful art and the fastest game in the world—in which players use an ash wood stick and a hard ball. Many argue with some conviction, and no small amount of fact to support their case, that Canada's national sport, ice hockey, has its origins in hurling. The word *puck* is derived from the Irish word *poc*, which is the action of striking the ball with a hurley.

In 1845, the civic fathers of Quebec City banned the playing of hurling in their narrow streets, while in St. John's, Newfoundland, hurling was being played as early as 1788 at the "Barrens" of the city. The ladies' version of hurling, Camogie, has had its presence on occasion in some of our Canadian communities.

The skilful play of Gaelic Football, which has dominated the sporting scene across the country in many Canadian cities, continues to be the greatest strength in modern times. Along with the two other Irish sports of handball and rounders, football has provided many wonderful memories, people and events for our Canadian-Irish sporting community to reflect upon and celebrate.

The presence of the GAA in Canada is a validation that a very important part of our cultural legacy lives on in a strong, healthy and vibrant fashion. To all those who have made this possible in Canada—the players, their families, the coaches, their clubs and members, the supporters and sponsors—congratulations! By your efforts, unselfish sacrifices and contributions, you have enriched our Irish presence and sporting culture *a mari usque ad mare* (from sea to sea) across this great country of Canada.

ACKNOWLEDGEMENTS

It has been a privilege to gain further knowledge about the Canadian-Irish sporting community. Through the cooperation of so many people in Canada, the United States and Ireland, too many to name, it has been a treat to speak with all who have participated in the interview process or in the sharing of publications during my time of research. Your pride and enthusiasm about the GAA and your local clubs were very evident. I have been humbled in learning more about the playing of our Irish games in our great country of Canada.

I want to thank two sponsors who have both made tremendous contributions to the publication of this book: **West Limerick Holdings Limited** – President Thomas O'Flynn and the **Canadian County Board of the GAA** – Chairman Brian Farmer.

It was my parents who introduced me to the games with the members of the Vancouver Irish Sporting and Social Club who would gather at John Hendry Park. The hurling sticks and Gaelic footballs were always at the ready in the boot of the car every weekend. Many good friends spent time in teaching me the skills. Friends like Brendan Burns, Peter Ferguson and Pat Burns. Thank you for sharing your time and talent.

I hope you, dear reader, bring to my attention corrections with the history of the Gaelic games in Newfoundland, Ontario, Quebec, Manitoba, Alberta and British Columbia. Your information will help with future editions. Irish sports in those provinces and territories not mentioned—the Yukon and Northwest Territories, Nunavut, Saskatchewan, New Brunswick, Nova Scotia and Prince Edward Island—await your contributions to canadagaa@gmail.com

I regret any errors or omissions. Those who have never made mistakes have never attempted or accomplished anything. "A nation reveals itself not only by the men it produces but also by the men it honours, the men it remembers." (John F. Kennedy)

North Vancouver, B.C.
2008

ACKNOWLEDGMENTS

...

Maria Vancouver, B.A.
2006

NEWFOUNDLAND

Early map makers and explorers give credence to the legend that St. Brendan the Navigator, with seventeen "hurling" monks, reached *Terra Repromissionis Sanctorum* (The Land Promised the Saints) in the early days of the sixth century. The story of their voyage in a leather-hulled *curragh* is told in an old Irish saga, "The Voyage of St. Brendan, the Abbot." There has been also some indication that Irish settlements may have existed in the St. Lawrence Valley between 875 and 900 AD. How else might one explain lacrosse, akin to hurling, witnessed by the early French explorers, being played along the banks of the St. Lawrence by the Mic Mac Amerindians and other tribes? Historians relate that the Mic Macs wore crosses on their playing tunics. Isn't "Mic Mac" the Gaelic inverse of "Mac Mic," meaning the "son of the son"?

The history of the Irish in Newfoundland dates to 1595 with the first written record of trade ships that sailed between Ireland and Newfoundland. In 1622, an Irishman was reportedly found hunting beaver with Native Americans. This was an isolated incident, but, by 1675, Irishmen became frequent visitors and inhabitants of the place they called *"Talamh an Éisc,"* the "Island of Fish." Many Irish came with the idea of working the fishing boats and eventually returning to Ireland. In the end, many remained. So many, that by 1731 the majority of the male population in Newfoundland were Irish Catholics. By the 1760s, there were more Irish Catholics on the island of Newfoundland than in any other colony in the New World.

During the 18th century, the British government enforced strict Penal Laws, outlawing the practice of Catholicism in Newfoundland. Roman Catholics were permitted to erect small chapels in Ireland, but this was forbidden in Newfoundland until Liberty of Conscience was proclaimed in 1783, effectively lifting these laws.

First Hurling Match

The earliest games of hurling in North America occurred in St. John's in 1788. The games were often played on a tract of land called the "Barrens," nine acres of land on the highest ridge overlooking the town. Many of the earliest settlers to St. John's came from the southeast of Ireland, primarily Waterford, Wexford, Carlow, Tipperary, Cork and

Kilkenny. The only place that had a presence outside of these counties was Dingle, in Kerry.

Loyalty to one's county and factional fighting were common among the immigrants. Nicknames that were common included the "Yellow Bellies" from Wexford, the "Whey Bellies" from Waterford, the "Clear-Airs" from Tipperary, the "Doones" from Kilkenny, and the "Dadyeens" from Cork. The spirit of these factions must have played a serious role in the games of hurling that were organized.

In a letter to His Excellency Governor Elliot in the middle of 1788, Bishop James O'Donel, a native of Knocklofty, County Tipperary, and the first bishop to be appointed in Newfoundland, sought to distance himself from any responsibility for riots in the settlement of Ferryland. These arose as a result of differences between the followers of a maverick priest from County Kilkenny, Fr. Patrick Power, and supporters of O'Donel. He wrote:

> As for my part on't, it cane be well attested that I have been lucky enough to prevent these disputes everywhere my voice cou'd reach those four years past, for I left no means untried to level those distinctions of Provinces, and to prevent my flock from attending hurlings in the spring of the year, which were generally productive of these riots. For there is a deep rooted malice in the hearts of the lower class of Irishman to each other from the great abuse and horrid mangling they have received from time to time in those Provincial Quarrels.

No doubt, the game of hurling took precedence over the ecclesiastical concerns!

Bishop Michael Fleming

By 1796, Irish Catholics comprised nearly two-thirds of Newfoundland's population. In 1830, Newfoundland was the hub of England's empire, but the Irish Catholics who underpinned this prosperity with their manual labour were barely tolerated. In 1836, more than 400 settlements were listed with the Irish and their offspring, composing half the total population.

Due to the persistent efforts of Waterford-born Bishop Michael Fleming, of St. John's, who petitioned the British government from 1834 until 1838 for an Irish site, in May 1838, the "Barrens" were granted to the Catholic Church where the present day St. John the Baptist Basilica Cathedral now stands.

When Archbishop John Hughes, of New York, arrived in St. John's for the consecration in September 1855, he was very impressed by the size and extent of the Basilica. Returning to New York, he was inspired to build St. Patrick's Cathedral, the only Irish-built cathedral in North America to eclipse Newfoundland's St. John's Cathedral in size.

Fleming's arrival in Newfoundland brought a systematic expansion of institutional Catholicism. This included the construction of new parish churches, the subdivision of existing parishes into new parishes, the recruitment of Irish priests, and the introduction of two religious orders (Presentation and Mercy) of Irish women to teach young female children.

Fleming took pains to visit out-ports in Newfoundland during the winter of 1835, and he lived in a fishing room at Petty Harbour, administering the smallpox vaccine to the whole community of Catholics and Anglicans. He even remained in quarantine with them when no other physicians or clergymen would go there.

Fleming is also credited with creating the "Pink, White and Green" tricolour flag of Newfoundland. During annual wood hauls for the Anglican cathedral and Roman Catholic cathedral, considerable rivalry developed between the two groups. The Protestant English marked their woodpiles with the pink flag of the Natives' Society, while the Catholic Irish used green banners. The threat of violence was such that Bishop Fleming intervened and persuaded the two groups to adopt a common flag, on which the pink and green would be separated by a white stripe to symbolize peace. The pink symbolized the Tudor Rose of England (the Protestants) and the green symbolized St. Patrick's Emblem of Ireland (the Catholics). The white is taken from St. Andrew's cross—the patron saint of fishermen and Scotland.

September 9, 2005, was the 150th anniversary of the consecration of Fleming's cathedral. A plaque was unveiled by the Historic Sites and Monuments Board of Canada, designating Bishop Fleming as a person of Canadian national historic significance.

To Fleming's memory, this hurler's prayer:

> *Grant me, O Lord, a hurler's skill,*
> *With strength of arm and speed of limb;*
> *Unerring eye for the flying ball,*
> *And courage to match them what'er befall,*
> *May my stroke be steady, my aim be true,*
> *My actions manly, my misses few;*
> *And no matter what way the game may go,*
> *May I rest in friendship with every foe.*
> *When the final whistle for me is blown,*
> *And I stand at last at God's judgment throne;*
> *May the Great Referee when he calls my name,*
> *Say, "You hurled like a man; you played the game."*

CANADA

Ireland

Although concentrated in Ireland, the Gaelic Athletic Association (GAA) is one of the world's most vibrant sporting and cultural organizations. Founded in 1884 it manages the ancient Irish games of Gaelic Football and Hurling and has a significant presence in many parts of the globe. Its amateur ethos, its firm rooting within communities, the passion its games generate and its widespread acceptance as much more than just a badge of Irishness, all combine to create its uniqueness.

In Ireland, Gaelic games frequently attract live audiences of over 83,000 people and during certain weekends in any one year Gaelic Football or Hurling will attract the largest live sporting audiences in the world. Participation as well as excellence is a core principle of the GAA and an inclusive "games-for-all" ethos pervades all levels of the GAA. In the same way, the Association looks beyond the games and actively fosters and promotes Irish culture and heritage.

The basic unit of the GAA is the Club, which is based on attachment to local community and to place. Clubs are not just in, but are of communities and typically field a range of teams, at all age levels, and for men and women, boys and girls. Clubs are grouped within their Counties. Counties in turn sit within Provinces and the entire Association is then governed at a central/national level.

The GAA is a wholly amateur, community-based, volunteer-driven and altruistic movement which believes Gaelic activities can improve the quality of individual and community life.

County Board

The GAA, as it applies to Canada, is the Canadian County Board, Incorporated (CCB). The basic aim of the CCB is to preserve and promote Gaelic Games and pastimes in Canada.

The GAA in Canada has always functioned as more than just a sports body. It is a social club, a labour clearinghouse and a point of contact for the Irish community. If any Irish person needed work, a place to live, friends to go for a drink with in a strange town, or anything else, the GAA was the network that people got into, and it remains so to this day.

The founding of the CCB took place on Sunday November 15, 1987. The meeting was chaired by GAA President Dr. Mick Loftus, of Crossmolina, County Mayo. Among those in attendance were Toronto's Cormac O'Muiri, Ottawa's Pat Kelly, Montreal's Paul Moran and Paddy Dunne (R.I.P.). The first elected officers were Toronto's Paul Kennedy as Chairman, Vancouver's John O'Flynn as Secretary and Ottawa's Michael Connolly as Treasurer.

Others who have served on the County Board since its foundation include Diarmuid O'Connor, Noelle Russell, Sean Harte, Matthew Healy, Fionnuala McGovern, Pat Donnelly and Billy Millar.

Over twenty years later, the 2008 County Board consists of President Brian Farmer (Toronto-Durham Robert Emmets), Vice President Jarlath Connaughton (Ottawa- Gaels), Treasurer Eddie Mangan (Toronto-Durham Robert Emmets) and Secretary John O'Flynn (Vancouver- Harps), with over 525 registered players from four provinces within Canada: British Columbia, Alberta, Ontario and Quebec.

Before the CCB, Canadian clubs participated in the North American County Board Championships, but the problem of operating under different sets of by-laws and the complexity of border crossings were always viewed as significant obstacles.

The CCB is a democratic organization comprised of the following units: Clubs, Divisional Boards and County Committee.

Toronto Divisional Board: Toronto, Brampton, Durham, Ottawa and Montreal.
Western Canada Divisional Board: Vancouver, Calgary, Red Deer and Edmonton.

In nine cities across Canada are thirteen affiliated clubs: *Vancouver* Harps, *Calgary* Chieftains, *Red Deer* Eire Ogs, *Edmonton* Wolfe Tones, *Toronto's* St. Pat's Canadians, St. Vincent's, Gaels, St. Michael's, *Durham* Robert Emmets, *Brampton* Roger Casements and Michael Cusacks; *Ottawa* Gaels and *Montreal* Shamrocks.

The majority of clubs have both men's and women's teams, while a few clubs have flourishing children's programmes. There is an organization that is not presently affiliated but has demonstrated an interest for full membership, Les Patriotes de Québec, located in Quebec City.

North America's Oldest 7's Tournament

Since the inception of the Powerscreen International 7's Gold Watch Tournament in 1986, this competition has continued to be an excellent way for clubs from across Canada, Ireland, U.K., the Cayman Islands and the United States to end their playing season. The tournament provides a holiday setting over the Labour Day Weekend in Toronto, Ontario.

The following honour roll is evident of the class of clubs that have participated over the years.

Senior Men		Ladies	Jr. Men	Ladies
2007	St. Pat's College	Brampton	St. Pat's College	n/a
2006	Killyman (Tyrone)	Ottawa	Killyman	Brampton
2005	Elphin (Roscommon)	St. Joe's (Tyrone)	Brampton	Ottawa
2004	Ardboe (Tyrone)	Durham	Durham	
2003	St. Pat's College (Armagh)	Ottawa	St. Pat's College	
2002	St. Mike's	Durham	St. Mike's	
2001	St. Pat's College (Armagh)	Durham	Armagh Masters	
2000	Glen (Derry)	Durham	Durham	
1999	Cookstown (Tyrone)	Durham	Durham	
1998	Powerscreen	Cusacks		
1997	Powerscreen	Durham	Brampton	
1996	Powerscreen	Durham	St. Mike's	
1995	St. Mike's	Le Cheile		
1994	Toronto Gaels	Ottawa Gaels		
1993	Cavan (New York)	Le Cheile	Clan Na nGael	
1992	Powerscreen	Le Cheile		
1991	St. Joe's (Donegal)	Irish Canadians		
1990	St. Anne's (Dublin)	Le Cheile		
1989	Powerscreen			
1988	Clan Na nGael			
1987	Pittsburgh			
1986	Powerscreen			

Skydome Games

On March 18, 1990, history was made when the GAA football and hurling stars first came to the newly opened Skydome in downtown Toronto to put on an exhibition of Ireland's games. The stadium has an astro-turf playing surface with a retractable roof, which can be moved completely in 20 minutes. A jumbo screen with great resolution and a seating capacity of 53,000 meant that the Gaelic games were being showcased in a state-of-the-art indoor stadium for the first time ever.

The idea of bringing out two hurling teams to play an exhibition game began with a phone call from Joe Murphy of Murphy's Chips to Canadian County Board President

Brian Farmer about the possibility of staging Gaelic games in Toronto. Murphy also mentioned that he had also approached CEO John Dunne of A&P with the concept. Farmer then began the correspondence with Croke Park, and from these efforts the idea became a reality, with Gaelic Football being a part of the plan.

In time, the entire expenses for this event were met by the major sponsoring company, the Great Atlantic and Pacific Company of Canada Ltd, better known as A&P, the largest supermarket chain in Toronto, with over 200 outlets in the province of Ontario. The efforts of GAA members in Toronto and the Canadian County Board would further ensure the success of these Gaelic games.

Details were announced at the Canadian Embassy in Dublin on January 16, 1990. In attendance, at the press gathering, was the Chief Executive of A& P, John Dunne (Fenor, Tipperary); President of the Canadian GAA, Brian Farmer (Clonmore, Armagh); and Frank O'Rourke from the Bank of Ireland; John Dowling, GAA President (R.I.P.); and Canadian Ambassador Michael Wadsworth (R.I.P).

An tUachtarán John Dowling said, " We are very excited about this, not only from the point of view of giving Irish people in Toronto an opportunity to see Irish games being played by the best exponents of these games, but as well, to expose our games to people who may never have previously seen them. This is the international breakthrough we have been looking for!"

The Canadian Ambassador, a former professional Canadian football player, said, "In my short time in Ireland, I have observed how Irish people are so keenly interested in sport of all kinds and I welcome the opportunity as a Canadian representative to give my people at home an opportunity to see firsthand distinctive Irish games."

Canadian GAA President Brian Farmer said, "We are optimistic about the success of the hurling and Gaelic Football exhibitions in Toronto. Canadians will love the action and speed, and we hope this is the beginning of regularly scheduled matches in Canada. Canadian sports fans will appreciate the history and excitement of the occasion. Their stamp of approval will ensure the games become an annual event."

Promotional slogans filled the Canadian media with one hurling reference of "You think ice-hockey is Macho? Now see the real thing!" or about the event itself, "What could be more fun than a Domeful of Irishmen?" and "The 1990 St. Patrick's Day games, your chance to be Irish for a day!" Tickets were priced from $10.25 to $25.25 and a donation was made to the Ireland Fund of Canada from proceeds raised by the games.

On the day, March 18, 1990, the 1989 All-Ireland Hurling Champions, Tipperary, defeated the Bank of Ireland All-Stars 5-15 to 3-11. Dublin and Ulster Champions, Tyrone, played each other in Gaelic Football with Dublin being the winner in these St. Patrick's Day Irish games. The attendance was over 30,000 and the matches were televised by TSN in Canada and RTE back in Ireland along with media coverage by the

Toronto Sun and CFRB 1010. The Prime Minister of Canada, Brian Mulroney, provided a message of support and pride in his Irish heritage in the official programme that day.

The following year, on March 17, 1991, the St. Patrick's Day Canada Cup games were televised once more by RTE in Ireland and The Sports Network (TSN) in Canada. In the Gaelic Football match between Cork and the All-Stars, Cork won by 1-12 to 1-9. In the hurling game, the All-Stars had an easy 5-13 to 0-6 win over Cork. The attendance of 18,000 was considerably down from the previous year, though a truly professional approach had been taken by all those associated with the organization of the Gaelic games in Toronto. This would be the final year of the Skydome games in Canada.

Ladies' Football

What may have started as a group of women looking for a chance to play in the late 80's, has now grown into what is becoming the "better" half of the GAA in Canada. There are as many women Gaelic Footballers registered in Canada as there are men.

The contributions of women to the leagues they participate in are paramount—the ladies in Canada are not in the background, but are in the forefront of game development, coordination and activity. They work hard to create and grow club life, which is always a challenge as commitments to family are always a priority.

The challenges that clubs in Canada are facing have long been challenges of the ladies' teams. With immigration of Irish people to Canada on the decline, women have known all along that you need to look in your own backyard for talent.

With 90 percent of ladies' teams consisting of Canadian-born players, how do they retain them? How can clubs continue to grow? The answer lies in the volunteers and players themselves. The ladies never let an opportunity to recruit players pass them by—you never know who you may pick up along the way—and they are always willing to ask anyone, anytime, anyhow.

Canada was in attendance at its first Central Council meeting of the Ladies' Gaelic Football Association on July 30, 2007. President Geraldine Giles and Secretary Helen O'Rourke introduced Canadian County Board Secretary, John O'Flynn, to the delegates. John was called upon to speak about the Canadian Ladies' Football history that was being written during the fall of that year. Also, queries were made about the future International World Cups for overseas units.

North America's First Ladies Tour

On November 12, 1990, an organizing committee of Maureen Looney as Chair, Geraldine Duffin Rice and Julia Hughes as Vice Chairs, Nuala McNamara as Treasurer and Noreen Mitkov as Secretary was formed. The Ontario Women's Gaelic Football Club would plan to be the first ladies football team that would travel to Ireland from North America to tour Ireland playing Gaelic Football.

The dream would come true in 1992 with a match on August 8 in Dublin versus the Marino Ladies Gaelic Football Club (Est. 1986), August 12 in Westmeath versus Rochfortbridge Ladies Gaelic Football Club (Est. 1977) and August 15 in Cork versus Glanworth Ladies Gaelic Football Club (Est. 1984) who was the Cork Champions that year.

Toronto GAA President Sean Harte and Canadian County Board President Matthew Healy were particularly proud of these "Ambassadors" of the Association from Canada. Though ten of the players were Irish born most had only learned to play the game in Canada. The majority of the team was Canadian and the coach of the team was Steve Murphy (Cork) who had been a supporter and coach of Le Cheile.

The players on this historic team included Durham Robert Emmets' Theresa Bray (Antrim), Colleen McNamara (Toronto), Nuala McNamara (Dublin); Ottawa Gael's Paule Carrier (Quebec City), Sheena Cullen (Peterborough), Captain Breda Kelly (Galway), Nancy McCall (Gloucester, Ontario), Karen Moore (Montreal), Wilma Te Plate (Finch, Ontario), Nicky Watts (Truro, England); Michael Cusack's Kirsty O'Shea (Toronto); Irish Canadian's Denise Breau (Toronto), Rita Hickey (Toronto), Maureen Looney (Toronto), June McAlarey (Glasgow, Scotland), Ciara McNaughton (Belfast); Le Cheile's Cath Heaney (Armagh), Captain Geraldine Heaney (Armagh), Marg McLeod (Hawkesbury, Ontario), Captain Breda Murphy (Cork), Lori Nawrocki (Scarborough), Sharyn "Burne" O'Doherty (Toronto), Noreen O'Shea (Louth), Fionnuala Scott (Dublin), Petra Scott (Dublin) and the mascot - Kellie Scott (Toronto).

Though the fitness was there for the team, the skill set was still lacking and so there were three sound defeats to the Irish competition. What was certainly a problem for the ladies was the fact that the Irish teams were playing with size 4 footballs while the Canadians had been training and playing with size 5 footballs. Thankfully, an agreement was made to play with both sized balls for a half in each match as a compromise.

The Marino team in Dublin would then become the first ladies football club to travel to Canada. They would participate in the September 4 and 5, 1993 Powerscreen 7's along with matches in Toronto on September 8 and 12 and in Ottawa on September 14. Those in Canada who were instrumental in making the tour happen for Marino included Maureen Looney, Breda Kelly, Noreen McCann, Cath Heaney, Julie Hughes and Pamela Doyle.

An unknown poet from the Marino club wrote the following in tribute to those Canadian ladies who had made North American history in touring Ireland and paving the way for a return visit by an Irish ladies team to Canada:

Canada v Marino
August 1992
Take 2

At some mental hour of the morning in August 1992

We met at Dublin Airport with this crazy Canadian Crew
We said our "hello's" all nice and polite
Little did we know we were in for a fright

We decided these Canadians were really quite bizarre
When soon after breakfast they headed for the bar
To sort out their jet-lag we left them that night
But in the pub on Friday we put up a good fight

We went to O'Shea's for a chat and a pint
Some cracked under pressure at the eight or ninth
When closing time came we lashed out the door to
Barry's Hotel where we ordered some more

We partied all night and some of the morning
We left at half six when we all started yawning
"Are we off our heads, Jaysus, what did we do?"
"We'll never be sober for the match at two!"

Martyrs for the cause we arrived for the match
Bloodshot eyes, legs like lead, not a ball could we catch
For the 1st half neither goalie was busy
"cos it's hard to shoot straight when you're feeling that dizzy"

After a dodgy decision – a penalty- OH NO!
So up stepped big Heavey to face little Mo
"No problem" says Maureen "No problem with this"
"Ah Shag off" says Heavey "your taking the....Mickey!"

With her trusty right boot the net she did rattle
But straight after that it was back down to battle
We won by a point, we'd finish our mission
Thanks only to the ref and his Dodgy Decision

Out on the town again that night, Surprise, Surprise
A few pints and a bop with a band called "Allies"
It's a great ol' session, a good bit of fun
But you crack under pressure – I knew I should have been a nun

We left them on Monday – some of us had to work
But their Trail of Destruction went to Westmeath & Cork
The newspaper headlines the following morning –
CANADIAN TEAM CARRIES GOVERNMENT HEALTH WARNING

We look forward to Canada with our spines full of shivers
'cos we promised "our mammies", we'd look after our livers

We may need a transplant, so our name's on the list,
'cos once we hit Canada we know we'll be ....sober?

And so ended their Tour here – a mighty success
All the footballers in Ireland they put to the test
They played great football, they did themselves proud
And they can really party – this Canadian Crowd.

International World Cups

The first men's international football competition that Canada participated in occurred during the week of September 5-11, 1994, at the University College Dublin's Belfield Sports Complex. New York, London, Scotland, the North American Board and the Rest of Britain competed at the Irish Holidays International Football Competition.

The panel of players from the Toronto GAA that represented Canada included player/manager Cormac O'Muiri, Paul McElvanna, Gerry Douglas, Kevin Byrne, Eamon Murphy, Barry Farmer, Jason Coughlan, Charlie Doorley, Paul Loughnane, Stewart Martin, Brian McMahon, Gerry Healy, Wayne Kelly, Mark O'Brien, Steve Daly, Owen Dillon, Gerry Mullane, Jock O'Connor and Stephen Millar.

Toronto would not have an easy time of it with no victories to celebrate. The team returned to Canada considering the serious preparations and work that would need to be done for future competitions.

The Canadian Board would continue to work with the Toronto GAA in the organization of both men's and ladies' teams for the International World Cups in 1998, 2000 and 2002.

1998 **General Manager**, Brian Farmer; **Coach,** Diarmuid O'Connor; **Assistant Coach,** Mick Burke; **Selectors**, Bridget O'Toole, Noelle Russell, Elaine Mealiffe and Sinead Canavan.

In 1998, Canada took part in the International Tournament in Dublin and the opportunity for the ladies to play on Irish soil for the first time proved to be a great success. Bearing in mind that the Canadian ladies were used to playing men's rules and using size 5 balls in the Toronto league, they did very well and learnt from the experience. Canada made it to the semifinals and lost to the North American County Board.

From the Durham Robert Emmets, six players made the team; these included sisters Erinn and Kirsten Lynch, Sarah Gowdy, Sara Oliver, Samantha Williams and Kristine LaMonday. Unfortunately, goalie Sara Oliver broke her wrist in a Toronto championship match two weeks before the International tournament and did not play. On watching the games, Oliver felt her teammates did a good job. "For the most part we did well, considering we were almost all Canadian and inexperienced. Now that the rules and ball have changed here, I think that it will make a difference."

Selector Elaine Mealiffe was delighted with the tournament. "It was a fantastic experience for all involved. The magnitude of the tournament showed our Canadian girls just how big the sport of Gaelic Football is. The professionalism of the event was so impressive, from the accommodation and highly competitive games to the extra events and activities. It was something we had never experienced before. The tournament was nothing but a positive experience for women's football in Canada."

Daphne Ballard, of the Ottawa Gaels, was named Canada's MVP of the tournament and Lisa Langevin, Breda Kelly, Karen Moore, Shannon Draper, Jody Draper, Sue Lussier, Willie Te Plate (Ottawa), Julie Whitelaw, Robyn Meredith, Victoria LaRocque and Noelle Russell (Irish Canadians), Jeannine Vogan, Christine Howard, Nessa Maddigan and June Callaghan (Michael Cusacks) provided gallant support on the team.

The Canadian men's team of the red, yellow and green jerseys would lose to New York in their semifinal match. The following are remembered for their determined efforts that year: Brian Farmer, Bernie Dullea, Tommy White and Matt Healy (Team Officials); Darren Farmer, Barry Farmer, Brian Kelly, Billy McManus, Ollie Malone and Brian Healy (Durham Robert Emmets); Michael Colton, Gerry Healy, Dara Lynn, Barry O'Brien, Peter McGinnity and Sean Rohan (St. Pat's); Wayne Kelly and Dinny Calahane (St. Vincent's); Steven Millar, Damian Donnelly and Niall Donnelly (Gaels); Mike Burns, Jason Coughlan, Paul Farrell, Edwin Walsh, Paul Loughnane, P.J. Doherty and Gerry Douglas (St. Mike's).

2000 General Manager, Brian Farmer; **Manager/Coach,** Elaine Mealiffe (Durham); **Trainer,** Michael Gordon (Michael Cusacks); **Selector,** Karen Moore (Ottawa Gaels).

All the games were hosted by the Naomh Mearnog club at their beautiful facilities in the popular North Dublin seaside village of Portmarnock, from September 18 to 22. The 20 minute-a-side games were played on a five-round league basis with the top four teams qualifying for the semifinals and final playoffs.

In the red, black and green, the ladies' team had a fantastic performance where they made it to the semifinals against the North America Board. North America exerted early pressure by scoring five points in the first 10 minutes before Canada registered their first point by Sarah Gowdy. Breda Kelly claimed Canada's first goal with an excellent strike to the top left corner of the net, having taken a pass from Erinn Lynch. This left North America leading 2-9 to 1-1 at halftime.

Canada opened the scoring in the second half with a point from Lynch, and with Gowdy and Deanna Adams picking off two points. Though the last five minutes of the game belonged to Canada, Lynch finished the scoring with an excellently angled lobbed shot to the top right hand corner of the net; Canada lost 3-11 to 2-5.

Members of the team included Karen Moore, Selector (Ottawa Gaels); Megan Greer (Ottawa Gaels), Julie Whitelaw (Irish Canadians), Jeannine Vogan (Michael Cusacks),

Erinn Lynch (Durham Robert Emmets), Samantha Williams (Durham Robert Emmets), Sue Lussier (Ottawa Gaels), Sinead Gordon (Michael Cusacks), Noreen Gordon (Michael Cusacks), Tiffany Shirley (Ottawa Gaels), Breda Kelly (Ottawa Gaels), Trish Shaw (Durham), Willie Te Plate (Ottawa), Deanna Adams (Durham), Tara Ablett (Durham), Sarah Gowdy (Durham), Niamh Ruane (Ottawa), Daphne Ballard (Ottawa), Siobhan McQuarrie (Michael Cusacks), Petrina Scullion, Jodi Draper (Ottawa) and Fiona O'Carroll.

On the men's side, members included Durham Robert Emmets Darren Farmer, Mark Kerr, Brian Healey, Ollie Malone and Billy McManus; Ottawa Gael's Doug O'Connor, David Lambert and Blair Anderson; St. Mike's Gerry Douglas, Tommy Keane, Mark Burns, Paul Loughnane, Edwin Walsh, David Kinahan, Shane Harmon, P.J. Doherty, Paul McElvanna and Dan Fitzsimmons; Toronto Gael's Niall Donnelly, Cormac Monaghan and Damien Donnelly; St. Vincent's Eamon Durgan; St. Pat's Graham McCarthy, Bernie McDonnell and Gary Lawlor.

The team officials were coach/manager Bernie Dullea (St. Pat's) and selectors Danny Kinahan (St. Mike's) and Brian Farmer (Durham Robert Emmets).

2002 General Manager, Brian Farmer; **Coach,** Diarmuid O'Connor; **Assistant Coach,** Jarlath Connaughton; **Equipment Manager,** Lorraine Morley.

Results

Round 1 *Canada* (1-2) v (4-13) Rest of Britain
Round 2 *Canada* (3-11) v (1-1) Europe
Round 3 *Canada* (0-1) v (5-8) London
Round 4 *Canada* (0-2) v (3-9) North America
Round 5 *Canada* (0-1) v (3-14) Australasia

The 2002 squad that competed September 17 to 20 consisted of Erica Leder (Brampton), Wilma Te Plate (Ottawa), Suzie Battaglia (Ottawa), Lisa Connaughton, Captain (Ottawa); Sue Lussier (Ottawa), Tammy Blakeney (Ottawa), Kerry Mortimer (Ottawa), Dawn Price (Ottawa), Beth Miller (Ottawa), Sarah Gowdy (Durham), Shannon Murdock (Durham), Orla Smith (Michael Cusacks), Danielle Hurst (Michael Cusacks), Erin Gallagher (Michael Cusacks), Maureen Keane (Michael Cusacks), Fiona Latham (Michael Cusacks), Christine Howard (Michael Cusacks), Yvonne Morley (Michael Cusacks), Sarah Callanan (Michael Cusacks) and Jeannine Vogan (Michael Cusacks).

Though this tournament served as another developmental experience for the Canadian team, there was a growing sense that more needed to be planned, in the years leading up to the 2005 tournament, for improvement on the international stage.

Men's Bronze

For the men in 2002, the team from the Toronto GAA was selected by Bernie Dullea and Brian Farmer. The team advanced to the semifinals, following five tough rounds. In the end, they were defeated by the North America Board, who went on to win the competition. The Canadians ended the tournament with an impressive bronze medal.

Round 1 London 0-9 to 0-4 Canada, *Round 2* **Canada** 0-8 to 0-7 Scotland,
Round 3 **Canada** 2-13 to 0-5 Europe, *Round 4* NACB 2-9 to 0-7 Canada,
Round 5 **Canada** 3-8 to 0-8 Rest of Britain
Semi-Finals NACB 3-12 to 3-1 Canada

Shield Cup 2005

The Canadian ladies' squad that traveled to Dublin in 2005 was, for the first time ever, a team of players from the Toronto and the Western Canada divisions. A truly representative team, drawn from the clubs of Vancouver, Calgary, Edmonton, Durham, Brampton, Montreal, Ottawa and Toronto, competed and won the Shield Cup. Coach Jarlath Connaughton's and General Manager Brian Farmer's willingness to travel across the country to Vancouver to help select the best players was critical to the team's success. Players had to demonstrate their abilities and compete for one of 25 positions. Athleticism, sportsmanship and skill were needed to attract the attention of the management team. Of the final team members chosen, amazingly, only three were Irish-born!

The following sponsors will be remembered for their tremendous contributions to the success of the 2005 squad that won the Shield Cup: Karen and Sean Murphy of Kemptville Travel; Sean Harte and H&S Fleet Services; Michael Hurley and Hurley Corporation; Powerscreen Canada, the Canadian County Board, the Western Canada Divisional Board, the Toronto Divisional Board, and Brian and Patsy Dolan from A&P Dominion.

General Manager, Brian Farmer; **Coach**, Jarlath Connaughton; **Assistant Coach**, Paul Loughnane; **Team Manager**, Sinead Canavan; **Equipment Manager**, Lorraine Morley.

Roster

1	Ashley Visser	Durham Robert Emmets
2	Ainsley Baldwin	Edmonton Wolfe Tones
3	Tressa McMaster	St. Mike's
4	Maureen Keane	Michael Cusacks
5	Meghan Deeney	St. Mike's
6	Lisa Langevin	Ottawa Gaels
7	Sharon Higgins	Brampton Roger Casements
8	Erin Gallagher	Michael Cusacks
9	Daphne Ballard	Ottawa Gaels
10	Kathleen Keenan	Brampton Roger Casements

11	Sinead Fitzsimons	St. Mike's
12	Julie Mroczkowski	Durham Robert Emmets
13	Tara Phillips	Vancouver Harps
14	Cathy Jackson	Vancouver Harps
15	Mandy Tuohy	Calgary Chieftains
16	Colleen Whelehan	Edmonton Wolfe Tones
17	Sarah Callanan	Michael Cusacks
18	Erinn Lynch	Durham Robert Emmets
19	Mary Traynor	St. Mike's
20	Stephanie Fitzpatrick	Durham Robert Emmets
21	Kim Tulloch	Calgary Chieftains
22	Sara McTaggart	Ottawa Gaels
23	Patricia Staniforth	Montreal Shamrocks
24	Elaine Gilmore	Montreal Shamrocks
25	Carlin Acheson Johnston	Edmonton Wolfe Tones

Results:

Round 1 Australasia 1-13 (16) Canada 1-3 (6)
Round 2 New York 1-10 (13) Canada 1-3 (6)
Round 3 London 3-12 (21) Canada 0-2 (2)
Round 4 *Canada* 3-5 (14) Britain 1-5 (8)
Round 5 *Canada* 2-7 (13) North American Board 2-6 (12)
Round 6 *Canada* 4-12 (24) Europe 2-5 (11)

SHIELD FINAL
Canada 4-18 (30) Britain 3-08 (17)

Most Valuable Player of the Tournament - Erin Gallagher: Michael Cusacks

Post-Tournament Interviews

The following interviews of Coaches Jarlath Connaughton and Paul Loughnane were conducted by Father Liam Kelleher of Grenagh, County Cork and P.R.O. for the Cork County Board following the tournament.

Jarlath Connaughton

Fr. Liam: I would like to welcome Jarlath Connaughton here with the Canadian ladies' team. They were delighted to win the Shield Competition. First of all, maybe a small bit of background on your own involvement in ladies' football in Canada and maybe before you went to Canada.

Jarlath: Well, I played some Gaelic Football before I went to Canada. I played some inter-divisional football with the Gardai.

Q: Where are you a native of?
Jarlath: I am a native of Dublin, from the south side Drimnagh and immigrated to Canada with my family in 1990.

Q: Which part?
Jarlath: Ottawa where we still live. There is a team there, the Ottawa Gaels. I got involved with the club over there, and I began coaching the Ottawa ladies and they were already a fairly good team. We had a lot of success over the last eight years; we won the championship four times and the league championship four times, and two of the occasions, we won the double. Last time, over three years ago, I was assistant coach to Diarmuid O'Connor. The last two times over, we had no success. The ladies' football in Canada was just in its growth section, so this time round, I was asked to act as coach, to put together a team that could come here to have some chance. We knew Australia was a mighty uphill climb, but we came with the ambition to at least get into the playoff section of the competition.

Q: So what does it mean to have won the Shield Competition?
Jarlath: It means a tremendous amount to us. It will do wonders for development over there and just the fact that we were able to come over here and compete. Our ladies are from all over Canada, so it is very difficult to put a team together; it means an awful lot of travelling on my part. I went out as far as Vancouver and back as far as Montreal. Edmonton and Calgary are also represented. Six teams from Toronto are also represented. Ottawa and Montreal are also represented.

Q: Did you see all the players before the game?
Jarlath: Yes, I went and saw everyone play and based the selection on that, and of course none of the girls had really met at all or even spoken. We arrived here on Saturday last. There was some anticipation at how different players were, but they gelled really well. They came together and they practised and got used to how each player played the game. The Fingallian's, here in Swords, were very good to entertain us on the day we arrived, and gave us a run out so that we could stretch our legs and to see where we were with our panel of 25.

Q: It's been a long week now, are ye in the 7's as well?
Jarlath: Yes, we are in the 7's now, but we are enjoying it now, for the first competitive tournament is out of the way. And today, we just decided to come and enjoy the 7's and if we get a run of it, we will be even more delighted and even if we don't we will be happy to have had the opportunity to play in the competition against Irish girls, even though we are in the Junior section, but I think that is where our standard is at the moment.

Q: What about the cost of travel—how did you raise money for the trip?
Jarlath: Each player was responsible for their own airfare and we had accommodation for the first day and night. We had fund-raising functions, social evenings and a raffle with first prize being an airfare and two tickets to next year's hurling final, so different things like that were put together, and we were able to raise enough money to cover nearly all our travel costs.

Q: Have your soccer players and basketball players gelled better with ladies' Gaelic Football?
Jarlath: The crossover skills of basketball and volleyball, and sports like the Canadians play a lot, gel really well with Gaelic Football. I suppose it's the athleticism. The Canadians really love to be out there and run.

Q: Any of your family involved in Gaelic?
Jarlath: Yes, my son and daughter. My daughter has moved back here to Ireland. She hasn't got really involved. She was Captain of the Canadian team that came here the last time. My son plays with Halifax, so we are hoping to spread our tentacles way out to the East Coast. We are already at the West Coast.

Q: Leaving for Canada late in life, have you any regrets about going to Canada or the changes you can see from Ireland? What do you think of the changes coming back here?
Jarlath: The changes here—traffic is one that jumps off at you here in Dublin; expensive, we find it very expensive for an ordinary day living. I couldn't afford to move back here, especially in Dublin.

Q: How did you find Canada compared to Ireland?
Jarlath: It was strange for a while, different culture; different kind of people, friendly people, but a different kind to Irish people, but it is a very welcoming country.

Q: What would be your ambitions and hopes for Gaelic Football in Canada?
Jarlath: Well over the next five years, we'd like to try and work on a five-year increment; and over the next decade, I would like to see ladies' football develop to all the cities in Canada. I would just like to see it blossom.

Q: Generally speaking did the ladies enjoy their week?
Jarlath: They had a great time. The ladies' GAA looked after us really well; they set a great programme, ran smoothly, buses were on time. I couldn't say enough to praise them. I am looking forward to coming back in three years' time.

Paul Loughnane

Fr. Liam: Here with me, I have Paul Loughnane, who with Jarlath is in charge of the Canadian team who have done very well. They won the Shield yesterday and have done very well in the 7-a-side. So, Paul, you have a very chequered history, including winning a county senior football medal with Castlehaven in Cork. How did all this come about, so you might fill me in on this first of all?
Paul: Yes, I grew up in Birr, and my father was heavily involved with the hurling in Birr and my mom played Camogie there. When we moved to Canada, they got involved with St. Mike's in Toronto, and I started playing U-14 football, minor, and then I moved on to playing senior football.

Q: What age were you when you went to Canada?

Paul: I was nine. I was actually born in Toronto, and when I was two we moved back to Ireland; then we came back again when I was nine years old.

Q: You mentioned going back; when did you come back and play with Castlehaven?
Paul: I came over and played for three seasons. We won the county in 2003, and I was playing right halfback.

Q: What was the reason that you came back and played with them—was it an invitation or did you know one of the team or what?
Paul: Yeah, Dinny Cahalane, he would be a brother of the legend, Niall Cahalane. He was out in Toronto and told me that if ever I was going to play football in Ireland that Castlehaven was the team to go to. So I figured why not; it is as good as any team and worked out very well.

Q: And you played GAA and worked obviously; they gave you a job as well?
Paul: Yes, I worked as an electrician in Cork.

Q: When did you go back to Canada again?
Paul: April 2004, and I was straight back involved with the team, playing with my club, St. Mike's, and training and coaching the ladies' team and coaching at the underage level and at the schools.

Q: I am amazed that you have built up such an underage structure. This has only been happening quite recently that the younger players you're working with are from there, that you are no longer depending on people coming over from Ireland.
Paul: That's right. We haven't had the emigration really since about, I guess, the '80s. We recognise that the people of Toronto recognise that they weren't getting the people out. Developing Canadian talent was the only way to go. So it started off with the children of people there that had already played the game, getting their friends from school to join in as well. We had contacts inside the schools to teach it, as part of the Phys. Ed. classes, and now these youngsters are coming through and becoming the adult players in our leagues.

Q: How did you get involved with the Canadian team—obviously it is your first time?
Paul: Yes, I am. Because we are based so far apart (we could be 3,000 miles apart) we had to break it up into regions and train separately. So, I was in charge of training all the Toronto girls. We had six clubs in Toronto. There, the girls would come together and train on Friday nights, while Jarlath took the ladies from Ottawa and Montreal. The girls out West would get together, as well, to train in Edmonton. The fact that so many girls were from the Toronto region, I was asked to get involved and coach.

Q: What did the week mean to you so far?
Paul: It was outstanding to see these girls come over and play an Irish game when so many of them are Canadian-born. Some of them have no Irish ancestry at all, but it is sport at the end of the day, but it is not about being Irish. It is about ladies going out and competing in sport, and they have acquitted themselves very well. Some of them have

only been playing for a few years now and some only two to three years, and they looked just as strong as any of the other teams out there that might have had Irish girls that played their whole lives.

Q: Yes, they are very skilful and ye have a great goalkeeper, very like a soccer player. Did she play soccer?
Paul: Yes, she has a soccer background. She plays in the nets, but she can also play out as well. She plays out with her club, centre-half forward but because of her soccer background, we asked her, would she stand in the net, and she has pulled off some unbelievable saves for us all week, and her ability to clear the ball is great. She can kick the ball 50 to 60 metres—no problem to her.

Q: Men's soccer isn't as big in Canada as in the States, but is it strong in the women's?
Paul: Yes, the Canadian ladies' team is one of the best in the world. Not quite as strong as the one in the States, but very competitive with them. Probably a lot stronger than the men's team, I'd say.

Q: Does it get much support, because in the States, it gets huge support?
Paul: Yeah, the sport is growing all right, because they have had such great results in the last few World Cups and other international competitions. They can compete with the best in the world.

Q: Most of your clubs are integrated men and women.
Paul: That's right. Pretty much every club has a ladies' section.

Q: It's handy for fund-raising.
Paul: It is—all for club development. You can make it a real family atmosphere, when you are including everybody—ladies, men, underage. It brings so many other people into the club atmosphere.

Q: You are settled in Canada now; you don't intend to go back, when your playing career is over?
Paul: I still play with Toronto. I really miss the football here. You can't find a more competitive and intensive atmosphere in the world playing football than in Cork. I really enjoyed playing for my club in Toronto, and there are so many opportunities out in Toronto and you get a great summer, which is also a bonus. I was very torn leaving, but I am happy to be settled back in Toronto now.

Fr. Liam: I think that we will leave it at that; your team are waiting for you there, thank you very much and best of luck.

The West Awakes!

In 2003, a need was expressed by GAA clubs in British Columbia and Alberta that Gaelic sports in Western Canada should, once again, come under the wing of the Canadian Board. The development of Canadian-born players and ladies' football was a testament to how successful and popular the game could be; as a result, structure was required in the West.

A meeting of the Canadian Board, with representatives from the three western clubs, occurred in Edmonton, Alberta, on May 24, 2003, at the offices of Christy Whelehan's Celtic Homes. CCB Secretary Diarmuid O'Connor; CCB President Brian Farmer; Vancouver Irish Sporting and Social Club's John O'Flynn; Kate McNamee and Sean Quinn; the Edmonton Wolfe Tones' Christy Whelehan, Marvin Dentzien and Danielle Bodnarek; the Calgary Chieftains' Ronan Deane, Frank Campbell and Leanne Niblock were in attendance.

The agenda included the western GAA clubs' application for full membership with the Canadian Board. Shortly following the meeting, the Western Canada Divisional Board was formed. Elected were John O'Flynn as Chairman, Ronan Deane as Secretary and Danielle Bodnarek as Treasurer with Calgary's Kim Tulloch and Adrian Lagan and Edmonton's John O'Connor as Members at Large.

Twinning and Youth Development

In February 2004, CCB President Brian Farmer chaired a historic meeting, along with Ulster Secretary Danny Murphy (Newry, Down) and Vice Chairman Miceál Greenan (Drumconnick, Cavan), in response to Canada being twinned with the Ulster Provincial Council by Croke Park. Danny Murphy presented the *Strategy for High Performance Gaelic Football in Ulster (2003-2007)* and displayed CDs and materials recently developed. Many ideas were shared for potential agreements in coaching, refereeing and youth development.

One of the first actions, taken by the Ulster Council, was to send over two senior referees to refresh the seasoned Toronto referees and to train some brave new souls willing to tog out in black. An enlightening and very informative all-day session was conducted in May of 2004.

In January 2005, another meeting was coordinated by the CCB to discuss ways of developing Gaelic games in Canada, including networking with the GAA Head of Games Pat Daly (Tallow, Waterford) and the Chair of the Overseas Units, Gene Duffy (Crossmaglen, Armagh). Youth development funds were made available for local GAA communities. They were able to apply for these funds through the CCB and the Divisional Boards.

High Performance Director, Dr. Eugene Young, and Games Development Manager, Terence McWilliams, came to Canada twice in 2005 to deliver coach education sessions. As a result of their visits, the Toronto GAA had enough trained mentors to "coach" coaches and to help improve the overall calibre of coaching that is expected by today's athletes.

Congress and Charity

Canada has had representation at the annual Congress, held in Ireland over the years, with a maximum of four delegates. In April 2005, Lorraine Morley, Diarmuid O'Connor, Paul Loughnane and Brian Farmer represented Canada at Congress. In 2006, Brian Farmer was the only delegate in attendance, and in 2007, Toronto's Paul Loughnane joined Farmer at Congress.

In 2005, members of the Canadian and Toronto Boards of the GAA acted as "Guards of Honour," with hurling sticks, at the rededication of a Celtic cross at the new Irish burial section of the Assumption Catholic Cemetery in Mississauga, Ontario. There were over 450 people in attendance. Canada's first modern-day Irish burial site officially came into being to provide a final resting place for the descendants of St. Patrick's isle.

On May 2, 2007, Irish hurling player Tony Griffin launched his epic cross-Canada 7,000 kilometre cycling journey from Vancouver. His goal was to raise EU150, 000, and funds raised went to benefit the Lance Armstrong Foundation, the Irish Cancer Society and Ovarian Cancer Canada.

It was the untimely passing of his father Jerome—who died of lung cancer in 2005 as a result of exposure to asbestos in the construction industry—that led to Tony's ambitious undertaking. To accomplish his goal, he put aside his illustrious career as a Clare senior hurler and 2006 GAA All Star to "Ride for the Cure."

The night before his departure from Stanley Park, the men and women of the Vancouver Irish Sporting and Social Club hosted a brilliant fund-raising event at the Blarney Stone in Gastown. GAA clubs throughout Alberta, Ontario and Quebec involved themselves in supporting Tony's cause as he passed through their provinces. In the provinces where no GAA clubs existed, many former players of the Gaelic games introduced themselves to Tony along the way, in Saskatchewan, Manitoba and Nova Scotia.

Tony Griffin joined in a Gaelic Football match at Laval University: Les Patriotes de Québec versus the Montreal Shamrocks. The heat was stifling for players, and the final score was 25-13 for Montreal. There was a bit of a surprise in the *Poc Fada* competition, where Donal Lacey of Montreal won over Tony Griffin. Griffin was nonetheless very happy with the day's events and the money that was raised for his foundation.

The Canadian County Board made a generous contribution to Tony's foundation on behalf of all the members across the country. By June 24, the final day of the Canadian leg of the 7,000 kilometre Ride for the Cure, the Tony Griffin Foundation had raised over $600,000.

Websites and Committees

In 2006, the Canadian County Board created its first website for adults. In 2007, another website for children wanting to learn more about Gaelic games was created. On the children's site, one can find out exactly what is Gaelic Football; one can gain an understanding of the skills required and find out where one can play Gaelic Football in Canada. www.gaelicfootballforkids.com. For adults, information can be found at www.canada.gaa.ie where fixtures, news and links are readily available.

In compliance with Rule 61 T.O. 2007, the following committees were established:

2007 Competitions Control Committee: Chairperson Kevin Higgins; Secretary Lorraine Morley; Members Gabriel Hurl, Katie Higgins and Sean Morley.

2008 Competitions Control Committee: Chairperson Ronan Matthews; Members Damian Higgins, Sean Harte, Ken Ray and Steve Owens; Referee's Coordinator Kevin Higgins.

Responsibilities: The C.C.C. shall be responsible for all arrangements for, and control of, any matters arising from games under their jurisdiction, as determined by the County Committee, including disciplinary matters other than those functions reserved by the County Hearings Committee. They shall investigate and process matters relating to the Enforcement of Rules, including hearing objections and counter-objections in their respective areas.

Hearings Committee: Chairperson Cormac Monaghan, Secretary Diarmuid O'Connor. Members Mark O'Brien, Danielle Hurst and Mark Lannin

Responsibilities: It will serve as the Hearings Committee for all the divisions under the jurisdiction of the Canadian County Committee. It will adjudicate on all disciplinary matters where a hearing is requested relating to the Enforcement of Rules arising from matters under the jurisdiction of the County Committee.

Appeals Committee: Chairperson, Montreal President Mick Martin; Secretary, Durham President Alan Martina; and Calgary President Adrian Lagan.

Responsibilities: None shall be members of the Divisional Competitions Control Committee, County Hearings Committee or the County Committee, whose function will be to deal with any appeals arising from decisions of the County Hearings Committee or the County Committee. There shall be no appeal against the decisions of the Appeals Committee.

Godfather of Gaelic Games

One of Canada's godfathers of Gaelic games at the national and international level is Brian Farmer. Brian immigrated to Toronto in 1975, as a member of Powerscreen's international sales team. It is a measure of the progress he has made, both in work and within the GAA that he has served as Chairman of the Canadian County Board for over 18 years and as President and Marketing Director of Powerscreen for 37 years. Farmer once said, "Running a football team is no different to running a company. It's all about having people of the right calibre."

Brian has worked at taking the GAA in Canada to a higher level. "It's vital that we present the game to the Canadian public. We have two of the greatest field games in the world." The Toronto Irish Person of the Year Committee honoured Farmer in March 2006 by raising Ireland's flag at a public ceremony. As part of the month-long celebration of "Irish Heritage and Cultural Appreciation," Farmer dedicated the moment of the flag-raising "to the men and women of the Gaelic Athletic Association, and indeed to all, who gave their lives in the fight for Irish freedom, a 32 County Ireland, everything for which the flag stands for."

His vision, for the Gaelic Games in Canada, is in its continued introduction and play in the schools and community groups of Canada. The Irish community from east to west has been well served by Brian's outstanding years of leadership. The Canadian GAA's present day strength is reflective of this man's tenacity and pride for his sporting culture.

QUEBEC

MONTREAL SHAMROCKS

Of the 400,000 Irish serving with the armies of France in the 18th century, one Irish brigade landed in Quebec City. These men were dispatched to Montreal, to Kingston and to the border on Lake Champlain. Many of them married French Canadian women and were granted farms in Quebec (Lower Canada).

Quebec City was incorporated in 1833, and the census had the Irish at 25 percent of the total population of 32,000. The suburb of Sillery had a substantial Irish presence, and the number of Irish playing their native games in the city soon led to the authorities passing a by-law in 1845 that forbade hurling to be played in the narrow streets. There must have been some severe window damage happening for a by-law to be passed!

The game of hockey, as we know it today, was developed in Canada and the first official rules of hockey were also Canadian. These rules were published in 1877 in the *Montreal Gazette* newspaper, but hockey has its roots in a wide variety of similar sports played long ago in many different countries.

These early versions of hockey had many different names, depending on the country from which the player came. For the Irish, "hurling" is the natural connection. People from England called their version "bandy" or "field hockey"; to the Scots it was "shinty" and to the Americans it was "ice polo." Native Canadians played a game called "baggataway," while other Canadians called it "shinny." In Windsor, Nova Scotia, reference was made by Thomas Chandler Haliburton, a lawyer and journalist, to a hockey-like game, played by the Mic Mac Indians in the early 1800s, in which they used a "hurley" stick shape and a square wooden block.

When hockey was being played in Montreal in 1875, the players were not French speaking. They were mostly Irish Catholic students from McGill University. Two colleges, Ste-Marie and Mont St-Louis, both bilingual, formed the core of an Irish hockey club, called the Shamrocks. Though the Irish taught the French to play hockey in the college's yard rink, up until 1896, the Ste-Marie team was exclusively Irish. Some of the players included Harry Trihey, Arthur Farrell and Jack Brennan who would later star for the Montreal Shamrocks. Mont St-Louis had some French students on its team in 1895, including Louis Belcourt who would join the Shamrocks in 1897, but he was notably absent from the lineup when the team won the Stanley Cup in 1899 and 1900.

In 1898, the Irish built their own college (Loyola) and parted physical company with their French friends. The ties between the two would remain strong, however, and would play a critical role in the French gaining entry to Montreal's game. Not only did the first French players in the senior league play for the Shamrocks (Belcourt and Ernest Pagnuelo in 1897, Theophile Viau and Louis Hertubise in 1902), but perhaps even more indicative of the Irish support—and how crucial it was—is the fact that the Shamrocks always voted in favour of having a French-Canadian team join senior hockey ranks, while the other teams did not accept the French until 1905.

The nickname of "Jack Canuck" or "Johnny Canuck" is believed to have come from the name of the Irish province Connaught. French Canadians used the nickname when referring to those of Irish descent more than 200 years ago.

Gaelic Football had been played in the Montreal area since the early 1800s. An annual sports day, under the auspices of an Irish Redemptorist priest, Father Sean Kelly of St. Anne's Parish, and members of the St. Patrick's Society of Montreal, was held in Pointe Saint Charles beginning in 1834 to the end of 1841.

Grosse Ille and the Irish Memorial

The famine years in Ireland ushered in a decline in sporting activities. The primary concern of the Irish Quebec community was that of aiding the starving people of Ireland and assisting impoverished immigrants who had been able to escape certain death.

On the Feast of the Assumption, August 15, 1909, the Ancient Order of Hibernians in North America dedicated a huge Celtic cross on Telegraph Hill—the highest spot on an isolated island in the St. Lawrence River near Quebec. The island was Grosse Ille, and the cross was a memorial to the more than 5,000 exiles from Ireland's Great Hunger, *'An Gorta Mor,'* who perished there in 1847 when the island was a quarantine station. The dead (including the nurses, doctors and priests who administered to the dying) are buried, unidentified, in mass graves beneath a field whose undulating landscape ironically bears a striking resemblance to the vestigial potato ridges, called lazy beds, that they left behind in Ireland.

On March 17, 1996, the Canadian Government officially recognized the suffering of the Irish immigrants by renaming the island "Gross Ille and the Irish Memorial." On August 15, 1997, 150 years after the tragedy, GAA supporters from across the country gathered with 2,000 other people in Quebec for a special pilgrimage. At the re-dedication of the 1909 Celtic cross, those Quebecers, who administered to the dying and cared for the children left behind, were also remembered.

Gaelic Games Awake

When life improved for Irish Quebecers, happier pursuits returned. The skills of Gaelic Football and hurling were taught to Montreal school children, mainly the sons of Irish immigrants, by Presentation Brother Sebastian Rogers (Clare) and other members of the religious order in the early days of this century prior to the Great War, and between the two World Wars. Brother Andrew Hobbins, Provincial of the Presentation Brothers, was one of the greatest supporters of the Montreal GAA in later years.

Montreal GAA lore speaks of hurling being played on the frozen Lachine Canal in the 1930s, but more evidence exists from 1945 onward that Irish immigrants gave exhibitions of their native games at Fletcher's Field in Verdun and at the old Montreal Athletic Association grounds.

Martin Green—Montreal's Godfather

In 1948, serious consideration was given to the formation of a GAA club, and in the spring of 1949 a club was officially convened under the presidency of a Raheen, Galway man, Martin Greene (an immigrant of the 1920s). In May 1950, the club received official approbation from the President of the GAA, Michael Kehoe. Evidence suggests that additional support for the organization of Gaelic games came from members of the United Irish Societies of Montreal. The United Irish society's motto was "Faith and Fatherland" and it was headquartered at the Queen's Hotel. The Society celebrated the Centenary of St. Patrick's Orphanage (1850-1950) on its letterhead, which was used by Martin Greene for one of his many letters to Ireland, in which he appealed for support of the fledgling GAA club.

The Montreal Shamrock Hurling and Football Club assembled on weekends at the Stelco grounds, on Notre Dame Street, for sterling workouts. The Stelco grounds became unavailable in 1952 and so the Montreal Athletic Association grounds, on St. Catherine Street, were used together with Fletcher's Field, in Verdun, their old stomping grounds.

The club was able to form an inter-squad league, which consisted of five teams in hurling and four teams in football. In 1949, the club spent $181 to outfit the Padraic Pearse team at the Soccer Import Company, which was founded in 1920 by John F. Rooney (Airdrie, Scotland). The 1950 Padraic Pearse football team included Martin Dunn, Sean Grennan, Jim Dempsey, Ben Cramer, Mike Nelson, Andy Forbes, Ed Dempsey, Bill McGivinney, Jimmy Flynn and Sam Nelson.

In 1950, the GAA spent $184 to outfit the Wolfe Tones' members. The team included John Neason, Benny Flynn, Conn Flynn, Liam Chivers, John O'Connor, Ted Hamil, Jim Laverty, Mady Costelloe, Billy Crowe, John Sullivan and Micky McQuillan.

The Soccer Import Company continued in business through the owner's son, John D. Rooney, who was a member of the Montreal GAA up until 1967. John moved his family to Toronto and eventually closed the business in 1975. John's sons, John Joe and Andrew, would go on to play for Clan Na nGael and St. Pat's club in Toronto.

A July 1, 1950, inter-city hurling result saw the Shamrocks beat the Wolfe Tones at the Stelco Grounds, by fifteen points to five. In mid July of that year, Greene (who was also Vice President of the United Irish Societies of Montreal) went to Ireland for a family visit and attended to some GAA matters that are of significance for Canada.

Due to his correspondence with Croke Park, Greene was invited to attend the GAA Central Council quarterly executive meeting held at Croke Park on July 29, 1950, with President Michael Kehoe. At that meeting of the Central Council, Greene asked for support in supplying hurley sticks and medals to aid in the promotion of the games in the city of Montreal and throughout Canada.

The *Irish Press* wrote an article covering Greene's visit to Croke Park on August 1, 1950, and a picture of the Shamrock hurling team that was taken in Montreal was published by the newspaper. The photo shows Martin Glynn (Galway); Martin Smith (Galway); Pat Fahey (Galway); Tom Minogue, Captain (Tipperary); Con Flynn (Cork); Martin Greene, President of the Shamrocks; John Loye, Canadian-born President of the United Irish Societies; Ben Taylor (Galway); Joe Fahey (Galway); Christie Moylan (Galway); William Reidy (Clare); Frank Shaugnessy (Galway); John Mounsey (Tipperary); John Harty (Tipperary); Joe Geoghegan (Galway); and Pat Marnane (Tipperary).

Four members of the club who were not included in the picture, but were mentioned in the *Irish Press* article were Tom Gleason (Tipperary), John Connolly (Clare), John Duggan (Clare) and trainer Michael Trayers (Galway).

In the follow-up letters—from Greene and John Loye to Michael Kehoe at Croke Park, dated August 14, 1950; to Kehoe's residence in County Wexford, dated January 18, 1951; and to Mr. W. J. O'Keefe, Secretary of the GAA Central Council, dated August 5, 1951—it is unclear whether the hurleys or the medals ever made it! There is no mention of the hurleys in the letters of 1951; the medals seemed to be the main focus for the writers. But according to Galway man Paul Moran, who arrived in 1955 to Montreal, it was his understanding that the medals were played for in 1953.

Greene also spent part of his time in Ireland trying to induce the Central Council of Tipperary to send its hurling team, who were to meet New York in the National League Hurling final in New York's Polo Grounds on September 24, 1950, to play an exhibition match in Montreal before the team's return to Ireland. A letter, dated July 16, 1950, from the Shamrock Captain and Tipperary man, Thomas Minogue, asked the Chairman of the Central Council of Tipperary for support of Martin Greene and his efforts to promote hurling. There was no luck in Martin's pursuit of this grand idea for Montreal, but there is no doubt that Canada's presence on Croke Park's radar was high as a result of Loye, Greene and other Shamrock supporters.

Martin Greene was also corresponding with the GAA of Greater New York. He was looking for a response to his letter of August 15, 1950, sent to Mr. Joe Casey (Corresponding Secretary). Green was soliciting an opportunity to meet with local officials to discuss affiliation. He suggested that during the September 24, 1950, hurling finals that it would be appropriate for them to meet. It is interesting to see how Martin also asked to meet with the officials of the visiting Irish team. No doubt, Martin's plan was to see if the Irish team might come up to Montreal for a match before they took off for home!

Published GAA Action Photos

A Labour Day weekend of football and hurling took place in 1952 between the Montreal Shamrocks and Toronto's Eire Og at Oakwood Stadium. The football match was heavily one-sided in Toronto's favour as they won three goals and five points to nil. The hurling match was a much more competitive affair, with a 4-4 tie at the end of the day. A *Globe and Mail* photo of players from the two matches may be the earliest published documentation of Canadian GAA action.

John Hehir—Montreal to Boston

John Hehir, who arrived in 1953 to Montreal, recalls home and away challenge matches with Toronto's Eire Ogs where Toronto prevailed on both occasions. John left for Boston late in 1954, where he had a long and successful association within the American County Board from 1959 to 1978. At the age of 90, he is still widely respected for his contributions to the North American GAA over the decades.

Promotion and Matches

Efforts to promote the Gaelic games within Montreal were evident in a written response on July 26, 1954, from Tom Healy, on stationery from the House of Commons. The letter promised that the Superintendent of Television, Mr. Coleman, would film a future Shamrock practice, in order to give the Shamrocks some publicity on local Canadian television.

An August 1, 1954, Montreal All-Star Football team selection consisted of Brendan McCoy (Louth) in goal; the fullback line was Frank Smith (Cavan), John O'Connor (Kerry) and Pat Harrington (Limerick). The halfback line was Oliver McCartney (Antrim), L. Donnelly (Antrim) and T. Barry (Kerry). At midfield were J. McVey (Derry) and J. McRory (Tyrone); the half-forward line was Bill McGhee (Tyrone), Captain Joe Sloan (Antrim) and Jim Dempsey (Kildare). The full-forward line included Tom McErlane (Antrim), F. Doyle (Dublin) and P.Glennon (Galway). The subs for that day were S. Keogh (Wexford), T. Stritch (Cork) and T. Callaghan (Limerick). The team wore white jerseys with green crests and they took the pitch for a match at Loyola College with Toronto's Eire Og.

Other notable football players of that time included Eamon McGrogan, Jim Keely, John McGroary, Liam Shivers, John Neeson, Jim Flynn, Barry Flynn, Pete Smith (Cavan), Aaron McErlane (Antrim), Ted Hamil, Jeff Donovan and Montreal-born Ray Watkins

A Montreal All-Star Hurling team of August 1, 1954, had the following selections: Mattie McMahon (Galway) was in goal; the fullback line was Mike Cooney (Clare), John Hehir (Galway) and Jim Dillon (Clare). At halfback were John Fahy (Galway), J. Doherty (Kilkenny) and Dan Dillon (Clare). At midfield were M. Hogan (Tipperary) and E. Maher (Tipperary); the half-forward line was Tom Murnane (Clare), Andy McNamara (Limerick) and Pat Feeney (Galway). The full-forward line had Mike Mulqueen (Limerick), Eddie Cooney (Clare), and Stephen Fahy (Galway). The subs for that day were Tom Daly (Cork), Pete Glenane (Galway), Mike Duggan (Limerick) and Desi Vaughan (Clare). The team wore red jerseys with white collar and cuffs. J. Byrne from Rochester served as the referee for the match at Loyola College.

The strength of both the hurling and football teams in the greater Montreal vicinity continued to fruition in 1957, when both teams played Boston Galway in Boston. The members of the 1957 hurling team were: Dan Grace (Kilkenny) in goal; the fullback line was John Fahey (Galway), Pat Power (Kilkenny) and Ned Regan (Cork). The halfbacks were Brendan Glenane (Galway), Dan Dillon (Clare) and Tom Murnane (Clare). Midfielders were Dennis Baker (Clare) and Ed Healy (Kilkenny); the half-forward line was Joe Conroy (Kilkenny) Martin King (Galway) and John Pollard (Kilkenny). The full-forward line had Pete Glenane (Galway), Jim O'Brien (Clare) and Noel Carey (Galway). The subs were Des Vaughan (Clare) and George Mulqueen (Limerick). Other notable players of this time were: Paddy Fahy, Dennis Gray, Tim Moynaghan, Jim Eddie, Fred Dillon, Paddy Vaughan, and Mike Cooney.

During 1957, another influx of Irish immigrants brought new strength to the teams in Montreal. There were so many enthusiastic players that Montreal was able to field several intra-city squads from which the varsity team was chosen. Players practiced each weekend at Beaver Lake Park, which was located at the top of Mount Royal. Team names included the Wanderers (Andy Finnerty, Captain), Harps (Bill McGhee, Captain), Celtics (Denis Leyne, Captain), and the Paddies (P.J. Harrison, Captain).

Although the action on the field was quite physical, there was never any carryover off the field. Everyone got along well, because the common interest in Irish games gave each participant a great sense of camaraderie.

The 1958 football team, as chosen by a selection committee, included Eamon Dolan (Roscommon) in goal; the fullback line was Paddy Dunne (Laois), John Walsh (Laois) and Joe Deignan (Antrim). The halfback line consisted of Larry Donnelly (Antrim), P. J. Harrison (Roscommon) and Paul McErlane (Antrim). Midfielders were John O'Connor (Kerry) and Ned Healy (Kilkenny); the half-forward line was John O'Brien (Roscommon), Matt Dooley (Monaghan) and Andy Finnerty (Roscommon). The full-forward line was Peadar Tunney (Mayo), Jim Dempsey (Kildare) and Joe Sloan (Antrim). Subs were Joe Waldron (Roscommon) and Tom Barry (Kerry).

American County Board

The first American County Board Convention was held at the Sylvania Hotel, in Philadelphia, on February 7–8, 1959. Montreal's two delegates were Roscommon native and All-Ireland minor medal winner John O'Brien and Billy McGhee (Tyrone). Former Montreal resident and Boston delegate, John Hehir, was in attendance at the inaugural convention too.

A strong team sprang out of the Montreal league and they were able to beat Toronto's Eire Ogs in the American League Northern Division Championship. The game was played in Kingston, Ontario, on October 4, 1959. It was one of the biggest days for Irish football in Montreal because Toronto had always been a strong contender and Montreal's biggest rival. Some of the accomplished footballers who played for Montreal that day were John Walsh, Matt Dooley, Paddy Dunne, E. Donnelly, Liam Cotter, Denis Leyne, Brian McCrann, Tom Barry, Joe Waldron, John O'Brien, Billy McGee, Des Magennis, John O'Shea, Andy Finnerty and Ed McBrien.

Unfortunately, Syracuse filed an objection against Montreal in connection with a previous match between the two teams. Because the referee had not filed his report, the Northern Board voided the Northern Division final and reinstated Syracuse into a round-robin playoff. Montreal won the replay against Syracuse but was defeated in the Northern Division replay against Toronto's Eire Ogs at Loyola College. Montreal had been winning by two points, but a last-minute goal scored by John Duffy (Monaghan), from a 50-yard free, gave the victory to Toronto.

As a result, the Eire Ogs traveled west to meet the Los Angeles Football Club for Memorial Day weekend in 1960, instead of Montreal. Los Angeles agreed to pay half the cost of the Toronto team's fares. The game was refereed by former Mayo player Dr. Pádraig Carney. In a very competitive match, Los Angeles won by six points over the Eire Ogs. Many of the Montreal footballers suggested that they would have fared better in Los Angeles if they had been awarded the match on October 4, 1959!

The second American County Board convention took place in Montreal in 1960; John O'Brien was elected Registrar. The members of the 1960 football team were: Billy McGhee (Tyrone) in goal; the fullback line was Tony Ryan (Dublin), John Walsh (Laois) and Des McGuinness (Louth). The halfback line had Ed McBrien (Montreal), P. J. Harrison (Roscommon) and Liam Cotter (Meath). The midfielders were Matt Dooley (Monaghan) and Kevin Donnelly (Galway); the half-forward line was John O'Brien (Roscommon), Denis Leyne (Cork) and Joe Waldron (Roscommon). The full-forward line had Tom Barry (Kerry), Paddy Dunne (Laois) and Andy Finnerty (Roscommon). The subs were Tim Donaghue (Limerick), Frank Donnelly (Galway) and Dan Dillon (Westmeath).

The 1960 Shamrock hurling team included Dan Grace (Kilkenny) in goal; the fullbacks were Paddy Dunne (Laois), Pat Power (Kilkenny) and Mike Collins (Galway). The halfbacks were Liam Cotter (Meath), Ed Healy (Kilkenny) and Andy Irish (Kilkenny).

The midfielders were Dan Dillon (Clare) and Martin King (Galway); the half-forwards were Tom Murnane (Clare), Tim Donaghue (Limerick) and Denis Leyne (Cork). The full-forwards were Brendan Glenane (Galway), Tom Daly (Cork) and Pat O'Meara (Tipperary). The subs were Stephen Fahy (Galway), Des Vaughan (Clare), Mike King (Galway) and Paul Moran (Galway).

John O'Brien served on the American County Board in 1961. Montreal created a clubhouse on St. Catherine's Street, which served the members for a number of years. During the 1961 season, Montreal's football team played Syracuse in Albany, New York. The Shamrocks were leading the game by nine points with eight minutes left when a ferocious fight broke out. The game was called, and both teams were ordered to replay it three weeks later in Syracuse as an eight-minute game and the score would remain the same. At the appointed time three weeks later, on Sunday August 27, 1961, only the team from Montreal arrived at the field. They lined up and the referee threw in the ball. The game was awarded to Montreal who was then set to play Philadelphia that same day. Then the team from Syracuse, along with their supporters, arrived and pulled down the goal posts and they marched off the field with the posts in tow!

Since both Philadelphia and Montreal had traveled quite a distance to play their game, the teams decided to wait and see if Syracuse could be persuaded to return the missing goal posts. About an hour elapsed before the Syracuse fans returned with the goal posts, they had been cajoled into cooperating by the fans from Philadelphia. Montreal went on to beat Philadelphia 3-7 to 2-6. On the same day, the Montreal hurlers beat a team from Washington D.C. 3-10 to 1-7.

Senior Hurling Championship

Following an investigation that an illegal team had been fielded by Boston's Fr. Tom Burkes at Loyola Park, on September 17, 1961, Montreal's hurlers won the American County Board Senior Hurling Championship. A photo from that year has the following Shamrock players included: Denis Leyne, R.I.P. (Cork); Denis Baker (Clare); Pat Power (Kilkenny); Paddy Dunne, R.I.P. (Laois); Pat Baker (Clare); Steve Fahey (Galway); Tom Daly (Cork); Liam Cotter (Meath); Mike Collins (Galway); Ned Healy (Kilkenny); Brendan Glenane (Galway); Desi Vaughan, R.I.P. (Clare); Andy Irish (Kilkenny); Pat O'Meara (Tipperary); Martin King (Galway); Dan Dillon (Clare); and Jimmy King (Galway).

Ned Healy, Denis Leyne, Paddy Dunne and Liam Cotter, who were known as the "Big Four," had double duty in 1961, as they lined out again on the same day. The Shamrock's football team narrowly lost the semifinal to Boston Galway in a hectic match. Monaghan man Matt Dooley was selected as the best footballer of the year by his peers, and Ned Healy was chosen hurler of the year.

Martin King, who now resides in White Rock, B.C., still has the medal that was presented to him and his teammates following their hurling championship. He intends to display his medal at the 50th anniversary of the team's victory that is planned for 2009.

On Sunday June 3, 1962, the All-Ireland Football Champion County Down visited Philadelphia and a number of American cities during the previous week. The Down team played against various American All Star teams. Montreal's John O'Brien and Matt Dooley were among the Canadians selected. In 1962, John O'Brien was elected Secretary of the American County Board; he moved to Cleveland in early 1963 where he continues to contribute to the Irish cultural scene with an annual festival.

Broomball

In order to stay in shape through the winter, Montreal players played a game called broomball. It is a version of ice hockey that uses a large ball instead of a hockey puck, taped brooms instead of hockey sticks, and rubber shoes instead of ice-skates. The players were a very dedicated group, often playing in sub-zero temperatures. A very physical game, broomball gave each player a great deal of satisfaction and fun, and it kept everyone fit and active during the long, cold winter months.

The league consisted of four teams: St. Antoine Bulldogs (Paul Moran, Coach), Oxford Night Hawks (Andy Finnerty, Coach), the Verdun Braves (Mike Duggan, Coach) and the Decarie Flyers (Billy McGhee, Coach). The St. Antoine Bulldogs were the 1960 and 1961 Broomball League champions; the Oxford Nighthawks took the title in 1962 and the Verdun Braves in 1963.

Aussies and Irish Rules

At Clifford Park in Ville-Émard, on May 9, 1965, the Montreal Shamrocks played host to a visiting Australian Rules team from Melbourne. They played the first half under GAA rules, and the second half under Australian Rules. The score at the final whistle read: Montreal 29 - Melbourne 28. There were reports that some of the visitors thought the whistle to end the game had blown a minute too early because they had scored seven unanswered points in the closing minutes of the game!

World's Fair

In 1965–66, the Montreal GAA rallied local support against City Hall's plan to remove the Irish Commemoration Stone located at the north entrance of Victoria Bridge. City Hall appreciated the Irish stance in defence of one its historic monuments and offered the GAA a "Celtic Day" at the World's Fair Expo in 1967.

Ned Healy (President), Paul Moran (Vice President), Denis Leyne (Secretary) and Denis Baker (Treasurer) were the Shamrocks' officers. They and club supporters organized a memorable event for Canada's Centennial: they held a Gaelic Games celebration of hurling and football. It was organized for St. Helen's Island Park on September 2, 1967.

The Montreal Shamrocks and a Toronto Select Hurling Team combined to defeat the visiting Kilkenny Hurling Club of New York by a point, before several hundred fascinated spectators. The referee for the hurling match was Denis Leyne and the Canadian team, listed in the souvenir programme, consisted of L. Sheahan, L. Ryan, K. Larkin, J. Callahan, T. Keyes, D. Baker, T. Walsh, K. Loughnane, R. Walsh, T. Daly, D. Dillon, P. Mahoney, E. Healy, S. Bowles, E. Nevin, P. Leyne, P.Gavigan, P. J. Noone, B. Glenane, and J. Brosnan.

There is reason to believe that those listed on the programme may not have necessarily played that day, as the programme would have been made in advance and changes would have been inevitable. Toronto's Eddie Thornton played with the Canadian hurling team; he came in from Detroit for that particular weekend along with a few others.

On the same day, the Montreal footballers (with some additional players recruited from Syracuse) were narrowly defeated by a Toronto Garryowen team; Ned Healy was the referee. The Shamrock players were Rev. Bro. Andrew Hobbins, M. Dineen, P. Dunne, M. Kelly, P. Loftus, B. McCrann, B. McDonnell, T. Murphy, S. O'Connor, J. O'Connor, Rev. Bro. Victor (John O'Shea), M. Walsh, B. Sammon (MVP of the match), E. Stack, J. Malone, C. Sullivan, J. Synnott, B. Glenane, J. King and Rev. Bro. Marcellus.

The Toronto Garryowen team included M. McTeer, A. O'Brien, D. Hogan, E. O'Leary, B. Egan, P. Byrne, D. McCarthy, T. Flynn, L. McIlwee, K. O'Shea, T. Moran, A. Henderson, B. Gilroy, O. McInro, M. Hamill, D. Coleman, F. Smith, B. Slevin, D. Columb and E. Barry. Following the games an enjoyable evening was held at the Black Watch Armory on Bleury Street.

Milestones

On October 29, 1969, the club entertained the Kerry Senior Football Team, All-Ireland Champions, who were on their way home from their successful American tour. Trainer Jackie Lyne and the Chairman of the Kerry County Board expressed their gratitude and appreciation to the Montreal Shamrock Club for the reception and fraternity shown to the visiting champions.

On October 8, 1973, the Montreal Shamrock Hurling team captured an American League divisional title against a Cleveland, Ohio, team in a hotly contested game in Toronto. In August 1974, Montreal played host to an Irish Civil Service Football Team at Trenholme Park. This was the first time that a visiting Gaelic Football team from Ireland played in Montreal. Much publicity was given to that game by the media and several hundred spectators saw an excellent exhibition of Gaelic Football under floodlights. The fitter Irish squad was easily victorious over their hosts. Celebrations occurred in October 1974 when the Shamrocks captured the Toronto GAA Junior Hurling League.

From the mid '70s, Montreal was not attracting as many young Irish immigrants as Toronto, Boston and Chicago—cities that continued to be serviced by Aer Lingus. Accordingly, the club was forced to rely on its still-nimble, but more mature, veterans and their up-and-coming sons. Competition between traditional rivals from Buffalo,

Rochester, Hartford and Syracuse (teams affected by the draft and the Vietnam War) had to be abandoned in favour of classic games with Toronto, Ottawa and Hamilton.

35th Anniversary Celebrations

A two-day Gala Celebration was held, featuring games of football and hurling, to commemorate the 35th Anniversary of the Club and the Centennial of the GAA. There was a sumptuous dinner/dance at the Seville Holiday Inn on August 18, 1984. The executive members that year were President Paul Moran, Vice President Pat Dunne, Secretary Paul Loftus and Treasurer John O'Shea. The President of the GAA in Ireland, Paddy Buggy sent a heartwarming citation, which was presented and read at the banquet. Former members from as far away as Ireland, Los Angeles, Chicago, New Zealand, Australia and New York journeyed to Montreal and telegrams arrived from all over the world.

The '90s

In July 1990, Montreal traveled to Ottawa to play a game against St. Pat's of Toronto. Founding Canadian County Board president Paul Kennedy was playing in goal for St. Pat's, while the founding secretary of the Canadian County Board, Vancouver's John O'Flynn, played with Montreal. Though Montreal would lose the match, one player who stood out was Montreal-born Paddy Dunne Jr., son of Paddy Dunne Sr. (R.I.P.) and nephew of Frank Dunne (R.I.P.) in Vancouver. Paddy Jr. had played in Vancouver a few years earlier. It was good to see the strong east-west GAA connections that day.

Montreal Tournament

To celebrate the 125th Anniversary of the founding of Canada and the 500th anniversary of the founding of Montreal, the club sponsored a two-day tournament on May 16-17 1992, under the chairmanship of Irish community member Leo Delaney.

	Men	Ladies
2007	Durham	Ottawa
2006	St. Mike's	Ottawa
2005	St. Mike's	Brampton
2004	St. Mike's	Ottawa
2003	Ottawa	Ottawa
2002	St. Mike's	Ottawa
2001	St. Mike's	
2000	St. Mike's	
1999	St. Mike's	
1998	St. Mike's	
1997	St. Mike's	
1996	Brampton	
1995	St. Mike's	

1994	St. Mike's
1993	Durham
1992	Clan Na nGael

Golden Jubilee

The kick-off to the Montreal GAA Golden Jubilee celebration included a historic visit to Montreal on January 24, 1999, of An tUachtarán of the GAA, Joe McDonagh (Galway). He addressed more than a hundred members and guests at a celebration of the club at McKibbin's Irish Pub. McDonagh paid tribute to stalwart members like Martin Greene, Paul Moran, John O'Shea and Paddy Dunne, who, down through the years, promoted and nurtured the games and culture. He urged the current and future executives to "grasp the torch and carry it aloft to even higher and greater eminence."

The Shamrocks were proud to have two of their players, Murdoch Fitzgerald and Sean Heavens, selected in 2002 as part of Canada's men's team for the Gaelic Football World Cup. In 2005, Canadian-born Patricia Staniforth and Galway native Elaine Gilmore were selected for the ladies' Team Canada at the International Women's Tournament in Dublin.

Most years, Montreal participates in the Toronto GAA League, as well as in exhibition games in Quebec City and various tournaments, including the Feis Ville-Marie, Denis Leyne, and Powerscreen 7's. Games have been played on the John Abbott College grounds and at the Lower Canada College.

Montreal will host its 184th annual St. Patrick's Day Parade in 2008—it seems clear that the Irish have been warmly embraced within Quebec's culture.

Presidents of the Montreal GAA

Name	Years	Name	Years
Martin Greene (Galway)	1949–1951	Eddie Dempsey (Kildare)	1952–1953
Martin Greene	1954–1955	Mike Cooney (Clare)	1956–1957
Dan Grace (Kilkenny)	1958	Sean Fitzgibbon (Westmeath)	1959
John O'Brien (Roscommon)	1960–1961	Paul Moran (Galway)	1962
Denis Leyne (Cork)	1963–1964	Paul Moran (Galway)	1965
Ned Healy (Kilkenny)	1966–1967	Pat Leyne (Cork)	1968–1969
John Keenan (Dublin)	1971	Pat Short (Dublin)	1974–1981
Paul Moran	1982–1984	Patrick Dunne (Laois)	1985–1987
Gerry Hughes (Antrim)	1988–1991	Peter Moran (Montreal)	1992–1994
Vince Cahill (Limerick)	1995–1997	Cathal Marlow (Tyrone)	1998–2000
Patrick Mahon (Down)	2001–2002	Micheal Martin (Cork)	2003–2005
Conor Brogan (Tyrone)	2006	Micheal Martin	2007

Canada's Other Official Language

Bienvenue à L'Association Athlétique Gaélique de Montréal (GAA). Le Montréal GAA était établi en 1948, avec le but de promouvoir les deux sport nationaux de l'Irlande — le football gaélique et le hurling — au près de la communauté Montréalaise. Le Montréal GAA organise aussi, plusieurs événements sociaux, incluant la diffusion en direct par satellite des championnats "All-Ireland" de football gaélique et de hurling durant la saison estivale. Nous accueillons toujours des membres nouveaux, en particulier ceux qui sont nouveaux à ces sports. Et rappelez-vous: Vous n'avez pas besoin d'être Irlandais— nos équipes féminines et masculines contiennent des membres de plusieurs différentes nationalités. Si contribuer à Montréal GAA vous intéresse, soit en temps que joueurs ou membre social, s'il-vous-plait! Contactez-nous: www.montrealgaa.com

LES PATRIOTES DE QUÉBEC

Les Patriotes de Québec Gaelic Football Club was founded in February 2006 in Peter Farrell's Nelligan's Pub Irlandais, 275 rue St. Jean, Québec. What started as a few lads hitting a *sliotar* around the Plains of Abraham was soon to become a living GAA club with a group of Irish, Québécois and Canadian friends, who wanted to promote and develop Gaelic games in Quebec City and assist the Irish and other new arrivals to integrate and assimilate into Québécois society.

The name of the club was decided upon as a mark of respect to the original Les Patriotes de Québec who were Irish and Québécois, and who fought together in the 1837 rebellion against the British. The name also reflects the demographics of the province where 40 percent of Québécois claim some Irish ancestry.

It wasn't that Gaelic sports were anything new to Quebec City! In fact, it is documented that the games were being played 100 years ago (according to the archives of the Québec Chronicle Telegraph). Before that, in 1845, a law was passed in Québec City forbidding the playing of hurling in city streets.

The original members, at the formation of the club, were Sean Bannon (Belfast), Cillian Breathnach (Kerry), Darragh Murphy (Dublin), Peter O'Farrell (Sligo), Pierre-Loup Boudreault (Québec), and Jean-Sébastien Gagnon (Saguenay, Québec). The committee that was elected later that summer was: President, Cillian Breathnach; Vice President, Darragh Murphy; Secretary, Jean-Sébastien Gagnon; P.R.O., Jeremy Peter Allen (Québec); Recruitment Officer, Sean Bannon; and Player's Representative, Alexis Giroux.

The club received assistance from Sean Bannon Sr. of the Antrim County Board and Damien Bannon of St. Paul's GAA (Belfast), who kindly donated a set of playing jerseys for the fledgling club. Les Patriotes received great support and help in their establishment through Conor Brogan, Redmond Shannon and Michéal Martin of the Montreal Shamrocks.

First Match

On May 7, 2006, the Shamrocks traveled to play Les Patriotes de Québec at the stadium in Laval University in Quebec City. In this, the first game to be played in over a hundred years, the Shamrocks proved too strong (7-7 to 5-4) for Les Patriotes, but this did not deter the players. After all, it was the first time that most of Les Patriotes de Québec had ever seen, never mind played Gaelic Football. Team members that day included Darragh Murphy, Sean Bannon, Cillian Breathnach, Patrick MacSweeney (Cork), Jean-Sébastien Gagnon, Pierre-Loup Boudreault, Maxime Boily (Quebec), Francis Fortin (Quebec), Jérôme Fortin (Quebec), Matt Pieri (England), Chris Brooke (Australia), Katrina Beck (Germany), Matteo Camporanese (Italy) and Katie Marsh (Vancouver).

Later that month, Les Patriotes de Québec went down to Montreal for their tournament and they were placed with a group of Shamrocks to form a "B" squad. On July 8, Les Patriotes brought a full team to Montreal and played on a pitch in N.D.G. (Notre-Dame-de-Grâce). Again the team was well beaten, but they were learning all the time and the non-Irish started to get the hang of the game.

In August, a match was played on the sports ground at McGill University. Improvements were noticeable, and there were new additions to the club: Jeremy Peter Allen, Florent Ruyet (France), and Jaye Macumber (Australia). Still, yet again, the Shamrocks' experience won the game.

The final game of the year was on September 23 at the Base de Plein in Ste. Foy, Québec; this match was for the inaugural Provincial Cup. The side that lined out that day included Darron Taylor (USA), Michal Pawica (Poland), Trent Clarke (Newfoundland), Jeremy Peter Allen, Matt Pieri, Jérôme Fortin, Florent Ruyet, Alain Lachance (Québec), Cillian Breathnach, Jaye Macumber, Darragh Murphy, Rémy Bourdillion (France), Jean-Sébastien Gagnon, Alexis Giroux (Québec), Maxime Boily, and Francis Fortin.

It was a competitive match, as the gap between the two sides had been greatly narrowed. Les Patriotes de Québec had a rock-solid defence; Jeremy Peter Allen played fullback and was commanding in that position. Allen won "man of the match" and the Montreal Shamrocks won the Cup 5-5 to 3-3.

Première Victoire des Patriotes de Québec!

Ce Samedi, 8 Septembre, Les Patriotes de Québec ont réalisé un exploit. À leur deuxième année d'existence, ils ont remporté la Coupe du Québec de football gaélique, en affrontant les Shamrocks de Montréal, un club qui existe depuis plus de soixante ans. La marque finale est de 4-5 pour Québec à 2-4 pour Montréal, soit 4 buts et 5 points (ce qui donne un total de 17) pour Les Patriotes de Québec; 2 buts et 4 points (pour un total de 10) pour les Shamrocks de Montréal.

Les Patriotes de Québec deviennent ainsi la première équipe francophone en Amérique du Nord à remporter un trophée au football gaélique. Le match a été chaudement disputé devant près d'une centaine de spectateurs à l'Université Laval. Après la première demie, les deux équipes étaient nez à nez au pointage (1-1 Québec; 1-2 Montréal). Dès le début de la deuxième demie, Les Patriotes de Québec ont marqué un but décisif. Les joueurs ont su faire preuve de discipline et d'agressivité, ce qui leur a permis de dominer complètement leur adversaire et de remporter la victoire.

On September 8, 2007, Montreal and Quebec met to compete for the Quebec Provincial Cup. The venue was Laval University, the site of Les Patriotes' first game. A crowd of 86 spectators gathered to cheer on the home side. Though the matches played during the summer had all gone in Montreal's favour, Les Patriotes were more determined than ever not to let it slip away from them, as had happened in the past, and especially not in front of the home crowd!

The match started with Montreal notching up the first score, a point from 20 yards. The Quebec team was far from deterred by this, though, and soon began to repay the favour "en masse," as they say in La Belle Province. Despite the best of efforts, Montreal still led at halftime, a lead that was far from the gaping canyons that separated the teams in previous matches. The constant training since the formation of Les Patriotes was beginning to pay dividends.

The second half saw some intense play from both sides. Whatever was said at halftime to Les Patriotes, it seemed to have worked, and the familiar second-half Les Patriotes slump did not make the slightest appearance. Les Patriotes de Québec came out with guns blazing and a rally of goals and points were clocked up. This second half was reminiscent of some of the tougher games once played; despite some heavy tackles, both teams managed to keep their composure. Damien Rooney (Dublin) and Peter Farrell shared the refereeing duties by taking a half each.

The game finished 4-5 to 2-4; this time, however, it was Les Patriotes who lifted the trophy! One year and seven months after the formation of the team, and one year and four months after their first match, Les Patriotes de Québec had finally succeeded: North America's only Francophone Gaelic Football team had taken a championship cup home.

Coached by Darragh Murphy, the players from that historic day included Michal Pawica, Jérôme Fortin, Sheldon Clarke, Jean Pouliot (Quebec), Cillian Breathnach (MVP), Jaye Macumber, Stéphane Gitareu, Marc-Olivier Dalpé, Jacky Assayag, Jean-Sébastien Gagnon, Sean Bannon, Alain Lachance, Florent Ruyet, Maxime Boily, Alexis Giroux, Darron Taylor, and Stephen Clarke (Down).

Quebec Provincial Cup

2007 Les Patriots de Québec   2006 Montreal Shamrocks

Affiliation and Beyond

In November 2006, the club sent Darragh Murphy and Jeremy Peter Allen to attend the Toronto GAA's A.G.M., and inquiries were made regarding affiliation within the Canadian GAA. As Quebec City celebrates the 400th anniversary of its founding in 2008, the committee that continues to build the Gaelic games includes President, Jaye Macumber; Vice President, Jeremy Peter Allen; Secretary, Catherine Doré; Treasurer, Conrad Castilloux; Administrators, Jean-Sébastien Gagnon and Peter Farrell; and Player's Representative, Darron Taylor.

ONTARIO

TORONTO GAA EIRE OGS

After the unsuccessful Irish Rebellion of 1798 (when the Irish in Ireland fought against the continuing domination of the British), immigrants from Ireland began coming to Canada in great numbers. Still more arrived after a famine in 1822, and soon settlements could be found at Prescott, Kingston, Cobourg, York (Toronto) and London. It was not long before both Upper Canada (Ontario) and Lower Canada (Quebec) had larger Irish populations than either the English or the Scottish. Of the 38,000 who arrived in Toronto in 1847, more than 1,000 died from typhus.

Like all other Canadian pioneers, the Irish learned to help one another. In Ireland, economic and religious differences caused much heartache and trouble for the Irish. Sometimes these problems remained even after the Irish arrived in Canada. Still, it is celebrated that all of the Irish contributed over the years to the establishment of our Canadian nation.

In the early 1930s, attempts were made to organize Gaelic games to be played at High Park, but the Toronto city fathers would not allow sporting activities to occur on Sundays. This thwarted the attempts of people like Tyrone man Patrick Canavan. The war years meant that there would be no GAA activities of note; it would be after the global conflict that the games would come alive.

The beginnings of the Toronto Gaelic Athletic Association started in 1947, when Michael Walsh (Mayo) got people together to kick a ball about in Riverdale Park. Toronto's first and only club for a number of years, Eire Og, was born by Labour Day 1952 where two matches of football and hurling between Montreal and Toronto were played at Oakwood Stadium in Toronto. Other visiting teams from Detroit, Chicago and Boston would visit the city for games at Millen Stadium, which was sometimes used instead of Riverdale Park.

Continental Zones

An tUachtarán, Michael Kehoe of Wexford, a man concerned for the difficulties besetting the fledgling GAA centres scattered throughout North America, used his persuasion and ability to correct a long-standing inequity. At the urging of the officers from various North American cities, in 1950, the Central Council established the National Council GAA of the United States. Three separate divisions called Zones were created by the National Council; New York was classified as Zone 1, Midwest as Zone 2 and New England as Zone 3. Each Zone was granted provincial status with the parent body in Ireland.

Representatives from Chicago, Pittsburgh, Detroit, Buffalo and Cleveland formed the Midwest States Championship, while teams in Toronto, Rochester, Montreal and Syracuse made up the eastern half of the Midwest Championship.

As the Midwest and New England zones completed their play-off schedule, *Nua Eabhrach* withdrew from the organization; this dealt the Inter-Zonal competition a mortal blow. The zones were a failure partly because of the financial difficulties of transporting teams such vast distances, but mainly because of the withdrawal of New York, who regarded the zones as a burdensome imposition.

Toronto's football team of 1953 won the Midwest at their first attempt and retained the championship until deposed by Chicago in 1956. In 1953, a Midwest Football selection beat a New England selection on a score of ten points to nine in Boston and was declared the first All-American Champions. Toronto's three all-stars were Leitrim's Paul Reynolds (R.I.P.), Sean McFearon and Kevin Nolan. In 1954, a Hartford Gaelic Football Club won the New England title only to lose by one point to Toronto's Eire Og in a regional playoff.

On August 12, 1956, a Midwest All-Star Gaelic Football team defeated New England in Cleveland by a score of 21 to 14 to be crowned the All-American Senior Champions. Toronto's all-stars on the team were John McHugh, Frank O'Kane, Jim Malone, John Duffy, Brendan Keogh (Vice Chairman of the Midwest Council) and the Captain, Dominic Kilroy.

Detroit won the senior championship in 1957 by defeating Eire Og by a score of 2-6 to 1-3, on a snowy day in Buffalo. Detroit's Pádraig Pearse member Dan P. O'Kennedy (R.I.P.) composed a poem called:

DETROIT MEN ARE CHAMPIONS

*The month was October, the year '57
When Detroit and Toronto prepared for the fray
The place was at Buffalo in a beautiful stadium,
That those teams played great football on a cold bitter day.*

(Chorus)
There are victory bells ringing, the fans are all singing,
The Final is over but not so the fun
Oh! The girls are so happy, the boys were so snappy
"Detroit are the Champions." The battle is won.

The crowd often wondered why our backs never blundered
How our midfield men called every tune of the play,
Though Toronto were stick, our forwards were tricky
And got passed to raise flags that carried the day

The Toronto Eire Og footballers must have gotten wind of this poem as they returned in 1958 to beat Detroit by 2 points. There is no poem to be found about that Canadian victory!

A 1958–1959 Eire Og team photo included those who tasted victory over Detroit: Jack Reidy, Mike O'Mara, Danny Roche, Pat McClearn, Oliver Gilligan, Joe Kennedy, Mike O'Leary, Brendan Power, Larry Morrin, Maurice Houlihan, Pete Nolan, John Sinclair, P.J. Brosnan, Pat Lanigan, John Gilligan (who owned the Toronto Maple Leaf Ballroom), Eddie O'Brien, John Hurley, Phil Walsh, Pat Mahoney, Tommy O'Connor, Pat O'Mara and Billy Grant.

Between the inception of the 1950 National Council GAA of the United States and the formation of the American County Board in 1959, games between the Midwest teams were closely contested. Often the difference between defeat and victory occurred on the last kick of the ball. Chicago probably held the upper hand over these years; Pittsburgh and Toronto's Eire Og vied for a close second place. The 1955 Toronto hurling team won the Midwest and retained it every year until the competition was discontinued.

Foundation and Beyond

At the first American County Board Convention, which was held at the Sylvania Hotel in Philadelphia on February 7–8, 1959, Toronto's two delegates were Mike Lawlor (Clan Na nGael) and John Sinclair. This was a significant event in the history of the GAA in Canada, and in all the cities where the games were played outside of New York and New Jersey. It brought all of North America into the GAA family officially, with direct affiliation to Central Council, representation at Congress and an allotment of All-Ireland tickets to the finals each year.

The Midwest teams from Buffalo, Rochester, Syracuse, Montreal and Toronto eventually evolved into the Northern Division with the American Board formation. Later, Toronto and Hamilton were delegated to a separate division, leaving the four remaining teams.

The games in 1959 saw Toronto's Eire Og hurling team beat Detroit's Pádraig Pearse by a point at home. Boston Galway would beat the Toronto selection in the semifinals of the championships in Syracuse later that year.

Toronto's football team beat the teams of Cleveland, Buffalo, Detroit, Chicago and Hartford in 1959, but was beaten by Montreal on October 4 in Kingston, Ontario, for the Northern Division Championship. The final was declared void by the American County Board due to an objection by Syracuse over a previous match with Montreal. The added issue of the referee failing to file his report in time also meant that Toronto had a second chance, and a replay of the game was ordered.

Montreal and Syracuse squared off in their replay match, which Montreal won. So the two rivals from Ontario and Quebec met up once again! The Shamrocks were winning by two points, but a last-minute goal scored by John Duffy (Monaghan) from a 50-yard free, gave the victory to Toronto!

Toronto vs. Los Angeles

Peter Roche (Glenmore, Kilkenny) who now lives in White Rock, B.C., hung on to an original souvenir programme of the first American County Board final. Peter, who played hurling with Kilkenny, New York and Los Angeles in the 1950s and 1960s, as a habit, always saved the programmes of matches he attended in the United States. Nearly 48 years later, a programme for Toronto's Eire Og championship match resurfaced due to Peter's good graces.

Since winter had fully set in by November 1959, the American County Board football final was put off until the Memorial Day weekend of 1960. Los Angeles was the West Coast Champion and agreed to pay half the cost of the Eire Og airfares so they could compete for the first American County Board Championship.

There was a welcome dance for the Toronto team on Saturday, May 28, at the Sheraton West Hotel in California. The game was scheduled for Sunday, May 29, at the Cantwell High football field in Montebello, California. The game was refereed by former Mayo player, Dr. Pádraig Carney, a resident of Long Beach, California.

The Toronto team's jerseys were maroon and white. Pat Egan was manager and Liam Friel was trainer. Pat Kinsella played goal; the fullback line was Jimmy Slane, Jim McDonogh (Captain) and John Duffy, who had broken the hearts of Montreal fans in late 1959 with his last minute goal. The halfback line had Sean Murtagh, Pat O'Flynn and Tony McKenna. Midfielders were Danny Church and Cyril O'Brien; Ray Logan, Aidan McCormack and Tommy O'Connor played half-forward. Full-forwards were Gerry Campbell, John Murphy and Tony Bambrick. The three subs were Dominic Kilroy, Mike Howley and Pete Kelly.

The Los Angeles team wore blue and white jerseys. They had four priests playing on the team that day, and a chaplain on the sideline! There was some speculation that Toronto wouldn't have a chance because of all the spiritual firepower, but the loss by six points to L.A. spoke well of Toronto's good efforts that day. There was a banquet at the Blarney Castle Restaurant, and a victory dance at the Larchmont Hall where the trophies were presented.

Heydays of the '60s

Toronto was a popular destination for Irish immigrants during the 60s, especially for those who wanted to avoid the US Army draft for the Vietnam War. Another incentive was the fact that the Canadian government assisted skilled immigrants. These factors contributed to the formation of GAA clubs such as St. Vincent's, Clan Na nGael, Garryowen, St. Pat's, St. Mike's, Robert Emmets in Hamilton and the Sean Souths. The pioneer Eire Ogs, who were a selection of Toronto's best throughout the 1950s, and had brought so much pride over the years to the Irish of Toronto, disbanded after the 1961 season.

During these banner years for the GAA in Toronto, the playing venues for games were High Park and Lawrence Park Collegiate. In 1961, an All-Star Toronto football team was formed with the likes of John Duffy, Pat O'Flynn, Aidan McCormack, John O'Brien and Matt Dooley. The team traveled to Iniskeen in Monaghan, Parnell Park in Dublin, Castlebar in Mayo and finally to Kerry, where some hard matches were played.

Dances were held most Saturday nights; one St. Patrick's Day the GAA banquet attracted up to 1,100 people for dinner and 1,300 for the dance afterwards. Those who attended enjoyed the music of Larry McKee and the Shandonairs, along with the famous Tara Show Band featuring Eddie Thornton, one of Toronto's finest hurlers. Some of the ladies connected to these social events included Nora McGuire, Madeline Hurley and Maura Convery.

Sunday, September 1, 1963, was a gala day for the Toronto GAA as they played host to a football and hurling selection from Boston and celebrated the eleventh anniversary of the Association. The organizing committee consisted of Mike Reilly (Westmeath), John Boyle (Donegal), Jim McKenna (Tyrone), Malachy Gribbon (Antrim), Bob Fulton (Dublin), Toronto GAA President Phil Walsh (Waterford), Mike Shanahan (Cork), Kevin Molloy (Dublin), John Shanahan (Cork), Dan Ryan (Kerry), Brian Smith (Antrim), Brendan Keogh (Galway), Larry Morrin (Laois) and Vincent Howard (Limerick).

The order of events at Varsity Stadium included the following: Tug-O-War Semi-Finals, Long Kick – Football, 56lbs. Distance, 100 yd Dash, 1st half of Football, Ladies' 60 yd Dash, 2nd half of Football, 100 yards Veteran's Race (Over 40), Relay Race, Long Puck – Hurling, 1st half of Hurling, Tug-O-War Final and the 2nd half of Hurling. Selections were played by the Toronto GAA Pipe Band during the intervals and the presentation of trophies took place that evening at St. Mary's Hall. The city's television, newspaper and radio media covered the Irish games.

The members of the Toronto football team were: Tom Jones (Kerry) in goal; the fullback line was Andy Byrne (Wicklow), Tony McKenna (Tyrone) and Ron Cooney (Roscommon). The halfback line had Tom Murphy (Cavan), Sean Multagh (Roscommon) and Joe Gogarty (Meath). The midfielders were Brendan McHugh (Sligo) and Jim Egan (Galway); the half-forward line was Tom White (Cavan), Brian McEniff (Donegal) and John Smith (Antrim). The full-forward line had Aiden McCormack (Longford), John Keane (Kerry) and Sean Costello (Dublin). The subs were Des Heffernan (Dublin), Danny Church (Dublin), Des McNabb (Down), Tom Flynn (Armagh), Colum Curry (Cavan) and Danny Columb (Longford). The team manger was John Boyle (Donegal) and the referee for the day was Ray Logan (Antrim).

The members of the Toronto hurling team were: Pat Mahoney (Kerry) in goal; the fullback line was Larry Morrin (Laois), Pat McLaren (Galway) and Eddie O'Brien (Tipperary). The halfback line had Chris Kirby (Limerick), Joe Kennedy (Limerick) and Bill Costelloe (Laois). The midfielders were Pat Joe Brosnan (Kerry) and Matty Woodgate (Kilkenny); the half-forward line was Kieran Larkin (Tipperary), Dermot O'Neill (Dublin) and John Hurley (Cork). The full-forward line had Jim Larkin (Tipperary), Tony Keyes (Tipperary) and Gerry Brosnan (Kerry). The subs were Fred Dillon (Clare), Bill O'Brien (Tipperary), Brendan Daly (Westmeath), Martin Shaughnessy (Kilkenny) and Pat Lanigan (Kilkenny). The team manger was Billy Roche (Limerick) and the referee for the day was Mike Lawlor (Kilkenny).

Toronto's organizing committee wrote at the eleventh anniversary of the founding of the GAA in Toronto: "The growing pains are now gone and at last we have succeeded in acquiring premises of our own at 186 Bay Street. You can enjoy dancing at the Club every Friday, Saturday and Sunday night. A bowling league commences in September each year and attracts hundreds of players to the alleys on Sunday nights. Last winter our band enthusiasts got going and a Pipe Band was formed. These are but some of the ways in which you can enjoy yourself when you join one of the Toronto Clubs."

One of the many highlights enjoyed by Eire Og was an invitation from John 'Kerry' O'Donnell of Gaelic Park, New York, fame in 1963. In a generous gesture, O'Donnell offered Toronto three dollars for every dollar raised by the team for travel expenses. The football team put on a great display against formidable opposition, and the hurlers gave a spirited performance against a star-studded local side—if Toronto fielded six County players, "Nua Eabhrach" had fifteen to match!

In 1964, Mike Reilly of the Garryowen club became President of the Toronto GAA. He was a driving force for the next six years, with the able assistance of Ray Logan (Clan Na nGael), Des McNabb (Clan Na nGael), Aidan O'Brien (Clan Na nGael), Dermott Hogan (Clan Na nGael), Michael Bellew (St. Vincent's) and Dermott "Red" O'Neill (St. Vincent's). The Toronto GAA thrived, and all three clubs fielded junior and senior teams. One highlight was the visit to Toronto by the All-Ireland Hurling Champions from Tipperary in 1964.

Toronto's Shamrock Camogie Team

Madge Galligan (Meath) was the key organizer behind Toronto's Shamrock Camogie team that formed in 1967. The Shamrock's often played the Young Ireland's Camogie team, which was based in Brooklyn, N.Y. The American team suffered continuous losses to the ladies of Toronto from 1968 to 1970. The Young Irelands won the American County Board Championship in 1972 over Toronto, for the Molson Shield, which was the top Camogie award on the continent at that time. The Shamrock's would stop playing in 1974.

Players of these glory years for camogie included Liz O'Grady (Offaly), Agnes McGlade (Tyrone), Francis Keely (Dublin), Kitty O'Toole (Offaly), Kitty Daley (Offaly), Joan and Marie Hamill (Antrim), Bernadette McMahon (Belfast), Joyce Martin (Dublin), Ann Mulvaney (Cavan), Trudie Reelis (Mayo), Kathy Knott (Toronto), Nuala McNamara (Dublin), Bridie Costello (Galway), Alice Jordan (Kilkenny), Maura Leahy (Dublin), Joan Caulfield (Dublin), Anne and Bonnie Coyle (Tyrone), Clare Carty (Offaly), Phyllis Breslin (Dublin), Slyvia Bonnie (Dublin), Patricia Egan (Meath) R.I.P., Dympna McGuinness (Wexford), Margaret Dwyer (Kilkenny), Maureen Walsh (Kilkenny), Bernadette and Sheila Kilcawly (Sligo), Chris McMahon (Clare), Liz Dolan (Meath) and Kitty, Hannah and Mary Murphy (Kilkenny). Kitty (Freely) Murphy served as a captain for a few years and the team was coached by Chris Kirby (Limerick) and Teddy Hurley (Cork) R.I.P.

Sheila and Elizabeth Costello (Toronto) revitalized the game in the early '80s but there were no teams around to compete with and it was very difficult to find players. Those that played were often Canadian born except for a few of the vintage Shamrock players that would kit up. These grand efforts were not able to regain the glory days of the Shamrocks and camogie has become a distant memory.

Hurling

Hurling was in its prime, in Toronto, during the late sixties and early seventies when County players were living in Toronto. Some of these players included the likes of Barney Moylan (Offaly), Patsy Fagan (Westmeath), Paddy Dwyer (Tipperary), Gerry, Brendan and P. J. Brosnan (Kerry).

Characters were plentiful; John Gilligan was a tremendous fullback for St. Vincent's and players like Ray Logan (Antrim), Tommy White (Cavan), Eddie Nevin (Carlow), Paddy Gavigan (Westmeath), Billy Costelloe (Laois), Phil Walsh (Waterford) and Mickey Hamill (Armagh) rounded things out.

In 1968, Toronto's Garryowen hurler and footballer, David Church, was elected Secretary of the North American County Board (NACB) and re-elected in 1969 to serve another term. David and his four brothers were active with the Garryowen club throughout the years.

The 1970s

In 1970, Toronto hosted its first NACB Convention, after Garryowen won another hurling championship that year. The GAA purchased a Scotch Presbyterian Church and Hall, at Landsdowne and College, for $155,000 that year. Unfortunately, zoning and other problems forced the Association to resell it one year later. At the 1972 NCAB convention, a rarity occurred, two Toronto GAA members were elected — Vice-Chairman Brendan Barry and Registrar Frank Murphy. At this time, football and hurling was being played at Northern Secondary High School. The teams that used this field were Garryowen, the Sean Souths, St. Pat's, St. Mike's and St. Vincent's.

In 1973, Detroit won the divisional championships and went on to defeat both Chicago's St. Brendan's and Toronto in the divisional playoffs to qualify for the Senior Football final in Boston. Detroit did the same again in 1975 when they beat Toronto in a semifinal for the senior football championship.

The 1974 NACB convention was held in Canada for the second and final time. The event convened in Hamilton, where the GAA originated with the Robert Emmets club in the early spring of 1966. The year 1974 was significant for Toronto's Garryowen club, as they won their third and final American County Board Hurling championship. The following year, Toronto's St. Michael's won their first hurling championship. A second hurling championship was awarded in 1978; St. Mike's along with members of Toronto's St. Pat's shared in the victory that day.

Toronto's Mike O'Driscoll was elected as American County Board Vice Chairman in 1976 and was re-elected in 1977. He would hold the distinction of being the last Canadian to serve on the executive. Other Canadians in attendance at the 1977 convention meeting in Detroit included Dessy Toner (Clan Na nGael), Noel White and Dan Boland (Sean Souths), Mike Casey (St. Patrick's), D. J. Kellehar (Ottawa Gaels) and Tony McEvoy of St. Mike's. The 1977 Junior Hurling Champions were Toronto's Sean Souths and Junior Football Champions were Toronto's St. Vincent's.

The Toronto league moved their base of operations to Lawrence Park Collegiate and, because of a rental fee, the GAA had to charge admission, which was collected at times by Sean Costelloe Jr. in 1977.

In 1979 in Sarnia, Ontario, a young group of Irishmen, who worked in the chemical industry, formed a junior team. This team was part of the Great Lakes Division that consisted of four teams: Detroit Pádraig Pearse, Michigan Gaels, Sarnia and a hurling club called James Connolly. The Michigan Gaels won the league and went on to play Ottawa in the next round. The Sarnia team was short-lived and some of the players went on to play with Detroit.

In 1981, the Garda Club from Dublin traveled to Toronto to play a selection team in football. Toronto was captained by St. Mike's Eddie Mangan (Dublin) and coached by Brian Farmer (Armagh) and Seamus O'Kane (Derry).

From 1980 onwards, clubs were playing 13 a side football and 11 a side hurling. Sadly, the Toronto GAA went through significant change which included the end of competitive hurling in 1983. As president of the Toronto GAA, the Irish Canadians' Pat Morrison Jr. sent an All-Star team to the North American County Board semifinals in 1985. The team was led by St. Mike's Pádraig Kelly.

The 1989 Toronto GAA executive included Cormac O'Muiri, John Tobin, Tonya Dempsey, Petra Scott, Angela O'Muiri, Gerry Heuston, Billy Millar, Brian Farmer, Patrick Hegarty, Paddy Thornton, Sue Hughes, Danny Columb Jr. and Hugo Straney. A special effort to revive hurling was notable from Larry Sheehan, Kevin Loughnane, Chris Gaffney and Tom Kelly.

1991 Tour

On September 9, 1990 Toronto President Cormac O'Muiri and dedicated GAA members hosted the Tyrone Senior County Champions, Coalisland Fianna. The Toronto Select Captain was Clan Na nGael's Finbarr Sheehan (Cork); Footballer of the Year for the past two years. Unfortunately, it would be Coalisland's Captain, Damian O'Hagan, who would hoist the A & P Dominion Cup from Mr. Brian Dolan R.I.P. (Roscommon).

A year later, Toronto GAA President Sean Harte, Cormac O'Muiri and Brian Farmer would be key catalysts in making the first tour of a Canadian squad to Ireland. The first match of the tour on Saturday, September 14 1991 started with a cheese and wine reception followed by Dublin's famed Artane Boy's Band leading the teams to the Stewart Hospital Grounds to play St. Patrick's of Palmerstown (est. 1961).

With team manager Billy Millar assisted by selectors Brian Farmer and Sean Harte, the following lined out for the Toronto Selection: 1) P. Brady (Dublin), 2) M. O'Brien (Laois), 3) L. Belton (Longford), 4) P. Burns (Cork), 5) Captain C. O'Muiri (Palmerstown) 6) C. Doorley (Offaly), 7) G. McConville (Tyrone), 8) F. Sheehan (Cork), 9) B. Loftus (Ohio, Cleveland), 10) G. Mullane (Limerick), 11) C. McElvanna (Antrim), 12) C. Shields (Dublin), 13) E. O'Boyle (Longford), 14) B. McCreesh (Fermanagh) and 15) P. McElvanna (Antrim).

Substitutes included R. Boyd (Mayo), J. Tobin (Waterford), K. Daly (Ottawa), G. McSweeney (Dublin), M. Callanan (Cork), C. Maguire (Toronto), D. White (Cork), T. Finnigan (Cavan), D. Barr (Tyrone), M. Dullea (Cork), B. Dullea (Cork), S. Hayes (Toronto) and L. Fitzpatrick.

Toronto beat St. Patrick's by nine points on that historic day and many will never forget the gracious hospitality by the Assistant Secretary of the St. Patrick's GAA Club, Seamus O'Muiri R.I.P. (Dublin), who had the added pleasure to watch his son, Cormac, captain the Toronto team to victory. It was a special moment for both father and son that day.

Of added interest was a camogie match that preceded the football where the referee was Phyllis Breslin of St. Brigid's Club in Blanchardstown who was no stranger to Toronto. Phyllis had spent some years in the 60's and 70's living in Toronto where she played camogie with the Shamrock's for a number of years.

The team traveled to play its second game against a West Cork selection from Newcestown. Toronto won the match in wet and soggy conditions on a last minute goal by Tyrone's Danny Barr. The Chairman of Newcestown G.F.C. said it was "a great comeback win from a disciplined and determined Toronto side."

The team stayed at the Munster Arms in Bandon, Cork and for Toronto's Dullea brothers, Finbarr Sheehan and Diarmuid White, being near their home parishes was a vey special time.

On September 29, 1991 at the Fr. Peter Campbell Park in Coalisland, County Tyrone the touring Toronto Selects tried to regain the A & P Dominion Cup back from their hosts. Coalisland put on a show in the days leading up to the match that included a band parade right after the local mass which was headed by the Coalisland Silver Band to the pitch. The match went into overtime and Toronto lost by 3 points. The local 'Tyrone Democrat' noted the surprisingly high standard of play by the men of Toronto.

By the time the team made it to Belfast for a hastily scheduled match versus St. Paul's, a road weary Toronto team lost in a see-saw battle. A sincere comment by the late GAA President, John Dowling, brought a lift to the team as they winged their way home "a very good Toronto Team and capable of competing in any senior league here."

In the 1992 and 1993 playing seasons, the Kitchener Celts participated in the league. Great service was provided by Pat Landy and Gerard Douglas in the short life of this club.

AIB GAA and Dublin Master's Tour

On Monday August 1, 1994, a Toronto select team of over 40's, played the Dublin Masters and won 1-20 to 3-8. With the Dublin team was former GAA President Mick Loftus who had chaired the founding meeting of the Canadian County Board in 1987. The Dublin Masters would travel on to Ottawa where they would win their only match of the Canadian tour.

On Sunday October 2, 1994, a travelling party of 60 or more from the Allied Irish Bank GAA club were hosted by Toronto GAA's President Cormac O'Muiri. AIB's tour had included stops in New York, Chicago and San Francisco. So the Canadian brand of Gaelic Football and hurling that was played that day saw a great display of skill for all to enjoy.

The New Millennium

A Mississauga ladies Gaelic football club was formed in 1999 with Siobhan McQuarry and Gary Flynn providing the leadership for this short lived club. In 2001, a *Toronto Irish News* photograph showed the "Old Brigade" at Centennial Park: Tommy Corcoran, Mike Normoyle, Dan and Jim O'Brien, Paddy Gleeson and Pádraig Kelly lit up the photo.

In 2004, highlights for the Toronto GAA were some exhibition matches that were played with the Irish naval crew of the *L.E. Niamh* in June and with the Garda GAA in October. Activities organized in 2005 included a Toronto GAA hockey challenge between the clubs of East and West Toronto, and an organized indoor Gaelic Football season at the Hangar in Downsview Park. In October 2007, a team from Killalla played a men's team of Toronto all-stars. The cohesive Toronto team easily defeated the visitors from County Mayo.

Youth Development

A Minor Board was formed in 1985 to help develop a youth programme. In 1986, a banner year, four teams competed. All of the participants were Canadian-born and they showed great enthusiasm for the sport. Some of those who assisted or served on the Minor Board included Albert Sloan, Billy Millar (Antrim), Florrie O' Donoghue (Kerry), Frank Smyth, Eddie Mangan, Kevin Loughnane (Offaly), Brendan Rossiter (Dublin), Sean Keogh (Dublin) and Billy McKnight (Belfast).

New York would travel to Toronto to play a Minor Board Select Team on May 24, 1992, and the league continued to thrive up until 1994, when it ceased operations.

In 2002 the game of Gaelic Football was first introduced into the elementary schools in Toronto. A U-14 team traveled to the World Championship in Dublin with the Canadian men's and women's teams. The U-14's gave a great display; they brought home a silver medal for their efforts.

In May 2004, with local interest and assistance provided from Croke Park, coaches from the West-Midlands GAA-Birmingham arrived in Toronto. Simon Pearson worked with twenty elementary and four high schools in the Toronto area, while John Quinn worked with two high schools in Brampton and five high schools in Durham. Chris Bolger and Lisa Mangan headed east to Ottawa, where they provided support to the schools there. Three of the four Toronto-area high schools (Michael Power/St. Joseph, Phillip Pocock and Bishop Allen) participated in a great tournament. The scores were close and the games exciting.

Youth programmes for the GAA, in 2006, occurred every Sunday morning at Centennial Park, starting at 11:00 a.m. Boys and girls, from ages 4 to 16, participated. Through May and June, students in elementary and high schools were given instruction during Physical Education classes. They also had the opportunity to represent their school at tournaments run by the Toronto GAA.

In late May, the high school tournament was held at Centennial Park. Former St. Pat's player Pat Grant, a teacher at Bishop Allen, ran training sessions after school and coached his team to a championship in the boy's division. The girl's coach at Philip Pocock, Adriana Fennelli, involved with the programme for a few years and a player with Durham, coached her school's team and they won the girls' division championship.

An elementary school tournament was held at L'Amoreaux Park in Scarborough for the East End Schools, and in Centennial Park for the West End schools. In the East End, St. Joachim emerged victorious in the junior and senior boys' division, while St. Malachy was crowned champion in the girls' division. Katya Gauci coached the St. Joachim teams—no doubt she got some pointers from watching St. Mike's and her husband Pat Leahy play. The team from St. Malachy was coached by former Clan Na nGael player John Cawley. St. John Vianney continued their dominance in the West End by winning both the boys' and girls' divisions. They beat young squads from Regina Mundi in both finals. Many of the participating students expressed interest in playing with the Toronto GAA and some will, one day, realize their dreams.

National Games Development Officer, Paul Loughnane, made contact with other schools during his tenure; these included Havergal, St. Mary's in Cobourg, Dante Alighieri, St. Mike's College, Neil McNeill and Cardinal Newman.

In 2007, very successful youth programmes were being developed with the Durham "Shamrocks" and Brampton "Rebels." Parents looking for an affordable activity that would keep their children active have been able to find it, due to the commitment of GAA supporters in these regions.

In 2008, the appointment of Lorraine Morley as a National Games Development Liaison will be supported by the efforts of Regional Development Officers Lorraine White (Durham), Damian Higgins (Brampton) and Mark Lannin (Ottawa).

Continental Youth Championships

Since 2004, Jarlath Connaughton from Ottawa has served on the Steering Committee of the O'Neill's Continental Youth Championships (CYC). As a result, Ottawa and Toronto have had representative teams compete in the championships in New York '04, San Francisco '05, Boston '06 and Chicago '07. Paul Loughnane has served as a referee at a number of these championships, along with Ottawa's Mark Lannin and Dermot Guinnane and Vancouver's John O'Flynn. 2008 will see Canadian youth from Toronto and Ottawa participating in Philadelphia for the fifth CYC.

Today

The Toronto Divisional Board of the Gaelic Athletic Association (GAA) is a volunteer, not-for-profit organization that oversees and maintains the membership and game of Gaelic Football in Toronto, Ottawa and Montreal. There are a total of eight men's and five ladies' teams. The clubs are the Brampton Roger Casements, Durham Robert Emmets, Michael Cusacks' Ladies, Ottawa Gaels, Montreal Shamrocks, St. Vincent's, St. Mike's, St. Pat's and the Toronto Gaels. The volunteers organize tournaments, league games, coordinate referees, and instill a passion for sport and fun. All league games are played in a public park called Centennial in Etobicoke, a suburb of Toronto. The games are played on Sunday afternoons from May through September, except for those games played in Ottawa and Montreal. Centennial Park is a huge open space with a hill at the side and a few benches on the other. A cultural space for the Irish!

Those that are leading Toronto's way into 2008 include Mike O'Driscoll, Stephen Owens, Gabriel Hurl, Kathleen Keenan, Alan Martina, Ronan Matthews, Damian Higgins, Mark Lannin and Kieran Ryan.

Toronto GAA Presidents

1961 Mike Walsh	1962 John St. Clair
1963 Phil Walsh (Waterford)	1964 Michael Reilly (Westmeath)
1965 Michael Reilly	1966 Michael Reilly
1967 Michael Reilly	1968 Michael Reilly
1969 Michael Reilly	1970 Michael Reilly
1971 Michael Reilly	1972 Tom Kelly (Galway)
1973 Tony Lee (Kerry)	1974 Brendan Barry (Dublin)
1975 Brendan Barry	1976 Brendan Barry
1977 Mike O'Driscoll (Cork)	1978 Mike O'Driscoll
1979 Mike O'Driscoll	1980 Brian Farmer
1981 Pat Donnelly (Antrim)	1982 John McGlynn (Tyrone)
1983 Dermot Ryan	1984 Paddy Morrison Jr.
1985 Paddy Morrison Jr.	1986 John Horgan
1987 Paul Kennedy (Dublin)	1988 Cormac O'Muiri
1989 Cormac O'Muiri	1990 Cormac O'Muiri
1991 Sean Harte	1992 Sean Harte
1993 Enda McGuinness	1994 Cormac O'Muiri
1995 Billy Millar	1996 Mick Burke
1997 Bridget Burke	1998 Matt Healy
1999 Pat Donnelly (Antrim)	2000 Pat Donnelly
2001 Klaus Oberparleiter (Toronto)	2002 Cormac Monaghan
2003 Cormac Monaghan	2004 Cormac Monaghan
2005 Paul Loughnane (Toronto)	2006 Sinead Canavan (Toronto)
2007 Sinead Canavan	2008 Mike O'Driscoll

North American County Board Senior Hurling Championships

1961 Montreal Shamrocks	1965 Garryowen
1970 Garryowen	1974 Garryowen
1975 St. Mike's	1978 St. Mike's/St. Pat's

Toronto Men's Football Champion		Men's Football League Winner
2007	St. Vincent's	Durham
2006	St. Mike's	St. Mike's
2005	Durham	St. Mike's
2004	St. Mike's	St. Mike's
2003	St. Vincent's	Durham
2002	St. Vincent's	St. Mike's
2001	St. Mike's	St. Mike's
2000	St. Mike's	St. Vincent's
1999	St. Mike's	Toronto Gaels
1998	St. Mike's	St. Mike's
1997	St. Mike's	St. Mike's
1996	St. Mike's	St. Mike's
1995	St. Mike's	St. Mike's
1994	Toronto Gaels	Toronto Gaels
1993	Durham	Durham
1992	St. Vincent's	Ottawa
1991	St. Vincent's	St. Mike's/Clan Na nGael
1990	Toronto Gaels	St. Mike's
1989	Clan Na nGael	Toronto Gaels
1988	Clan Na nGael	Toronto Gaels
1987	St. Pat's	Toronto Gaels
1986	St. Mike's	Clan Na nGael
1985	St. Pat's	St. Mike's
1984	St. Mike's	St. Vincent's
1983	St. Vincent's	St. Vincent's
1982	Clan Na nGael	St. Vincent's
1981	Clan Na nGael	St. Vincent's
1980	Clan Na nGael	St. Mike's
1979	St. Mike's	
1978	Garryowen	St. Mike's
1977	St. Mike's	St. Mike's
1976	St. Mike's	
1975	Garryowen	
1974	St. Mike's	Clan Na nGael
1973	St. Mike's	
1972	Garryowen	
1971	Garryowen	
1970	Clan Na nGael	
1969	Garryowen	Clan Na nGael
1968	Garryowen	
1967	Garryowen	
1966	Clan Na nGael	Clan Na nGael
1965	Garryowen	Clan Na nGael

1964	Garryowen	
1963	Clan Na nGael	Clan Na nGael
1962	Clan Na nGael	Clan Na nGael

Toronto Ladies' Football Champion	**Ladies' Football League Winner**
2007 Ottawa	Durham
2006 Ottawa	Ottawa
2005 Michael Cusacks	Michael Cusacks
2004 Ottawa	Ottawa
2003 Michael Cusacks	Michael Cusacks
2002 Ottawa	Ottawa
2001 Ottawa	Ottawa
2000 Durham	Ottawa & Michael Cusacks
1999 Ottawa	Durham
1998 Durham	Durham
1997 Durham	Le Cheile
1996 Le Cheile	Le Cheile
1995 Le Cheile	Le Cheile
1994 Le Cheile	Ottawa Gaels
1993 Le Cheile	Michael Cusacks
1992 Le Cheile	Le Cheile
1991 Le Cheile	Le Cheile
1990 Le Cheile	Le Cheile
1989 Le Cheile	Irish Canadians
1988 Le Cheile	Irish Canadians

2007 Toronto GAA Individual Awards

Under 14 player of the year (Male): sponsored by Danny Quail Masonry, **Brian Ast**, Brampton Roger Casements;

Under 14 player of the year (Female): sponsored by Danny Quail Masonry, **Mary Fabris,** Brampton Roger Casements;

Under 21 player of the year: (Female) sponsored by the Toronto GAA, **Elizabeth Sheridan,** Brampton Roger Casements;

Under 21 player of the year (Male): sponsored by The Toronto GAA, **David Gallagher,** St. Pat's;

Senior Men's player of the year: sponsored by Grace O'Malley's Irish Pub, **Ken Ray,** St. Vincent's;

Senior Ladies player of the year: sponsored by Grace O'Malley's Irish Pub, **Daphne Ballard,** Ottawa Gaels;

GAA Person of the Year: sponsored by Ireland Canada Chamber of Commerce, **Damian Higgins**, Brampton Roger Casements;

Senior Merit Award: sponsored by McGlynn and Sparrow, **Eddie Mangan,** Durham Robert Emmets.

2007 Grace O'Malley's Irish Pub Toronto Ladies' All-Stars

Anto Marsden, Noreen Gordon, Sarah Callanan and Leslie Zamich of the Michael Cusacks; Ashley Visser, Abbie Visser, Lorraine White, Erinn Lynch and Heather Woodward of the Durham Robert Emmets; Lisa Connaughton, Daphne Ballard, Lisa Langevin and Dawn Price of the Ottawa Gaels; Sinead McElvanna and Ciara Fitzsimmons of St. Mike's.

2007 Grace O'Malley's Irish Pub Toronto Men's All-Stars

Barry Farmer, Colum Savage and Sean Mangan of the Durham Robert Emmets; Shane Boyd, Sean Egan, Ken Ray, Tom Curtin and John Paul Horgan of St. Vincent's; Ruairi O'Brien, Tommy Keane, Pat Leahy, Paul Loughnane and Edwin Walsh of St. Mike's; Kieran Ryan of St. Pat's and Dermot Guinnane of the Ottawa Gaels.

2006 Galway Arms Toronto Men's All Stars

Barry Farmer, Durham Robert Emmets; Doug O'Connor, Ottawa Gaels; Thomas Keane, St. Mike's; Noel McGinnity, Ottawa Gaels; Kieran Ryan, St. Pat's; Ken Ray, St. Vincent's; Paul Loughnane, St. Mike's; Colum Savage, Durham Robert Emmets; Oliver O'Hanlon, Ottawa Gaels; Pat Leahy, St. Mike's; Dermot Guinnane, Ottawa Gaels; Edwin Walsh, St. Mike's; Bryon Mallon, Brampton Roger Casements; Damian Higgins, Brampton Roger Casements; John Creery, Durham Robert Emmets.

2006 Galway Arms Toronto GAA Ladies' All Stars

Anto Marsden, Michael Cusacks; Noreen Gordon, Michael Cusacks; Ashley Visser, Durham Robert Emmets; Lisa Connaughton, Ottawa Gaels; Heather Woodard, Durham Robert Emmets; Lisa Langevin, Ottawa Gaels; Lesley Zamojcz, Michael Cusacks; Daphne Ballard, Ottawa Gaels; Erin Gallagher, Michael Cusacks; Sinead Whelehan, St. Mike's; Sarah Callanan, Michael Cusacks; Dawn Price, Ottawa Gaels; Siobhan O'Muiri, St. Mike's; Erinn Lynch, Durham Robert Emmets; Kathleen Keenan, Brampton Roger Casements.

2006 Toronto GAA Individual Awards

Under 14: Sarah Fabris, Brampton Rebels; James Kenny, Brampton Rebels
Under 21: Siobhan O'Muiri, St. Mike's; Edward Donnelly, Toronto Gaels
Senior Ladies' MVP: Sinead Whelehan, St. Mike's
Senior Men's MVP: Dermot Guinnane, Ottawa Gaels
Senior Merit: Ben Smith, St. Vincent's
GAA Person of the Year: Lorraine Morley, Michael Cusacks

2005 Kemptville Travel GAA All Stars—Men

(Goal) J.P. Swaminathan, Brampton Roger Casements; (fullback) Thomas Keane, St. Mike's; Paul Reid, Toronto Gaels; Michael Silva, St. Mike's; (halfback) Doug O'Connor, Ottawa Gaels; Paul Loughnane, St. Mike's; Ken Ray, St. Vincent's; (midfielder) Oliver O'Hanlon, Ottawa Gaels; Colum Savage, Durham Robert Emmets; (half-forward) Darren Farmer, Durham Robert Emmets; Mike Hamill, Durham Robert Emmets; Damian Higgins, Brampton Roger Casements; (forward) Ned Flynn, Ottawa Gaels; Edwin Walsh, St. Mike's; John Creery, Durham Robert Emmets.

2005 Kemptville Travel GAA All Stars—Ladies

(Goal) Ashley Visser, Durham Robert Emmets; (fullback) Maureen Keane, Michael Cusacks; Celeste Morgan, Michael Cusacks; Stephanie Fitzpatrick, Durham Robert Emmets; (halfback) Noreen Gordon, Michael Cusacks; Lisa Langevin, Ottawa Gaels; Sinead Fitzsimons, St. Mike's; (midfield) Daphne Ballard, Ottawa Gaels; Erin Gallagher, Michael Cusacks; (half-forward) Kathleen Keenan, Brampton Roger Casements; Sarah Callanan, Michael Cusacks; Sharon Higgins, Brampton Roger Casements; (forward) Elaine Gilmore, Montreal Shamrocks; Erinn Lynch, Durham Robert Emmets; Siobhan McQuarrie, St. Mike's.

Toronto G.A.A. Woman's MVP Winners

1988 Bernadette Tuite & Lori Nawrocki	1989 Geraldine Heaney
1990 Geraldine Heaney & Maureen Looney	1991 Julia Hughes & Noreen O'Shea

ST. VINCENT'S

On November 27, 1959, a small group of young Irishmen gathered in the basement of 27 Galley Avenue, which was located in the Parish of St. Vincent dePaul in Toronto. This was where one of Toronto's first Gaelic Athletic Clubs was formed, on the 75th anniversary of the founding of the GAA in Thurles, and aptly named St. Vincent's Hurling and Gaelic Football Club.

That day in November, President Phil Walsh, Secretary Larry Morrin, and Treasurer Jim Kelly were selected by Con Barrett, Danny Columb, Bill Costello, Louis Delaney, Bill Farrell, John Gilligan, Maurice Houlihan, Vince Howard, Ricky Leahy, Bill Lehane, Paul McMahon, Eddie O'Brien, Jim O'Brien, Dermot (Red) O'Neill, Harold Parker, Martin Shaugnessy and Phil Walsh.

The team jerseys were donated by Louis Delaney and Paul McMahon, two Canadians of Irish descent. Nora McGuire, who was a dressmaker by trade, sewed the first set of shorts and mended shirts when needed. The first club banquet was held at the Canadian Hotel on Dundas Street. Women such as Lena Columb, Janet Barrett, Kathleen O'Brien, Kay Boyle, Ann Mulhall, Ann Callaghan, Ethel Costelloe, Doreen Hayes and Virginia McIntyre often catered the food for all club socials and dances.

Hurling Successes

St. Vincent's was a resounding success in hurling during the 1960s. In a six-year period, captained by Eddie O'Brien, St. Vincent's captured six league and five championships. O'Brien would win 21 medals playing for Toronto and St. Vincent's. A Toronto select team photo from the '60s was comprised mainly of St. Vincent players. The photo included Larry Morrin, Pat Lannigan, Phil Walsh, Maurice Houlihan, Stan Maher, Pat McLaren, Danny Roach, Tony Keyes, Dermot "Red" O'Neil, Brendan Power, Oliver Gilligan, Bill Costello, Mike O'Leary (Trainer), Johnny Hurley, Jim O'Brien, P. J. Brosnan, Eddie O'Brien, Danny Columb, Jimmy Larkin and Gerry Brosnan.

A founding father of the St. Vincent's Club, Jim O'Brien, wrote the following poem after a classic Championship hurling match with Garryowen:

St. Vincent's Song

The 3rd of September was the day of the year
When Garryowen and St. Vincent's once more did appear
For the championship of Toronto in old Toronto Town,
When the laurels of Garryowen, St. Vincent's brought down.

Just about 3 o'clock at the venue we found
About 50 spectators had gathered around
When Garryowen came on for to die or to do
And the colour they wore was that famous light blue.

Next came St. Vincent's, men of great fame,
In the States and throughout Canada had earned their name,
Led on by the Captain, so fearless and bold
And arrayed in their jersey the Green and the Gold.

Now that day in High Park sure the sight it was grand.
As the two teams lined up at the rear of the band.
And to march to the line like their fathers of old.
We felt proud of St. Vincent's the Green and the Gold.

As the teams lined up and the backs they went out.
The bookies grew hoarse as for bets they did shout,
"Even money—St. Vincent's" we soon heard them say
That the Champions of Toronto would carry the day.

Then the ball was thrown in and they started to play,
With the championship of Toronto in battle array
And the old rocky mountains re-echoed each clash,
Every hit on the ball, every clash of the ash.

Now these Garryowen lads pressed St. Vincent's all round,
But a stubborn resistance they very soon found,
From Larry Morrin and Con Barrett, the pride of a pack.
And St. Vincent's fit athletes they soon drove them back.

Then a foul on the right was St. Vincent's a free
The ball was soon placed by that good referee.
Red O'Neill rose and struck it, good Lord it did soar
And it crossed o'er the bar for St. Vincent's first score.

Now the tackling was keen and the hurling was fast,
We had thrills here in plenty right up to the last,
One fierce rush by Garryowen our backs failed to stave
But that gallant Eddie O'Brien made a marvellous save.

Now the work done by Columb at mid-field was grand,
And the cheers for that hero that came from the stand,
Will live in our memory until we are dead,
And the crimson-stained bandage he wore 'round his head.

And here's to you Kennedy and long may you reign.
You were the pride of Toronto and the star of the game,
And to you Martin Shaugnessy we'll never forget,
That grand pass from John Gilligan you banged to the net.

Three goals & seven points when the long whistle blew
To the spot where our flag lay unfurled we flew,
We flocked 'round our heroes and wished them good cheer,
And be champions of Toronto for many a year.

Now my tale is unfolded, the end it is near,
But one thing is certain; there's no cause to fear,
And the heart in our bosom will never grow cold,
While the stalwarts of ours wear the Green and the Gold.

Annual trips to Ottawa and Montreal, as well as treks to American ports of call—Pittsburgh, Cleveland, New York, Detroit and Boston—meant that many bonds of friendship were formed. Especially on the bus trips where confined spaces, long hauls, characters, decision making, even the odd explosion of frustrations meant that club members were more than friends; they were family in the fullest sense of the word.

The 1970s

An early '70s exhibition football game was played between Cleveland and St. Vincent's; the visitors won 25-16. One highlight included reaching the semifinals in 1972 with an 11-10 win over St. Mike's. Paddy Columb led St. Vincent's with a goal and a point.

Eamonn Boyle scored three singles, Ben Smith got two and Joe Cassidy and Pat Kelly had one apiece. Seamus Kane was the top scorer for St. Mike's with a goal. Frank Smith, Bill Flanagan and Dermot Coleman each scored two points and Mickey Hamill booted a single.

In 1976 in Syracuse, N.Y., St. Vincent's achieved their greatest accomplishment to date, when they became winners of the North American Board Junior Championship. They defeated the New Haven Gaelic Football club. St. Vincent's outstanding footballer for that decade was Joe Cassidy.

With the arrival of more emigrants, the ladies' committee was strengthened with the addition of Liz McEntire, Libby Mulgrew, Noelle Harte, Noreen Carolan, Ann McCallion, Margaret Lucey, Joan Burns, Margaret Keogh and Marion Sheridan. Maureen Horgan washed sweaters for many a season, as did Patsy Smith, but the most famous laundry mistress was Mrs. Aine "Coach" Kelly. She washed the gear so often that at one AGM it was proposed by her son, Wayne, that the club buy a washer and dryer for his mom!

Mary McGlynn kept watch at the door, on numerous occasions, and if one tried to get in without a ticket, "Watch out!" Mary Fay was a great writer and correspondent; she chronicled the history of the club through her famous newsletters.

The Fay, McKenna and McGlynn Cups

In a continuing effort to maintain friendship and camaraderie, St. Vincent's organized card parties and pub nights. One thing not wanting in the club was the member support. Whether it was babies' births, milestone birthdays, illnesses or bad spells, moving away or coming home, St. Vincent's looked after their friends.

St. Vincent's, and indeed all GAA clubs, were good to their own in times of need. In the space of 10 years, two young families who had immigrated to Canada were robbed of their fathers by sudden death. The bereaved widows with young children were offered loving and heartfelt support by the members of St. Vincent's. In addition, their husbands were remembered through the games in the form of memorial trophies—the Sean McKenna Cup was established in 1973 and the Maurice Fay Cup was established in 1977.

In 1994, Ed McGlynn died prematurely at the age of 33. In a loving tribute from father to beloved son, John McGlynn established the Ed McGlynn Memorial Cup, which is now awarded annually to the club's Footballer of the Year.

Youth Development

In 1979, while the veterans continued to compete in the park Sunday after Sunday, dads began teaching their sons to play the game. Danny Columb, Sean Harte, Jimmy Hayes, Mike Holly and Cormac O'Muiri taught the boys Gaelic Football. These activities were to develop into the Juvenile Programme under the tutelage and guidance of Billy Millar. Young boys, from the age of nine and up, joined the Juvenile Programme and this led to the establishment of the Minor Board in 1984. Some club members, including Wayne Kelly, who came up through the minor programme, were chosen to travel with the Canadian Men's Team to the international tournaments in Ireland.

Players who provided great leadership during these years for St. Vincent's included John Sharkey, Pat Kelly, Jim Garrity, Joe Gogerty, Ben Smith, Eddie Brett and John Horgan (Meath).

The '80s and '90s

Irish nannies started to arrive on the scene during the 1980s, often coming to Canada for a year or two of experience. Young men planned four- or five-year stints in Canada to raise capital with a view to returning to their homeland. Some of these Irishmen and women stayed: Teresa Kerr, Patricia O'Callaghan-Molloy, Kerry Nolan, Terry Cassidy, Rose Egan and Valerie Kelly. The women were able to carry on the tradition of a strong ladies' presence in the club.

St. Vincent's football successes in the 1980s were many. For the first three seasons, 1980 to 1983, St. Vincent's won the league. This success culminated in August 1983 when they won the elusive "double" with nine Canadian-born players on the panel. The score was 2-9 to 2-7 over Clan Na nGael. Players of note during that Championship victory were goalkeeper John Horgan, John McElvanny, Finbar Collins, Paddy Cullen and Joe Cassidy.

25 years and Micheal O'Hehir

For the club's 25th anniversary celebration in 1984, which was held at the Irish Canadian Aid and Cultural Society on DuPont Street, they won another "double" in football. It was a joyous reunion of founding fathers and a time for great nostalgia.

January 25, 1985, was a major day in Toronto when a press release announced the visit of the one and only Micheal O'Hehir. The release stated, "The most reputable voice in sports in Ireland ... an institution in European broadcasting ... the legendary figure representative of true journalistic skill." St. Vincent's GAA were the proud organizers of this event with John McGlynn, Seamus Mulgrew and Sean Harte at the helm. In O'Hehir's honour, they held a buffet and dance at the Rio Banquet Hall in Weston, Ontario.

The press release continued, "Not only did Micheal O'Hehir cover sports reporting, but he was called upon to cover other major events, including John F. Kennedy's historic visit to Ireland. He was the voice of 99 All-Ireland Finals between 1938 and 1985. His personal objective of dedicated broadcasting proved to be a major asset to the ever-demanding world of journalism.

Gaelic Developments

St. Vincent's was beaten in both the league and championship finals in 1986, but the team worked hard to maintain its strengths. Trips to the Catskill Mountains to play New York's Longford Club became an annual treat for St. Vincent's and friends. One year, when St. Vincent's was captained by Niall Bracken, they lost by two points to Longford after leading by five points late in the second half; they missed a penalty with seconds to go in the match.

In 1987 St. Vincent's were the McKenna Cup and Fay Cup winners and a team photo included Seamus Mulgrew, Patsy Sheridan, President John Horgan, Mike Costello, Liam Carroll, John O'Connell, Ray Tierney, Finbar Collins, Ken Kerr, Stuart Neely, Noel Casey, Peter Sheridan and Wayne Kelly. Missing from the team photo were J.J. O'Loughlin, Vice President Ben Smith, Secretary Mary Fay, Coaches Joe Kelly and Liam Callaghan and Past President John McGlynn.

Behind the scenes in Canada there was hard work going on in the larger GAA circles. For several years, John Horgan and John McGlynn endeavoured to establish ties between Canada and the heart of the GAA in Croke Park. St. Vincent's was proud to have had strong representation of its members among the Canadian leaders. The likes of Sean Harte, Danny Columb, Dan Ryan, John Molloy (Louth), Ken Kerr (Louth), Joe Kelly (Carlow), Niall Murphy (Dublin), Eamonn Boyle, Brad Reagan and the first club President, Phil Walsh.

Many daughters of club members have grown up to play Gaelic Football. These include June Callaghan, Aisling Smith, Orla Smith, Sinead Smith, Erin Horgan and Louise Sheridan.

St. Vincent's entered the '90s strong and confident. The Toronto Gaels defeated the club in the 1990 championship, but they bounced back to take the Gaels in the 1991 championship semifinal. St. Vincent's went on to defeat Clan Na nGael in a closely fought final in which Paddy Burns scored a last minute goal to clinch it for the lads in "Green and Gold" by a single point. An ecstatic Seamus Mulgrew lifted the championship cup that year.

In 1992, St. Vincent's defeated a strongly fancied Ottawa team in the championship semifinal. They followed this up by winning the final over St. Mike's—Martin (Frankie) Conway scored the magic point. The years 1993 and 1994 were equally good for St. Vincent's and their lineup of energetic and lively young footballers kept the club proud.

A lull for the club occurred during the 1995 and 1996 seasons, yet John Molloy was rewarded for his service with the GAA Person of the Year award in 1995. St. Vincent's returned to form in 1997 when the club reached the championship semifinal, yet again against St. Pat's. They won the match after playing in the quarterfinals against Durham less than 24 hours earlier. Another highlight for the club included winning the Owen Nolan Tournament in 1998, and Dinny Cahalane was named the GAA Player of the Year.

40th Anniversary

On March 27, 1999, the club celebrated its 40th anniversary with a banquet. The guest of honour was Meath football legend and All Star, Colm O'Rourke. In the souvenir brochure, the club remembered those who had passed on to their eternal reward. These members included Sean McKenna, Maurice and Greta Fay, Andy Byrne, Phil Walsh, Edward McGlynn, Dan Ryan, John Gilligan, Rick Leahy and Bill O'Connor.

Millennium Championships

In the new millennium, the club won the 2000 League and they followed up with 2001 and 2002 championship banners. The years 2005 and 2006 were good to the club with Denis Leyne tournament trophies to add to their mantle piece.

In the 2007 Toronto GAA Men's Championship match, the perceived underdog was St. Vincent's, who had placed second in League play. They played a highly fancied St. Mike's team. With 16 Championships and 15 League wins since 1965, St. Mike's had been on a mighty roll throughout the 2007 Toronto Championships with victories over powerhouse Durham and the Toronto Gaels.

In the first half of the Championship match, taking a halftime lead 1-5 to 0-3, St. Vincent's Toronto-born Sean Egan contributed 1-4. Midfielder Phillip O'Donnell (Donegal) and the Longford Slasher's Aidan Gillarahan played "out of their skins," according to St. Vincent's Coach John Molloy.

St. Mike's Championship hopes took a blow with the loss of Toronto-born Paul Loughnane at the cornerback early in the first half. St Vincent's added only one more point in the second half, but the first half damage proved vital as St. Vincent's won 1-6 to 0-7. St. Mike's saw inspirational second half play from Toronto's Dave Kinahan and Kerry's Pat Leahy, but it was a losing cause.

St. Vincent's Coach John Molloy was over the moon after the victory and acknowledged that the team had lost its first-half strength. Still, they hung on in the second half, despite the fact that St. Mike's pushed hard in the final minutes. Since the club's founding in 1959, this was the sixth Toronto Championship for St. Vincent's; they also won five League banners. St. Vincent's looks forward to the future with an enhanced team of great players, including the leaders of 2008 - Uachtaran: Gabriel Hurl; Leas Uachtaran: Shane Boyd; Runai: Ken Ray and PRO/Registrar: Sean Egan along with the support of the old guard who keep things going in the background.

GARRYOWEN

There is no doubt that one of the celebrated clubs in Toronto GAA history was the Garryowen club. They won three NACB Senior Hurling Championships in 1965, 1970 and 1974. The club was formed in 1959 and early members included Pat Joe Brosnan (Kerry) and Cork's Mike O'Leary (first President); other club Presidents were: Tommy

White (Cavan), Paddy Fagan (Westmeath) Colum Curry (Cavan) and Mike Reilly (Westmeath). Mike Reilly also served, capably, as the Toronto GAA President from 1964 to 1970.

Other notable members included Eddie Nevin (Carlow), Seamus Lavery (Antrim), Paddy Burns (Kildare), John Shannon (Cavan), Tony Moran (Cavan), Dermot McCarthy (Cork), B. Slevin, Mickey Gordon (Meath), John Woods (Meath), Mickey Doherty (Donegal), David and Danny Church (Dublin), John Boyle (Donegal), Billy Roche (Limerick), Phil McCotter (Derry), Jack Balfe (Kildare), Mike Byrne (Kildare), Tony McKenna (Tyrone), Albert Sloan, Pat Donnelly and Gerry Flanagan.

Hurling players of 1970 included goalie Pat Mahoney (Kerry); Tom Connolly (Galway); Tom Deniffe; Gerry Brosnan, R.I.P. (Kerry); Pat Gavigan (Westmeath); Tony Lenihan; P.J. Noone; Eddie Thornton (Westmeath); Paddy Fagan (Westmeath); Tom Dermody (Tipperary); Jimmy McVeigh, of Windsor House fame; present-day San Francisco residents Pat Joe Brosnan (South City), footballer Kevin O'Shea (Fermanagh), Joe Uniacke (Limerick-San Francisco), Joe Casey (Kerry-San Francisco) and Glen Fitzsimons (Daly City).

Garryowen fielded football teams that won nine Toronto championships between 1964 and 1978. A Garryowen panel team that played on September 2, 1967, at Montreal's Expo included M. McTeer, A. O'Brien, D. Hogan, E. O'Leary, B. Egan, P. Byrne, D. McCarthy, T. Flynn, L. McIlwee, K. O'Shea, T. Moran, A. Henderson, B. Gilroy, O. McInro, M. Hamill, D. Coleman, F. Smith, B. Slevin, D. Columb and E. Barry. In 1971, the team lost a NACB semifinal match in Philadelphia to the Philadelphia Tyrones.

In June 1973, Garryowen won both its hurling and football games against St. Mike's in the junior league. The hurlers won 20-6 and the footballers won 14-2. Gerry Mangan and Dan Kavanagh scored two goals each in the hurling, while J.B. Kelly and Kevin Dunne had a goal each for St. Michael's.

In the football match, Tommy White, Alan Henderson and Mike Gordon each scored goals for Garryowen. Mike Normoyle and J.B. Kelly each scored a point for St. Mike's. The standard of Garryowen football was excellent throughout the years. In 1984 the historic Garryowen ceased as a club.

CLAN Na nGAEL

In 1961 a third team was formed and joined St. Vincent's and Garryowen in Toronto. With Eire Og team connections, the founding members of the club (renamed Clan Na nGael in 1962) were Mike Walsh R.I.P. (Galway) who was the club's first president; Des McNabb (Down); Brendan Power R.I.P. (Limerick); Bob Fulton (Dublin); Ray Logan (Antrim); Tom Walsh (Mayo) and the late Frank Murphy (Newmarket, Cork).

Wearing the colours of Cork, the club thrived right from the start. From Kilkenny came hurler Pat Lannigan and Mike Lawlor, Ron Cooney, Kevin Larkin, hurler Johnny Hurley

(Cork) and from St. Vincent's, Sean Costello. Sean would serve as player, coach, manager, president, financier, employer and general factotum during the life of the club. His brother Tony also served in a variety of capacities including team manager for a number of years.

The Club's first trophy was the championship in 1962. The game was played at Earlscourt Park. Two additions to the team that day were the newly arrived Brian McEniff and John Rooney, R.I.P. (Sligo). Brian McEniff played on four championship and league winning teams, until he left for home in 1965 due to his father's passing. McEniff's sons later made their own pilgrimages to Canada in the years that followed and they played on Clan Na nGael's teams. A fitting tribute and acknowledgement towards Canada's GAA scene was when McEniff brought the Sam McGuire Trophy to Toronto in 1993, where it was fêted during a memorable weekend. Brian, an hotelier from Bundoran, had managed Donegal's All-Ireland football victory in 1992.

Mike O'Driscoll

In the early 70s, Skibbereen born Mike O'Driscoll was a major influence, an outstanding contributor and a fine dual player. Mike has done every job and filled every position in the club from player to coach, he has been manager, president, secretary, treasurer, referee and delegate; he was even chairman of the Toronto Board for a few years and for the North American Board. Once again, in 2008, Mike has taken on the role of Toronto GAA President.

'60s and '70s

Players who are remembered from the '60s and '70s include Dermot Hogan, Pat Kehoe, Jack Callinan, Simon McNamara, John Cawley (Cork), Jimmy and Billy Egan (Ballinsaloe, Galway), Brendan McHugh (Donegal), Aidan O'Brien (Dublin), Brendan Holly (Antrim), Jim Long (Cork), John Hearne (Waterford), Matt McAteer (Down), Jim and Ciaran Larkin (Limerick), Lua and Sean Ryan (Tipperary), Christy and Brendan Daly (Offaly), Sean Conroy (Offaly), Liam Keely (Dublin), John Byrne, Eamonn Monaghan (Dublin), Paddy Monaghan (Longford), Terry Little (Dublin); Aonghus O'Leary, R.I.P. (Kerry); Bob Fulton and Frank McElroy (Tyrone), Sean Cooper and Sean Comerford, R.I.P. (Wicklow); Mike and Tommy Walsh (Mayo), Joe McNulty (Armagh), Jim Graham (Armagh), Tom Dwane and Joe Roche (Kilkenny), Pat McClaren and Larry Sheehan (Galway), Stan Maher (Clare), Brendan Power (Limerick), Liam McCartan (Down), Gerry O'Donoghue (Kerry), Mike McGrath and Ken Reid (Tipperary), Joe Murphy (Cork), Pearse Walsh (Mayo), Jim Mimnagh (Longford), Liam Kerr and Dessie Toner (Armagh), Bobby and Tommy Mulvey (Leitrim), Neil Duggan (Cork), Seamus Keown (Down), Stephen Rice (Down), Shay McCafferty (Antrim), Clem Fitzsimons (Down), Steven Kane (Down), Damien Watson (Down), Ciaran O'Driscoll and D.J. Kelleher (Cork), the Treacys from Tipperary, Emmanual Canavan (Down), Declan Lynch (Dublin), Liam Kerr (Armagh) and Jim McAleer (Tyrone).

The Costello crew contributed from the '70s to the mid '90s, including Robert and Sean (not forgetting Sheila and Eileen); and Maureen and Tony's son, Joe. Danny Pankhurst, Jim Scott, Brian Weir and Charlie Maguire are Canadians that made many contributions over the years. In addition, Ken Murphy (Dublin) and Pat Morrison Jr. (Mayo) made many positive contributions to the Toronto GAA.

'80s and '90s

A 1980 team photo included Joe Walsh (Toronto), Niall Duggan (Cork), Pat Morrison (Mayo), Jim Fitzgerald (Kerry), Sean Byrne (Dublin), Jim Parks (Antrim), Leo McKee (Antrim), D.J. Kelleher (Cork), Mark McElheeny (Cavan), Manual Canavan (Antrim), S. Costello (Galway), Tony Costello (Kildare), Des Lynch (Dublin), S. Costello (Toronto), Bob Mulvey (Leitrim), Tommy Mulvey (Leitrim), Des Toner (Armagh), Matt McAteer (Down), Brendan Keenan (Down) and John Fitzgerald (Kerry).

The 1987 League Champion Clan included President Mike O'Driscoll (Cork), Ollie Coughlan (Offaly), J. Tobin (Waterford), P. McCusker (Tyrone), S. Byrne (Dublin), S. O'Sullivan (Cork), F. Sheehan (Cork), Treasurer John Fitzgerald (Kerry), M. McElhenny (Cork), Joe Thornton (Mayo), Jim Fitzgerald (Kerry), J. Curran (Meath), A. Costello (Kildare), D.J. Kelleher (Cork), M. McElhenny (Cavan), D. Mason (Tipperary), C. Maguire (Toronto), G. O'Riordan (Cork), A. Murphy (Cork), S. Costello (Toronto), J. Costello (Toronto) and J. Garrity (Galway). Aidan Murphy served as the club's secretary that year.

The 1988 team went undefeated for the entire season; they lost the league title on a technicality, but they won the League Cup over St. Mike's and the championship over Ottawa. In September of that year, the team participated in the International 7's final. They met the Powerscreen team led by Kevin McCabe, an inter-county player who traveled from Ireland. It was a close game throughout, but Clan Na nGael eventually ran out the winners by two points and became the first Canadian team to win at this prestigious tournament.

A 1988 photo of the Championship team included Mike O'Driscoll (Cork), Tony Costello (Kildare), Damian McHugh (Derry), Joe Thornton (Mayo), Sean Byrne (Dublin), Jim Fitzgerald (Kerry), Brian Croly (Dublin), John Fitzgerald (Captain-Kerry), Mark McElhenny (Cork), Dermot Mason (Tipperary), Finbarr Sheehan (Cork), Ollie Coughlan (Offaly), Sean Costello (Galway), Aidan Murphy (Cork), Mark McElhenny (Cavan), Diarmuid White (Cork), G. Maguire (Toronto), Joe Costello (Toronto), Sean Costello Jr. (Toronto), Louis Dekhors (Dublin), John Tobin (Waterford), Jim Garrity (Toronto) and Danny Pankhurst (Toronto).

Bernie Dullea (Cork) served as a player and unofficial photographer for the team on many occasions. Among the players profiled in a 30th anniversary programme for the club in 1991 were Brian Loftus (Ohio), Brian O'Connor (Meath), Don White (Limerick), Brendan Tunney (Dublin), Paul McGee (Donegal), Pádraig Sheehan (Cork), Colm

Hyland (Dublin), Sean Byrne (Dublin), Finbarr Sheehan, Martin Dullea (Cork), Ray Boyd (Mayo), Danny Donoghue (Cork), Neil Duggan (Cork) and Lloyd Daly (Dublin).

In 1994 the Dublin Masters visited Toronto and Ottawa. Former Clan Na nGaels that were with the touring team included John Gibbons (Mayo) and Sean Byrne (Dublin). The secretary for Clan Na nGael was Limerick's Don White.

Presidents of Clan Na nGael

1961–62	Mike Walsh, Galway	1963–65	Frank Murphy, Cork
1966–67	Brendan McHugh, Donegal	1968	Al O'Leary, Kerry
1969	Aidan O'Brien, Dublin	1970–71	Lou Doody, Dublin
1972–73	Mike O'Driscoll, Cork	1974–76	John Cawley, Cork
1977–78	Frank Murphy, Cork	1979	Seamus Keon, Down
1980	Ted Tracey, Tipperary	1981	Sean Costello, Galway
1982–83	D.J. Kelleher, Cork	1984–86	Jim McAleer, Tyrone
1987	Tony Costello, Kildare	1988	Mike O'Driscoll, Cork
1989–91	Matt Healy, Kerry	1992–94	Sean Costello, Galway

Honour Roll

Championship Cups: '62, '63, '66, '70, '71, '76, '80, '81, '82, '88, '89
League Cups: '62, '63, '65, '66, '69, '74, '85, '87, '88, '91
Other: Tommy Flynn Cup '72, '73, '74; Jr. Football '74, '76 ; Jr. Hurling '76
Hamilton Feis, Ottawa 7-a-side '79; Toronto 7-a-side '79; Powerscreen 7-a-side '88, '93 and Montreal 1992

SEAN SOUTH'S

Sean South's was formed in the mid-1960s. It was both a hurling and Gaelic Football club that had a strong connection from Limerick supporters. It would seem, from the records, that there were no championship or league victories during its years as a club, but the many competitive matches played brought much respect from the clubs that they faced.

In a May 1972 league game, Sean South's defeated Clan Na nGael 20-18. Liam Hipwell scored two goals in the last five minutes to secure the victory. John Archibold had a goal and two points and Ciaran Donnelly scored three singles. Gerry Gallagher and Tony Tigue each scored two points, and Alec Quinn and Louis Connolly added singles. Billy Egan topped Clan Na nGael with two goals and three points; Paddy King (Toronto) and Jim Graham (Armagh) had a goal each; Chris Daly, Tom Walsh and Arenas O'Leary scored singles.

On May 5, 1973, Sean South's lost both the hurling (15-9) and football (12-8) doubleheader to St. Vincent's. Jimmy Rochford paced the Sean South's with five singles; Pat Kennedy had a goal and Tom Purcell scored a single point. Larry Cleary led St.

Vincent's with two goals; Tom Gilligan a goal and a single; John McGivern hit four singles and Eddie Brett had one point.

St. Vincent's had to hang on for the win in football; Ben Smith scored a goal and a point to lead the team. Pat Kelly kicked two singles and John McGivern, Gerry Mullins and Joe White had one each. Sean South's' top scorer was Tom Purcell with a goal and a point, while dual player Liam Hipwell scored two singles, and Tony Tighe, Chris Kearney and an "Aidan" had a point each. It is uncertain when Sean South's ceased as a club, but memory suggests it was in 1979.

ST. MICHAEL'S

A group of Irishmen in the Club Canadiana started St. Mike's in 1965. Present at the first meeting were Frank Murphy, from Clan Na nGael; and Joe Carty (Galway) R.I.P., John Kane, Mickey Hamill (Silverbridge, Armagh), Tony Keys, Madge Galligan, and Mike Reilly, from the Garryowen club. Eddie Flynn was St. Mike's first president.

In their first year, St. Mike's entered teams in football and hurling. The original colours for St. Mike's jerseys were red and white. This was changed to black and white after the red dye faded in the wash to produce pink jerseys!

The club's first football game was played to a draw with Garryowen and the club's first banquet was held in 1965 in the Range Restaurant at Dundas and Bloor St. This started a tradition in holding an annual banquet to celebrate the glories and defeats of the previous season.

The St. Mike's social scene included functions at the: Club Kingsway, Club Canadiana, Masaryk Hall, Moose Hall, PBA Hall, Parkway Club, the party room at 24 Mabelle Ave., the "Funeral Room" or "Hole in the Wall" on Annette St, the Wedgewood Restaurant, the Irish Centre, the Lakeshore Lion's Club and the Bowling Alley that was run by Dermot (Red) O'Neill who was also the first goalkeeper in both hurling and football for St. Mike's.

In 1967, the club won its first trophy, the Expo Cup. The game was played in Hamilton against Hamilton's Robert Emmets. Players on the 1967 team included Joe Gogarty (R.I.P.), Mickey Hamill, Gene Smyth, Denis Kelly, Bill Kiernan and Bill Flanagan.

Gene's brother, Frank Smyth, was regarded as one of the most outstanding footballers in Toronto in the late sixties and early seventies. Frank held various positions in the club and was president in 1970.

Tommy Flynn, who played minor football for Armagh, was on the first St. Mike's football team along with his brothers. He came from Forkhill and at the young age of 22 was killed in a construction accident. Leaving behind a wife and child, the Toronto GAA named the Flynn Cup in his memory so that it would be awarded to the senior football league winner each year.

The first hurling victory came in 1968 when they won the championship and league in Lawrence Park. The club repeated these Toronto victories in 1969. A hurling team photo from that year included Kevin Loughnane, Micky Duane, Barney Moylan, Shem Walsh, Danny Kinahan, Jimmy Rochford and Joe Kenny, among others. One of the celebrated selectors of St. Mike's hurling was Frank Rafter and a notable member, Liam Cotter, a dual player, who helped to write the constitution for the Toronto GAA.

A photo taken at a 1969 banquet included Pat Reilly, Dave Power, Richie Walsh, Mike Bellew, Larry Carroll, Tony Keys, Jim Howley, John Campbell, Kevin Dunne and Gerry Judge.

Joe Carty, who hailed from Galway, was one of the founding members of the club, a hurler and an executive member of the Toronto GAA. An avid supporter, Joe was sure to be in the Park every Sunday, cheering on St. Mike's. He died in May of 1969 and the Carty Cup was named in his memory and played for on a number of occasions.

A 1972 football team photo included T. Deagan, Mickey Hamill, Sean Keogh, Cathal McCormack, J. O'Connor, Dick Burns, K. Farrell, Dermot Coleman, Bill Flanagan, Bill Black, Seamus O'Kane, Jerry Judge, Frank Smyth, Oliver McEnroe, Danny Kinahan, Joe Kenny, B. Killeen, Patsy McLarnon and Colm Lagan.

The Junior Hurling League winners of 1973 included Paddy Thornton, Martin Molloe, Pat Reilly, Joe Gogarty, Joe Kenny, Joe Roach, John Campbell, Larry Carroll, Cathal McCormack, Padraig Kelly, Eddie Duffy, Danny Kinahan, Mick Duane, Bill Flanagan, Mike O'Brien, Kevin Loughnane and Shem Walsh.

The late Paddy Thornton, otherwise known as the "Lad", arrived in Canada from Tullamore, Offaly in 1967. He joined St. Mike's in 1968 and held numerous executive positions over the years. Paddy played hurling and football for the club and was known as the "man in the gap".

From 1973 to 1977, St. Mike's was the strongest club in Toronto, winning four football championships and three hurling championships. The 1974 football team that won the double included players such as Seamus O'Kane, Dermot Coleman, Mickey Hamill, Dan Kinahan, Martin Coyle, Mike Elliot, Patsy McLarnon and Padraig Kelly.

Denis and Padraig Kelly were very involved with St. Mike's over the years. Denis took more of an active role in the running of the club while playing both hurling and football. Padraig, by all accounts, enjoyed the "hard hitting" and played football when men were men and women were scarce. According to Padraig, "There's no need for any man to go gray in this country."

Probably the most outstanding win for the club was in 1975 when they beat the Harry Bolands of Chicago, in the final of the North American Senior Hurling Championships. They won by five points; the game was played in Lawrence Park. Dan O'Brien

(Kilkenny) captained the St. Mike's team and Martin Loughnane was the outstanding player of the game. A most memorable point, by Mike Normoyle in the second half, helped clinch the game.

The players featured in the 1975 championship hurling photo were Martin Loughnane, Eddie Mangan, Danny Kinahan, Dermot O'Neill, Joe Roach, Patsy McLarnon, Mike Normoyle, Mike O'Brien, Mike Guinan, Larry Sheehan, Shem Walsh, J.B. Kelly, Dan O'Brien, Kevin Loughnane, Art Harvey and Mickey Hamill.

St. Mike's was the third Canadian club to win the Senior Hurling Championship after Montreal (1961) and Garryowen (1965, 1970 and 1974). In 1978, bolstered by players from Toronto's St. Pat's club, St. Mike's won their second and final NACB Senior Hurling Championship.

The O'Brien brothers, Mike, Jim and Dan, hailing from Castlecromer, Kilkenny played an integral role in the club, both on and off the field. On the field, they captained many of the fine St. Mike's hurling teams. During the early '80s when footballers were scarce, the club could always call upon the O'Brien brothers to play. Mike and Jim both served as presidents of the club and Dan held numerous positions on the executive.

Bill Flanagan

The Clara, Offaly, native Bill Flanagan immigrated to Toronto in 1966. He began playing with St. Mike's. During his tenure, the team won a number of city championships in both codes. Toronto hurlers that impressed Bill included Barney Moylan, (St. Rynaghs, Offaly), Pat Kirby (Clare), Kevin Loughnane (Birr) and Danny Kinahan (Clara). The best footballers included Antrim pair Billy Millar and Pat Diamond, Kevin Kilmurray (Offaly) and Frank Smyth (Kildare).

Bill lost a North American Junior football final in Pittsburgh, playing "under an alias" for Hamilton-Robert Emmets in the early '70s. A highlight of Bill's GAA career was playing for St. Mike's against Garryowen in an exhibition hurling match at the Canadian National Exhibition Stadium (CNES) in Toronto. St. Mike's won the game and Bill was carted off the field on a stretcher with a head injury before full-time.

In Buffalo, N.Y., at a football tournament in the early '70s, a selection team from Toronto traveled to play the local teams along with Boston and Detroit. Toronto won the competition and Bill collected the MVP award. He sent the trophy home to the Headmaster in Clara, NS, and asked that it be presented to the best footballer in the school that year. The award went to a lad named Damien Flattery who later played football for Offaly.

Bill officiated at many matches. His highest honour was being in charge of the 1973 North American Senior Hurling Final between St. Pat's, Toronto and Galway, Boston. Galway won the match. Bill moved to California and recently served on the San Francisco GAA Board Development Fund Committee, which rose over $30,000 in 2007.

The '70s

From 1974 through to 1980, the football club imported a lot of players from its "farm" team in Draperstown, County Derry. Most notable being Jimmy Kennedy, Emmett O'Kane, Enda McMaster, the 'Bush' Kelly, Kenny Bradley, Gary Lagan and Brendan (Crimby) O'Kane.

The 1975 senior football team members for St. Mike's included Seamus O'Kane, Martin Coyle, Brendan O'Kane, Pat McKeown, Mike Elliot, Richard Connolly, Kenny Sarrich, Danny Kinahan, Mickey Hamill, Dermot Coleman, Emmett O'Kane, Patsy McLarnon, Kenny Bradley, Padraig Kelly, Eddie Mangan and Jimmy Kennedy.

Patsy McLarnon arrived in Canada in the late sixties from Swatragh, Derry and played both hurling and football for St. Mike's. Patsy made a great contribution to the club during the seventies, when he served as president in '74, '76, '77 and '79. During these years the club would win many honours in both grades. Patsy returned to live in Derry in 1979.

Maureen Houlihan immigrated to Canada from England and was the club secretary from 1976-1978. She was very active in the organization of many social events and a vocal supporter of the teams.

St. Mike's took a bold move in 1977 when the football team traveled to Ireland to play five games against local sides in Swatragh, Clara, Draperstown, Downpatrick and Clonmore. The tem was joined by former players who had returned to Ireland and St. Mike's went on to victory in three of the matches. The trip was organized by Brian Farmer, Patsy McLarnon and Mickey Hamill.

The 1977 senior football team included Joe Houlihan, Jimmy Kennedy, Brian Farmer, Eddie Mangan, Patsy McLarnon, Richard Connolly, Brendan O'Kane, Hugh McGrogan, Ken Sarich, Dan McNamara, Mickey Hamill, Mickey Kane, Brendan Walls, Padraig Kelly, Sean Hopkins, Dan Kinahan, Martin Loughnane, Pat McKinney and Seamus O'Kane.

Late 1979 saw the arrival of Cormac O'Muiri (Dublin). Immediately Cormac involved himself in the running of the club from day one after being contacted by Mickey Hamill. Cormac would later extend this involvement to the running of the Toronto GAA, the founding of the Irish Canadian's club and the Toronto GAA Minor Board.

Angela (Howley) O'Muiri was born and raised in Toronto to Jim (Galway) and Mary Howley. Angela is so good with her memory, and goes so far back, that she can remember when club members like the Loughnanes, Hamills, Rochfords and the Elliots got married! Angela has been actively involved in the club in many capacities and served as president in 1988.

Eddie Duffy, a native of Drumlosh, Roscommon, immigrated to Canada in 1957. He made his hurling debut in the early '70s with the St. Mike's juniors and enjoyed a competitive game of handball. A bus driver for Gray Coach, Eddie was the usual chauffeur for the out of town trips for GAA clubs and St. Mike's to places like Boston, Montreal, Hamilton and Detroit. Eddie was always right in there with the lads and wouldn't be happy until he got someone uptight over something he said. Sadly, in 1976, he died at the age of 50 and is remembered with fondness by St. Mike's.

'80s and '90s

Ena O'Brien (Galway) was the first female president in 1981 and 1982. Pauline (Duffy) Prior was born and raised in Toronto, daughter of Lena and the late Eddie Duffy. She held several positions in the club, notably, being the first Canadian born president of the club in 1984. Under her leadership, the club won the Senior Football Championship, League and the McKenna Cup. The league was captured by beating Clan Na nGael, a major victory for the club considering that two of their top players, Jimmy Kennedy and Danny Kinahan, were absent. Mickey Hamill scored a goal in this game to clinch the victory.

Jim Stack, who hailed from Kerry, arrived in Toronto in 1957. Although he never played for the team, Jim could be found in the Park most Sundays, "sitting on the hill", with his pipe in hand, watching the boys. According to Mickey Hamill, Jim was a "great observer" of the game. Jim was able to talk about the minor incidents in a match for weeks on end. Although a very quiet, peaceful man himself, he enjoyed the odd confrontation during a game. A long time employee of Molson's, Jim passed away in 1983.

Sean Kelly was the first Canadian to play for St. Mike's in the late'70s and may have been the first Canadian to play in league football. Although he was not always selected in the first 15 to play on a Sunday, Sean could always be counted on to play if required. He sat on a number of St. Mike's committees, but his claim to fame is the singing of "Spancil Hill" at many a party after the games.

In 1986 St. Mike's would win the football league, championship and McKenna Cup with players that included Gabriel Rushe, Colm Flynn, Kenny Sarich, goalkeeper Mike McCusker (Cavan), Eddie Mangan, Cormac O'Muiri, Jimmy Kennedy, Dan O'Brien, Dermot Coleman, Brian McMahon, Gerry McFarland, mid-fielder Tomas Finnegan (Cavan), Nishie Farmer, Brian Power and Danny Kinahan.

A memorable game that year was when the club traveled to Ottawa to play in a league game. St. Mike's were losing by ten points at half time but came back to win by a large margin, thanks to the sharp shooting of Gerry McFarland, Brian Power and Ignatius (Nishie) Farmer. The craic that night in the Blackburn Arms in Ottawa included a number of victory songs that were composed and sung for the first time. Many of the players got their first taste of University life as the players stayed overnight on campus and were treated to an evening of song, bible readings and Dan O'Brien's snoring.

Colm Flynn penned the *Tales of a 1986'er* as part of the 25th Anniversary souvenir programme in 1990. Flynn wrote:

"There was moaning and gnashing of teeth. Yes, from Tunnyduff and Lacken to Tyholland and Connollys. Grown men cried in their beer. Old women lamented in cattle byres. It was happening again in 1986 – sure the brains of the country were leaving. Like hunted animals they skulked through Pearson International and dispersed, poor wretches, throughout the great metropolis of Toronto. But help was at hand.

Dutifully, and with an unselfish disregard for his kidneys, Mike Costelloe scoured the public houses of the city in search of these lost souls and located many. Those who he adjudged to be in reasonable health with all their faculties, he introduced to St. Mike's. There began one of St. Mike's most successful years and also a great year's crack.

As well as receiving great assistance in settling down in Canada the new members, eight players in total, were given a thorough background in club history. Stories such as that of Paddy Hegarty arriving from Poland (and learning to speak English from GAA members) were commonplace in the Harp & Shamrock, as new members entertained with such traditional melodies as "The Lonesome Cowboy" and Gerry McFarland's all time great "The Auld Ford Car". Another fun-filled gathering in '86 was our presentation get together for Gerry McFarland and Eddie Quigley in the Harp."

The late Paddy Hegarty actually came from Ballycastle, Mayo to Canada in 1956 and joined St. Mike's in 1968. He served in a variety of executive roles on the club and his most memorable game was a 1984 football match against the Irish Canadians in which Paddy got an assist to a point at the age of 60.

A 1987 men's team photo included D. Coleman, S. O'Kane, K. Sarich, D. Kinahan, Captain T. Finnegan, M. Elliott, President C. O'Muiri, R. O'Flynn, J. Connelly, C. Flynn, B. McMahon, S. McClone, T. Fiddeas, G. Rushe, M. Coghlan, N. Farmer, M. McCusker and E. Mangan. Other supporters of note that year were Secretary Angela Howley and Treasurer Ann Loughnane.

Danny Kinahan, who hails from Offaly, represented St. Mike's in both hurling and football. He won many individual awards in both grades and was also named as the GAA Footballer of the Year for 1987. Years later, Danny's son, David, would spend a few years playing with the Seattle Gaels on the West coast and successfully competed against the Canadian clubs of Vancouver, Calgary and Edmonton.

The 1988 St. Mike's banquet at the Lakeshore Lion's Club saw a photo of Mary Howley (R.I.P.), Bridie Stack, Bridget Bellew and Eileen Molloy sharing a laugh together. While out on the playing field some of the vocal supporters included Amanda Farrell, Kate Cunningham, Aileen Devine, Grainne (the Bat) Tyndall and Bernie (Badger) Tuite.

The A-Team arrived in town in 1989 that included Ciaran and Paul McElvanna from Antrim, Brendan and Peter Smith from Armagh, John and Pat Maguire from Armagh and Brendan O'Hagan from Armagh. With the arrival of Niall O'Connell from Dublin, St. Mikes captured the league and were semi-finalists in the championship and Powerscreen 7's. All of this took place under Coaches Brian Farmer and Seamus O'Kane, and trainer Cormac O'Muiri.

The St. Mike's 1989 Powerscreen International 7's Gold Watch Tournament players included John Maguire (Armagh), Ciaran McElvanna (Antrim), Peter Smith (Armagh), Raymond Cunningham (Down), Cormac O'Muiri (Dublin), Gerry McFarland (Monaghan), Brendan Keneally (Cork), Niall O'Connell (Dublin), Brendan Smith (Armagh) and Paul McElvanna (Antrim). Three St. Mike's players were part of the Powerscreen International team that won the tournament in 1989 with Eddie Mangan, Nishie Farmer and Peter Gilbourne, along with Manager, Brian Farmer.

1990 started with a 25th Anniversary banquet on April 14, with an executive that included Eddie Mangan, Gene Hickey, Mike McCusker, Paddy Thornton, Eamon Devine, Brendan O'Hagan, Kevin Loughnane, Dan O'Brien, Paddy Hegarty, Paul McElvanna, Brendan Smith and Mike Coughlan. That year and in 1991, the club would win the League.

A few dry years passed but the mid-'90s proved to be very successful for St. Mike's under the leadership of Cormac O'Muiri, Danny Kinahan, Kevin Loughnane, Mickey Hamill, Pádraig Kelly and Paul Loughnane. In 1995 the club picked up six trophies from Montreal, Powerscreen 7's, League, Championship, Owen Nolan and Denis Leyne. The club would go on to win the Senior Football Championships for five straight years (1995–1999).

Players that were together during these five championships were P. J. Doherty, Tony Doyle, Paul Loughnane, Edwin Walsh, Gerard Douglas, Paul McElvanna, Mark Burns, Larry McQuarrie, Charlie Maguire and Danny Kinahan.

Those with four championships were Damien Campbell, Jason Coughlan and Michael Hamill. Other St. Mike's players that contributed were Tommy Keane, Timmy Hamill, Kevin O'Driscoll, James Kennedy, Ruairi O'Brien, David Kinahan and Ray Moore. International players of note were Paul Dolan (Scotland), Mike Silva (Uruguay), Ike Husain (Guyana) and Julian Radlein (Jamaica).

Kenny "Crocodile" Sarich

Kenny Sarich hailed, not from any county in Ireland, but from the continent of Australia and played with St. Mike's for over 20 years. He was born in the town of Kalgoolie, near Perth. A millwright by trade, he immigrated to Canada in 1970. He was approached by Bill Flanagan to play Gaelic football and his first game was in September of 1970 in the position of goalkeeper. However, after a short period of time, and after injuring three of his fullbacks, Kenny was moved to an outfield position which he embraced readily.

Bridget Sarich, of German extraction, was club secretary in 1975 and could be heard on many a Sunday cheering "her Kenny" on. Ken also picked up the hurling stick and played in several junior hurling games. He captained the championship and league football victories in 1984 and was awarded the club sportsman in 1986. He remains a true "Aussie" legend with St. Mike's.

169 Westminister Avenue

A home for many St. Mike's players, "Westminister", as it was fondly known, was located in the Polish area of town, near High Park. Found by Eddie Duffy, Tony Duffy and Denis Kelly, the house was the locale for many parties, card games and meetings. It was a common sight to see a big pot of spuds on the oven along side a frying pan full of grease. To hide the beer and keep it cool at the same time, it was put into the cistern of the toilet.

The rent charged by the landlord, Metro, was based on a per head basis. He would arrive upstairs and the count the heads when many of the boys hid in the nooks and the crannies to keep the costs low.

It was said that seventy-five percent of the St. Mike's hurling teams of the late sixties and seventies were residents there. Among the many occupants were Kevin Loughnane, Jimmy Rochford, Eamon Quarney and one of the last occupants of the house, Emmett (Ganch) O'Kane, who wrote this poem:

Westminister Avenue

The last time I hit London town, I met up with a cabby
Who showed me all the sights around and one, Westminister Abbey
I could not look him in the eye, my gaze fell to the floor,
For it took me back to one June day in nineteen seventy four.

For on that morn I left my home and kissed my mother sadly,
And headed off, Toronto bound, with Randy, Geoff, and Bradley.
We flew across the many miles above the clouds and rain,
And descended to a waiting car, the driver Seamus Kane.

A Ford or Chevy, I don't know, which one that took us down,
One thing for sure, that shiny car seemed big as Draperstown.
We drove along the 401 and down the Gardiner flew,
And came to rest at 169 Westminister Avenue.

Jim Kennedy and Big Croomby lived there, Paddy Thornton and the likes
But the bond that kept the crew intact was playing for St. Mike's.

So in we moved and settled down, t'was two men to a bed
And on Saturday when Metro showed, the thing came to a head,

For on Friday night at the Man of Aran, the money it was spent,
And no one ever thought to save ten dollars for the rent.

The visitors came oft and soon from Kilkenny up to Cavan,
To see the boys and make some noise, McEvoy and Jimmy Slavin.
Then later on in that same year, when attendance it was saggin'
The ranks were swelled by the arrival of Dan Bush and Gary Lagan.

The years went by, some came and stayed, while others moved out faster,
But in seventy eight the crew was joined by Kojak and McMaster.

Let's not forget that wee back room where Padraig Kelly froze,
Nor sitting round the living room admiring Thornton's toes.
Lena Duffy baked our bread and sometimes for a change
Ten pizzas came from Jim and Dan above there at the Range.

To Lawrence Park in Hamill's truck we'd never miss a chance
Six in the back, three up front, Sean Kelly in short pants.
Shem Walsh called in a time or two and often in a pinch,
He'd line us up a bit of work pulling cables for Pat Lynch.

If only that old house could talk, the stories it would tell,
Paddy Hegarty, if he'd lived there, would send us all to hell.
So here's to all that lived in there or spent a night or two,
Let's not forget the crack we had at Westminister Avenue.

Kevin Loughnane, a native of Birr, played Minor and U-21 hurling for Offaly in the sixties. He joined St. Mike's after a short career with Clan Na nGael and is regarded as one of the most stylish hurlers to ever play in Toronto. His most memorable moment was spying Anne Coyle playing camogie in High Park, and a match was made. Kevin had the honour to serve as a linesman in the 1990 All-Star game at Skydome.

New Millennium

In 2000, St. Michael's defeated St. Vincent's (0-8 to 0-5) to capture their sixth championship in a row. In a game that featured great goaltending and tough defence, St. Mike's came back from a two-point deficit early in the second half to win the contest. A crucial point made by Dan Fitzgerald, his second of the game, started St. Mike's on their way to another comeback. Scores from Michael Hamill (0-3), Paul Loughnane (0-2), Dan Fitzgerald (0-2), Larry McQuarrie (0-1) contributed to the final score line.

The following year, St. Michael's defeated the Toronto Gaels to win their seventh championship in a row! With about five minutes to go in regulation time, it appeared that the streak was over as St. Mike's were down by three points, but Eanna O'Malley's tying point sent the game into overtime. Once in overtime, St. Mike's took the game to the

Gaels and won by four points. A goal by Tony Doyle and a final point by Dorion Foley sealed the win.

As for the men's team in 2002, they started the year by winning the Montreal tournament and the league title. However, disappointing losses, in the Denis Leyne tournament and the championship semifinals, did not sit well with many club members. These losses were wiped away by a determined group of players, who claimed the Powerscreen 7's Gold Watch Tournament. The club had a great Labour Day weekend that year, as the senior team defeated St. Pat's from Palmerstown, Dublin; and the junior team defeated Rockland from New York to win the gold watches. St. Mike's became the first club to win both the senior and junior titles in the same year.

The year 2003 marked the end of one era and possibly the beginning of a new one. For the first time in a long time, St. Mike's failed to win any major honours. The men's team did win the George Curry tournament, finished second in the league and lost the championship final to St. Vincent's in extra time. In the Powerscreen 7's, they lost in the semifinal of the senior division and they were finalists in the junior division. So close on many occasions but not quite.

The club traveled to Ireland on a very successful tour in May of 2003 and played games in Kerry, Cork and Dublin. They beat Beaufort in Kerry, lost to senior county champions Castlehaven in Cork, and lost to St. Pat's in Palmerstown. It was a great trip for all involved and will always be remembered.

The 2004 season began with the Montreal tournament; St. Mike's defeated the Edmonton Wolfe Tones in the semifinal and Ottawa in the final. St. Mike's had little trouble winning the league title with convincing wins over all opponents.

St. Mike's hosted the Denis Leyne tournament, and the men defeated Durham in the final. The women continued to make steady progress and won their first-ever trophy when they defeated Durham in the same tournament.

The championship season started with a quarterfinal match against St. Vincent's. The game ended in a tie, but it was ruled that ineligible players were fielded and thus St. Mike's progressed to the next round. St. Mike's played their most complete game in the semifinal against Durham, and they had a convincing win. The Ottawa Gaels provided good opposition in the final and, though St. Mike's struggled in the first half, they eventually gained the upper hand and claimed their eighth title in 10 years.

St. Mike's entered the Powerscreen 7's with the goal of making a clean sweep of all trophies, but Ardboe and Dungannon were to provide tough opposition. After winning their group, St. Mike's faced Ardboe in the semifinal. St. Mike's held an early lead, but Ardboe came back to tie the game and they eventually won the match in extra time. The junior team defied the odds by making it to the final where they lost a close game to Durham.

The St. Mike's men claimed the Montreal tournament in 2005 and had a strong league campaign where they finished at the top of the standings. They defeated the Toronto Gaels in the league semifinal and St. Vincent's in the league final. In the championship final, St. Mike's met Durham after defeating Montreal in the quarterfinal and Ottawa in the semifinal. In a close game, Durham was the deserving winner of the championship.

40th Anniversary

On May 28, 2005, St. Mike's celebrated their 40th anniversary with An tUachtarán, Sean Kelly in attendance along with guests from Ireland, the US and the four football provinces of Canada (British Columbia, Alberta, Ontario and Quebec). The Tommy Markham Cup for Ireland's minor football champion was on display during this memorable occasion. Many felt that it was one of the well-organized events by a GAA club in recent years.

Ladies' Football

The 2001 season saw St. Mike's field a ladies' team for the first time. Coached by Mark Burns, the women played with the same determination that is a trademark of St. Mike's. They represented the club with skill and fair play. The women continued their steady improvement during their second season and recorded some impressive victories in the league on their way to finishing fourth. They were defeated in the quarterfinal of the championship.

The ladies continued their steady growth in 2005, as they introduced a number of new players who made an immediate impact. As a result, the women's team made it to the championship final against the Michael Cusacks. St. Mike's were again unlucky not to take the honours in one of the best finals ever played in the city.

St. Mike's were proud to have four of their players, Meghan Deeney, Mary Traynor, Tressa McMaster and Sinead Fitzsimons, and assistant coach Paul Loughnane help Team Canada at the International Women's Tournament of 2005 in Dublin.

Though the ladies of St. Mike's have not won all available trophies, they are to be commended for their 2004 and 2006 victories at their own Denis Leyne Tournament. In 2007, the ladies finished the season on a high note by deservedly reaching the finals of the Powerscreen 7's, only narrowly losing out on the gold watches to the Brampton ladies.

Paul Loughnane

Paul Loughnane, whose father Kevin played on the 1975 NACB Senior Hurling Championship team, learned to play football in underage clinics run by the Toronto GAA. He moved on to play minor and senior football for St. Mike's. So far, he has won a minor championship and eight senior championships in Toronto. Paul also played in Ireland for three years with Castlehaven in West Cork; he was the right halfback when the club won the county final in 2003. He returned to Canada in 2004 and won Footballer of the Year in Toronto.

Paul has been very active in the coaching and the development of the underage and schools programmes in Toronto. He became President of the Toronto GAA in 2005. He also served as the National Games Development Officer from 2005–2007. Paul plays Aussie Rules football in between seasons and represented Canada at the International Cup in Melbourne. He was also honoured by being selected to the All-World team in 2005.

2007 and beyond!

St. Mike's annual presentation banquet was celebrated on Saturday, May 26th. This was the club's 42nd annual banquet and it was held at Strates Banquet Hall in Etobicoke. Special guests for the night included Father Gerry Scott, Sean Murphy (Irish Person of the Year) and his wife Karen, Brian Farmer (Canadian GAA Board President), Sinead Canavan (Toronto GAA President) and Ann McMahon (Mayo Person the Year).

St. Mike's hosted their annual 9-a-side tournament at the Crusaders Rugby Club in Oakville, Ontario, on June 30, 2007. Men, women, and youth all came together to showcase their football skills. Both St. Vincent's and the Michael Cusacks were back to defend their titles.

To start the day off, Paul Loughnane had the youth programme in full swing. It was a great display of future footballers for Toronto. Throughout the day, there were many fun activities that all the kids participated in.

When the youths cleared off the field, it was the ladies' turn to show their stuff. Teams included the Durham Robert Emmets, the Michael Cusacks, St. Mike's, Montreal, and the Banshees who came all the way from Pittsburgh. Durham and the Cusacks met in the final. The Cusacks came out strong, but Durham stormed back with three quick goals. In the end, Durham took the 2007 Denis Leyne Women's title, and the Cusacks' Erin Gallagher was named MVP.

The men's division consisted of St. Pat's, St. Mike's A and B, and defending champions St. Vincent's. There were hard-fought round robin games and St. Vincent's ended up on top, undefeated, with St. Mike's A close behind at 3-1. They met in the finals once again, and put on a great display of football for the huge crowd at the club. In the end, St Mike's - A pulled out the victory and took the 2007 Denis Leyne Men's title.

Throughout the day, there were numerous things happening besides football. There was a BBQ and live music by Comhaltas, and free pizza provided by Pizza Nova. Eamonn O'Loghlin from *Ceoil agus craic* broadcasted live from the club. O'Loghlin's *Toronto Irish News* magazine routinely promotes the games and in its March 2008 edition highlighted GAA stalwarts in a William Smith (Smitty) photo of John Byrne, Kevin Loughnane, Billy Kelly, Fr. Gerry Scott, Sean Harte and Cormac O'Muiri.

Following the men's final there was a "Poc Fada" competition where contestants lined up at one end of the field and tried to hit the sliotar as far as they could. The women's title went to Orla Ryan, member of St. Mike's ladies' team. James Tierney won the men's division.

Those that are taking the lead for St. Mike's in 2008 include Paul McElvanna, Ruairi O'Brien, Sinead McElvanna, Mike Silva, Cormac O'Muiri, Ronan Matthews, Kevin O'Driscoll, Ray Moore, Paul Loughnane and Tommy Keane.

Denis Leyne

Born in Ireland, Denis Leyne moved to Montreal at the age of 21. He was a prominent member of the Montreal Shamrocks and served with distinction. Denis moved to Toronto and sadly died of a heart attack in February 1995. Later that year, St. Mike's honoured his memory by creating a tournament in his name.

Denis Leyne Memorial Tournament

	Men	Ladies
2007	St. Mike's "A"	Durham
2006	St. Vincent's	Michael Cusacks
2005	St. Vincent's	Michael Cusacks
2004	St. Mike's	St. Mike's
2003	n/a	n/a
2002	Toronto Gaels	Durham
2001	St. Mike's	Durham
2000	St. Mike's	
1999	St. Mike's	
1998	St. Mike's	
1997	Durham	St. Anne's, Detroit
1996	St. Mike's	Durham
1995	St. Mike's	

St. Mike's Presidents

1965	Eddie Flynn, Armagh	1966	Eddie Flynn, Armagh
1967	Mike Bellew, Galway	1968	Mickey Hamill, Armagh
1969	Gene Hickey, Limerick	1970	Frank Smyth, Kildare
1971	Paddy Thornton, Offaly	1972	Paddy Thornton, Offaly
1973	Mark Buckley, Westmeath	1974	Patsy McClarnon, Derry
1975	Joe Houlihan, Kerry	1976	Patsy McClarnon, Derry
1977	Patsy McClarnon, Derry	1978	Emmett O'Kane, Derry
1979	Patsy McClarnon, Derry	1980	Paddy Hegarty, Mayo
1981	Ena O'Brien, Galway	1982	Ena O'Brien, Galway
1983	Enda McMaster, Derry	1984	Pauline Prior, Toronto

1985	Mike O'Brien, Kilkenny	1986	Jim O'Brien, Kilkenny
1987	Cormac O'Muiri, Dublin	1988	Angela O'Muiri, Toronto
1989	Mike Coughlan, Offaly	1990	Eddie Mangan, Dublin
1991	Mike McCusker, Cavan	1992	Cormac O'Muiri, Dublin
1993	Gabriel Rushe, Monaghan	1994	Gabriel Rushe, Monaghan
1995	John Murray, Derry	1996	Adrian Burns, Down
1997	John Murray, Derry	1998	Paul Loughnane, Toronto
1999	Paul Loughnane, Toronto	2000	Paul Loughnane, Toronto
2001	P.J. Doherty, Donegal	2002	Ray Moore, Toronto
2003	Tony Doyle, Wicklow	2004	Pat Leahy, Kerry
2005	Kerrie Burns, Down	2006	Kerrie Burns, Down
2007	Ruairi O'Brien, Toronto	2008	Paul McElvanna, Antrim

The Gene Hickey Award Club Supporter of the Year

1986	Jim & Mary Howley	1987	Paddy Hegarty
1988	Lena Duffy	1989	Mickey & Bina Hamill
1990	Joseph & Mary Gogarty	1991	Kevin & Anne Loughnane
1992	Paddy & Pauline Thornton	1993	Frank & Eileen Smyth
1994	Paddy & Anne McMahon	1995	Enda & Kathleen McMaster
1996	Shem & Iris Walsh	1997	Danny & Mary Kinahan
1998	Seamus & Ann O'Kane	1999	Ollie & Mary Coughlan
2000	Larry & Grace Sheehan	2001	Gabriel & Monica Rushe
2002	Ken & Bridget Sarrich	2003	Mike & Willa Elliot
2004	Eddie & Lynn Mangan	2005	Dan O'Brien
2006	Padraig Kelly	2007	Michael & Briege Bellew

Paddy Thornton Club Person of the Year Award

1986	Anne Loughnane	1991	Mike McCusker
1992	John Murray	1997	Pádraig Kelly
1998	Paul Loughnane	1999	Paul Loughnane
2000	Ike Husain	2001	Danny Kinahan
2002	Ray & Aishling Moore	2003	Cormac O'Muiri
2004	Pat Leahy	2005	Sean Harte
2006	Ciara O'Brien	2007	Ronan Matthews

The Dwayne Walsh Award Sportsperson of the Year

1970	Danny Kinahan	1973	Mickey Hamill
1975	Danny Kinahan	1976	Martin Loughnane
1986	Ken Sarrich	1987	Mike McCusker
1989	Ken Sarrich	1991	Tony Gill
1992	Dan Kinahan	1993	Eamonn Devine
1994	Bill Murphy	1995	Ike Husain
1996	Paul Loughnane	1997	Edwin Walsh

| 1998 | Charlie Maguire | 1999 | Mike Silva |
| 2000 | P.J. Doherty | 2001 | Tony Doyle |

2002	James Kennedy & Doreen Walsh
2003	Kevin O'Driscoll & Ciara O'Brien
2004	Paul McElvanna & Tressa McMaster
2005	Ruairi O'Brien & Nora Counsel
2006	Pat Leahy & Ciara Fitzsimons
2007	Paul Loughnane & Katie Higgins

Player of the Year

1968	*Barney Moylan (SH)	
1969	Danny Kinahan (SF)	Kevin Loughnane (SH)
1970	Danny Kinahan (SF)	Kevin Loughnane (JF)
1973	Seamus O'Kane (SF)	Kevin Loughnane (SH)
	JB Kelly (JF)	Jim O'Brien (JH)
1974	Seamus O'Kane (SF)	*Kevin Loughnane (SH)
	Kevin Loughnane (JF)	Paddy McMahon (JH)
1975	Martin Coyle (SF)	Shem Walsh (SH)
	Mike Guinan (JF)	Joe Houlihan (JH)
1976	Richard Connolly, Dan Kinahan (SF)	Dan O'Brien (SH)
	Dermot Coleman (JF)	Jim Kennedy (JH)
1977	Danny Kinahan (SF)	
1981	Danny Kinahan (SF)	
1984	Kenny Sarrich (F)	Kevin Loughnane (H)
1986	Gerry McFarland	
1987	*Danny Kinahan	
1989	Cormac O'Muiri	

1990	Tom Finnegan	*Under 21/ Minor/ U-14*
1991	*Keiran McElvanna	
1992	Mark Burns	Ray Moore (M)
1994	Adrian Burns	*Edwin Walsh (M)
1995	Gerry Douglas	Kevin O'Driscoll (M)
1996	Mark Burns	*David Kinahan (M)
1997	*Damien Campbell	Ruairi O'Brien (M) Michael Thornton (14)
1998	Michael Hamill	James Kennedy (M) Noel Kennedy (14)
1999	Edwin Walsh	
2000	*Mark Burns, Paul Loughnane	Tom Keane (21)
2001	Tom Keane	
2002	Eanna O'Malley	Seamus Grealish (21)
2003	Pat Leahy	James Kennedy (21) Justin Harte (M)
2004	*Paul Loughnane	*Justin Harte (21)
2005	Michael Silva	*Justin Harte (21)
2006	Ruari O'Brien	*Conor O'Muiri (21)
2007	Edwin Walsh	*Conor O'Muiri (21) Finbar McDonnell

	Ladies	**Minor/Under 21**
2002	Kerrie Burns	*Tressa McMaster (M) *Siobhan O'Muiri (14)
2003	Siobhan McQuarrie	Sinead Fitzsimons (M)
2004	Meaghan Deeney	Sinead Fitzsimons (21) *Mary Traynor (M)
2005	Siobhan McQuarrie	Sinead Fitzsimons (21)
2006	Sinead McElvanna	Siobhan O'Muiri (21)
2007	Kendra Mercer	Ashley Maalouf (21)

*Toronto MVP, **F**= Football, **H**= Hurling, **JF**= Junior Football, **JH**= Junior Hurling

Honour Roll

1967 Expo '67 Football Cup in Hamilton
1968 Senior Hurling Championship, Senior Hurling League
1969 Flynn Cup, Hamilton Feis Cup, Senior Hurling Championship, Senior Hurling League, Carty Cup (Hurling)
1970 Carty Cup
1971 Senior Football Championship, Hamilton Feis Cup
1972 Junior Hurling League
1973 Senior Football Championship, Junior Hurling League
1974 Senior Football Championship, Senior Football League, Senior Hurling League
1975 North American Championship Senior Hurling, Senior Hurling Championship, Carty Cup
1976 Senior Football Championship, Senior Football League, Flynn Cup
1977 Senior Football Championship, Senior Football League
1978 Fay Cup, North American League Senior Hurling (with St. Pat's) Championship
1979 Senior Football Championship, Senior Football League
1980 Flynn Cup
1981 Fay Cup
1982 Flynn Cup
1983 Senior Hurling Championship
1984 Senior Football Championship, Senior Football League, McKenna Cup
1985 McKenna Cup
1986 Senior Football Championship, Senior Football League, McKenna Cup
1989 Senior Football League
1992 Minor Football Championship
1994 Minor Football Championship, McKenna Cup, Montreal tournament
1995 Senior Football Championship, Montreal tournament, Denis Leyne tournament, Senior Football League, Owen Nolan (Brampton) tournament, Powerscreen senior 7's
1996 Senior Football Championship, Denis Leyne tournament, Powerscreen junior 7's, Senior Football League, Minor Championship
1997 Senior Football Championship, Montreal tournament, Owen Nolan (Brampton) tournament, Senior Football League

1998 Senior Football Championship, Montreal tournament, Denis Leyne tournament, Fay Cup, Senior Football League

1999 Senior Football Championship, Montreal tournament, Denis Leyne tournament, Owen Nolan (Brampton) tournament

2000 Senior Football Championship, Montreal tournament, Denis Leyne tournament, Owen Nolan (Brampton) tournament

2001 Senior Football Championship, Montreal tournament, Denis Leyne tournament, Senior Football League, Owen Nolan (Brampton) tournament, Heineken Cup

2002 Senior Football League, Montreal tournament, George Curry (Durham) tournament, Powerscreen senior 7's, Powerscreen junior 7's

2003 George Curry (Durham) tournament

2004 Senior Football Championship, Montreal tournament, Denis Leyne tournament (Mens), Senior Football League, Denis Leyne tournament (Ladies)

2005 Senior Football League, Montreal tournament

2006 Senior Football Championship, Senior Football League, George Curry (Durham) tournament

2007 Denis Leyne tournament.

HAMILTON ROBERT EMMETS

In the mid '60s, a group of young Irish immigrants began to gather weekly at Reservoir Park in West Hamilton to play their native sports. Fergus McNally, Tim O'Mahoney, Jimmy McCarron, Mike Milard, Pat Ryan and John O'Donnell were among those who planned for the GAA's presence in Hamilton. On a trip to Ireland in 1965, John O'Donnell brought back a set of hurleys. The Irish Canadian Club of Hamilton added their support to these early endeavours.

On March 6, 1966, in the Rainbow Room on Sanford Avenue, Tim O'Mahoney became the first President; Mike Magee was chosen Vice President; Bill Lucitt, Treasurer; John Ahearne, Secretary; and Eddie Powell was Equipment Manager. The first GAA social event was a Gala Dance held on April 30, 1966, at the Serbian Hall on Nash Road. Tickets were a tidy $1.50 each.

Hamilton approached the St. Patrick's GAA club in Buffalo to enlist support with their growth, and the likes of Mary Browne and Sean Coakley attended early meetings. It was agreed that the Buffalo GAA would help Hamilton to field their team in the Toronto league, and the Hamilton GAA would assist Buffalo in their North American County Board league play. The first group of players from Hamilton to assist Buffalo included John O'Donnell, Tim O'Mahoney and John Ahearne, who all found some time to attend a Carlton Showband dance at a place called the "Chuckwagon."

First Match

The first league game was played in High Park, on May 15, against Clan Na nGael. The season closed on November 12 with a trophy game in Sherman Park versus St. Vincent's. In the first year, the club had an amazing record with some splendid victories in both

Canada and the USA. The most prominent of these was a hurling win against Garryowen in the final league game of the season; the results of this match prevented Garryowen from winning the league.

From formation, the sporting and social events of the GAA brought the young Irish community of Hamilton and Buffalo together. There are many stories to tell of the games held at the only full-sized GAA field within the North American Board at Macassa Park, located on the mountain at Upper Sherman. The socials that followed in the downstairs of the Hillcrest after every game are legendary. In Buffalo, there was always a home-cooked meal at the old Bishop Duffy Centre catered with love by Mrs. Casey, Mrs. Moriarity, Mrs. Courtney and Mrs. Byrne. Everyone loved their homemade bread!

Hamilton players of 1968 were involved with Toronto's St. Pat's when they won a North American Championship. Hamilton's hurling team won a major 7-a-side tournament with victories over Toronto and Rochester one year. Throughout the club's history, games would be played in Buffalo, Rochester, Syracuse, Binghampton, Detroit, Pittsburgh, Cleveland, Montreal and Ottawa. The teams they faced included Toronto's Garryowen, St. Pat's, Sean Souths, Clan Na nGael, St. Mike's and St. Vincent's.

Other highlights for the club were the Hamilton Feis Games, hurling and football played on astro-turf at Hamilton's Civic Stadium (later renamed Ivor Wynne); the hosting and sponsorship of the Expo Cup in 1967; a 1973 CNE Stadium hurling match with the best of Hamilton and Toronto competing; and the 1974 NACB convention, which would be the last time a Canadian city would host this gathering.

35th Anniversary

The club continued a strong presence in Hamilton for approximately 15 years. The lack of young immigrants and the "maturing" of the players resulted in the demise of the team in the late '70s. However, the friendships formed remained strong and on August 18, 2001, a 35th reunion banquet was organized by committee members June and Michael (R.I.P.) Byrne (who won an All-Ireland Minor Football medal for Offaly in 1964), Helen and Mike Dunphy, Eithne and Harry Lynch, Hannah and Phil Slacke, Betty and Sean Browne, Pauline and Noel Ennis, Pearl and Jimmy Deane and Brendan Baragwanath.

Presidents that were honoured for their service included Tim O'Mahony, Jimmy Deane, Mike Dunphy, Joe Lynch, Gerry Murray, Sean Browne, Jude Malone and Jerry Kelleher.

Other members recognized for their service included John Ahearne, Ed Powell, Joe Vallely, Janie Smith, Jerry Cronin, Mike Magee, Michael O'Dea, C. O'Donoughue, Mike Martin, Seamus Daly, Bill Lucitt, Tim Lyons, Brendan Merriman, Mickey Keddy, Mark Synnott, Pat Cassidy, Larry Grace, Mike McGee, Phillip Cassidy, John O'Donoughue, Bernard O'Reilly, the Gills, John McIntyre, Dymphna Brown, Donna Haines, Brendan Daly, Seamus Kilmurray, Louis Barry, Jim Synnott, Sean Heagney, Sean Madden, Vince Conlon, Bernard O'Reilly, Harry Lynch, Jack Egan, Paddy Hough, Mick Donoughue, Sean Clements, Donaghy Brothers, Tom Jorden, Bro. Brendan, Christy Gaffney, John

Martin, Jimmy Gunning, Bertie Cronin, Malachy Smith, Jack Mahoney, Jimmy Deery and Gerry Murray.

ST. PATRICK'S

St. Patrick's Gaelic Football and Hurling Club was formed in March 1968. All of the founding members were previously with the Garryowen club. Due to a massive influx of people from Ireland to Toronto in the late '60s, it was felt that there was a need for another GAA club in Toronto. The new club was based in the West End of Toronto; founding members included Vice President Eddie Nevin (Carlow), Secretary Jimmy Mullins (Laois), Delegate John Keane (Kerry), Treasurer Syl Bowles (Limerick) and President Father Gerry Scott (Roscommon). The following year the President was Frank Sheehan (Cork); Katie Gilroy, R.I.P. (Cavan), served the club with distinction in these early years. St. Pat's first games were played at Neil McNeil High School against Garryowen. The participants were as follows:

Football Team	Hurling Team
Frank Sheehan, Cork	Mick Ryan, Limerick
Paddy McCormack, Kildare	Gus Walsh, Cavan
Mick Casey, Louth	Mike Hanniffy
Joe Casey, Kerry	Mike Fahy, Galway
Donie Fitzpatrick, Cavan	Larry Bowles, Limerick
Hughie Fitzpatrick, Cavan	Syl Bowles, Limerick
Ed Nevin, Carlow	Paddy Dwyer, Tipperary
Fr. Gerry Scott, Roscommon	Mike Carmody, Tipperary
Fr. Noel Martin, Roscommon	John Gilmurray, Longford
Mick Griffith, Kerry (R.I.P.)	Ed Nevin, Carlow
John Keane, Kerry	Sean O'Sullivan, Limerick
Mike O'Brien, Kildare	Dave Power, Tipperary
Patsy O'Brien, Kildare	Noel O'Halloran, Galway
Jim Maguire, Kildare	Brendan Sheerin, Kilkenny
Jim Mullins, Laois	Mike Woodgate, Kilkenny
Mick Donegan, Kerry	Oliver Cummins, Kilkenny
Larry Bowles, Limerick	D.Cummins, Kilkenny
John Gilmurray, Longford	John Carroll, Tipperary

In the very first year the club reached the football championship final and was narrowly beaten by Garryowen. St. Pat's went from strength to strength; they had great hurlers from all the hurling counties, and players from nearly every county made up the football teams. The club members enjoyed playing the game at the highest level with competitive sportsmanship and they enjoyed camaraderie during the many organized social functions. Indeed, St. Pat's was instrumental in bringing the famous "Bothy Band" on tour to North America in 1976.

Club members in **1968** included Jim Foley (Carlow), Peter Gilbourne (Limerick), Pat Griffith (Laois), Ernie Kennedy (Cavan), John O'Connor, (Limerick), Donal O' Donoghue (Kerry), Des O'Halloran (Cork), Brian Smith (Cavan), Seamus Smith (Cavan), Dominic Toomey, Pat Touhy (Laois), Ed Tracey (Tipperary), Joe Tracey (Tipperary), Liam Wade (Derry), Sean Wade (Derry), Ed Walsh (Wexford), Gus Walsh (Cavan), John Young, John Burke (Galway), Mike Cahill (Tipperary), Pat Callahan (Cork), Joe Carey (Limerick), Mike Kelly (Carlow), Tony Duffy (Galway) and Larry Dwyer (Kilkenny).

1969 members included Damien Byrne (Mayo), Tommy Byrne (Meath), Joe Cagney (Limerick), Tom Cahalane (Galway), Larry Cleary (Tipperary), Jim Cooney (Clare), Declan Corrigan (Louth), Olly Coughlan (Offaly), Vincent Coyne (Roscommon), Eddie Creed (Cork), Lorcan Cribben (Offaly) (President), Frank Devlin (Derry), Pat Diamond (Antrim), Pat Donovan (Cork), Frankie Doyle (Carlow), Benny Drumm (Leitrim), Pat Foley (Carlow), Tom Kelly (Wexford), Aiden Manning (Donegal), Tom Mulvaney (Meath), Larry Murphy (Wicklow), Ned Murphy (Limerick), Richard McCarthy (Tipperary), Colman McSweeney (Cork), Colm O'Brien (Cavan), Sean O'Sullivan (Limerick), Mickie Reilly (Cavan), Mick Ryan (Limerick), Tom Carthy (Roscommon), Mike Ryan (Waterford) and Vincent Sheahan (Cork).

In the **1970** Carthy Cup—played in 1971—St. Pat's team that year consisted of Sean O'Sullivan (Limerick), Brian Shouldice (Tipperary) (R.I.P.), Ken Walsh (Kilkenny) (President 1974), Noel Rohan (Kilkenny), Syl Bowles (Limerick), Larry Bowles (Limerick), Paddy Dwyer (Tipperary), Jim Foley (Carlow), Joe Cagney (Limerick), Joe Mulcahy (Limerick), Mike Carmody (Tipperary), John C. Ryan (Tipperary), Tom Dawson (Limerick) and Eammon McGrath (Limerick).

Club members of **the 70s** included Dan Ryan (Tipperary), Matt Smith (Cavan), Martin Hyland (Cavan), Billy McHugh (Mayo), Liam Mullins (Laois), Mickey Mullins (Laois), Mike Mulvaney (Meath), John Molloy (Galway President) (R.I.P.), Seamus Moran (Dublin), Maurice Lynch (Limerick), Jimmy Madden (Tipperary), Dermot Kavanagh (Dublin), Eamonn Greenan (Cavan), Tom Dawson (Limerick), Pat Dermody (Carlow), Joe Uniacke (Galway), Pat Uniacke (Galway), Vince Ward (Tyrone), Tom Whelan (Laois), Dermot Ryan (Tipperary) (President), Hughie Ryan (Offaly), Jack Ryan (Tipperary) Joe Ryan (Tipperary), John Scully (Laois), Sean Shanahan (Tipperary), Ciaran Tuite (Longford), Charlie Quinn (Offaly), Mick Quirke (Kerry), Tommy Rafter (Offaly), Brian Plunkett (Dublin) (President), Ann Power (Tipperary) (Secretary), Pat Power (Tipperary), Dave Power (Tipperary), Gerry O'Leary (Dublin), Eamonn O'Loghlin (Clare) (President), Paddy O'Neill (Cavan), Jerry O'Reilly (Dublin), Joe O'Reilly (Dublin), Neil Owens (Roscommon), Sean McCarthy (Dublin), Sam McCauley (Wexford), Joe McCole (Monahan), Mike McCormac (Mayo), Steve McCrudden (Dublin), Seamus McEnroe (Monahan), John Morley (Mayo) (President), Sean Morley (Toronto/Mayo) (President), Nick Morrisey (Offaly), Joe Mulligan (Offaly), Jack Murphy (Cork), Maurice Murphy (Cork), Tommy Murphy (Cork), Niall Leahy (Cork) (R.I.P.), Ed Leen (Kerry), Jonathan Lynn (Kilkenny), Joe Maguire (Kildare), Kevin Maguire (Kildare), Liam Maguire (Toronto), Pascal Malone (Kildare), Gus Moffat (Dublin), John Grant (Longford), Danny Garry (Limerick), Pauric Gavin (Galway), John Fehan (Cork), Luke Flanagan (Roscommon), Fr. Paddy Flatley (Galway) (R.I.P.),

Pádraig Burke (Cork), Seamus Burke (Galway), Tommy Callanan (Galway), John Campbell (Limerick), Mike Carthy (Roscommon), Gerry Cassidy (Tyrone), Patsy Colgan (Offaly), Dr. Paddy Crowley (Cork), John Cummins (Toronto), Seamus Curran (Kerry), Dave Curtin (Cork),Tommy Daly (Tipperary), Dr. Pádraig Darby (Cork), James Devane (Tipperary), Joe Diamond (Antrim), Liam "Doc" Doherty (Donegal), Dennis Fahey (Tipperary), Bill Farrel (Meath), Cathal Boyd (Mayo), Niall Bracken (Kildare), Sam Breen (Limerick), John Burke (Cork), Richard Bennett (Cavan), Bill Bergin (Offaly), Ciaran Bonner (Tipperary), Gunther Korniman (Germany) and Finian Leahy (Dublin) (R.I.P.).

In a senior hurling match in May 1972, St. Pat's trounced St. Mike's 24-12. St. Pat's Denis Fahy and Eamonn McGrath both had two goals and two points. Noel Romad scored two goals and two points, and Jack Ryan got a single. Seam McNamara led St. Mike's with two goals. Kevin Loughnane scored a goal and two points and Tony Keyes got a single.

In May 1973, St. Mike's avenged their loss with an 18-15 victory over St. Pat's. Joe Roche with two goals and four points was the winner's top scorer. John Uniacke, Paddy Gleeson and Denis Fahy scored a goal and a point for St. Pat's.

In June 1973 at Lawrence Park Stadium, St. Vincent's and St. Patrick's split a double header. St. Pat's won the hurling 21-18 and St. Vincent's won the football match 11-6. Goals, by Ciaran Bellew and Pat Kelly early in the second half, paved the way for St. Vincent's win in football. Seamus McKenna and Hubert Quinn had two points and Ben Smith had a single. Vince Ward led St. Pat's with a goal and two points and Matthy Smith kicked a single.

In the hurling game, Liam Mullins scored two goals and two singles to lead St. Patrick's. Denis Fahy scored five single points, Jack Ryan had a goal and two singles, and Paddy Gleeson had three singles. St. Vincent's Pat McIntyre replied with two goals, and John McGivern, Eamonn Bile and Larry Cleary struck for four points.

In the Toronto final against St. Mike's in 1974, St. Pat's win allowed them to advance to the NACB semifinal championships against Chicago's Harry Bolands. Players that won over St. Mike's included Paddy Gleeson (Tipperary), Tommy Callanan (Galway), John Ormond (Waterford), Dennis Fahey (Tipperary), Tommy Kennedy (Tipperary), Noel Rohan (Kilkenny), Sam McCauley (Wexford), John Molloy (Galway), Pat Power (Tipperary), Joe Uniacke (Galway), Syl Bowles (Limerick), Ken Walsh (Kilkenny) and Dr. Paddy Crowley (Cork).

St. Pat's won their semifinal over Chicago's Bolands and then competed in the 1974 NACB Senior Hurling Final; they lost narrowly to Boston Galway. Players in the final included James Devane (Tipperary), Tommy Kennedy (Tipperary), Joe Uniacke (Galway), John Ormond (Waterford), Maurice Lynch (Limerick), Ken Walsh (Kilkenny), Sam McCauley (Wexford), Jim Foley (Carlow), Paddy Gleeson (Tipperary), Noel Rohan (Kilkenny), Pat Power (Tipperary), Dr. Paddy Crowley (Cork), Dennis Fahey (Tipperary) and Tommy Callanan (Galway).

St. Pat's most glorious moment came in 1978, with select St. Mike's players, when they won the NACB Senior Hurling Final. This would be the fourth Canadian club, after Montreal (1961), Garryowen (1965, 1970 and 1974), and St. Mike's (1975), that would win a NACB crown. This was also the final year that a Canadian team took home a NACB Championship trophy.

St. Pat's endeavoured to support the Toronto Divisional Board in every way. The club appreciated the efforts of all involved, particularly Chairmen Brendan Barry and Mike O'Driscoll, for the commitment given to promoting the playing of the Gaelic games. Players also much appreciated the efforts of the many women who served on committees over the years, particularly Ann Power who was named Secretary of the "Century."

Players during **the 1980s** included Ciaran Farrell (Dublin), Brian Forrester (Dublin) (President), Henry Geraghty (Galway) (President), Geremy Glennon (Offal), Mick Glynn (Sligo), Fergie Gordon (Down), Colm Bonner (Tipperary), Cormac Bonner (Tipperary), Bernard Tully (Cavan) (Captain), Pat Moriarty (Kerry) (Treasurer), Joe Murphy (Cork), Garry McAullife (Kildare), Jerome McCann (Antrim), Finbar McCarthy (Cork) (President), Tom McGuinness (Derry), Benny McGuire (Louth), Joe McKenna (Monahan) (President), Jimmy O'Connell (Clare), Niall O'Connell (Dublin), Leo O'Shea (Kerry), Tony Pat (Galway), Paul Kennedy (Dublin) (President), Tommy Kennedy (Tipperary), Kevin Kilmurray (Offaly) and Dan Healy (Kerry).

In a 1981 senior hurling championship versus Garryowen, the following lined out: Pat Callahan, Dermot Ryan, Tommy Murphy, John Burke, Jack Murphy, Paddy Gleeson, Sean Shanahan, Jonathan Lynn, John Fehan, Cormac Bonner, Colm Bonner, Ken Walsh, Ciaran Farrell, Bill Bergin and Maurice Lynch.

1985 and 1987 were banner years for the club; they won the Toronto GAA men's championships in football. This was a magnificent time; St. Pat's brought athleticism and skill to their championship form.

The 1987 football championship team photo included Brian Forestal, Mike Conolly, Paul Kennedy, Finbar McCarthy, Steve Murphy, Ross McDonald, Eamon McGuinness, Niall Finnegan, Secretary Niall O'Connell, Dave Cashell, Ray Lockhart, Captain Ted Webb, Alex Morlay, Cathal O'Connor and President Eamonn O'Connor. Paul Moriarity served as the club's treasurer that year.

A 1989 St. Pat's Hurling team that beat St. Mike's included Ken Walsh, Jack Murphy, Tommy Murphy, James Devane, John Fehan, Sean Shanahan, Larry Dwyer, Paddy Gleeson, Dermot Ryan, Mick Ryan, Jonathan Lynn and Tom Whelan.

In July 1990, St. Pat's traveled to play the Ottawa Gaels in a one-point victory. Davey Carroll, who had played for a few years earlier in Vancouver, moved to Toronto that year and lined out for St. Pat's. He was an effective half-forward that day.

Ireland's "Celtic Tiger" had kicked in during the early 1990s and immigrants were in short supply. Players of the '90s who served the club included: Mike Burke (Laois), Gerry Hevey (Meath), Mike Hanniffy, Finbar Collins, Gerry Healy (Meath), Bernie Presthorn, Alan Hussey (Meath), and Canadians John J. Rooney (1995; Captain 2006) and Brendan Cahill (1998).

A meeting was held between the executive committees of both St. Pat's and the Irish Canadians in late 1993 at Jack Murphy's bar on Eglinton Ave. The clubs had done some indoor training together over the winter months and everyone seemed to get along. The teams decided to amalgamate so they could field a more competitive squad. This amalgamated team would eventually reach the championship finals in 1995 against St. Mike's.

1995 was the year the GAA Senior Player of the Year was awarded to the "Quiet Man", Joe Murphy. Joe was recognized for his years of hard work with the Association and in leading St. Pat's to their league cup win. A true sportsman, who demonstrated respect to both friend and foe alike, and was highly respected in return.

Players of the new millennium include: Paul King (Derry), Sean King (Dublin) and Shay Reilly (Dublin). Many Canadians have contributed to St. Pat's including Kieran Ryan, Captain (2000); Liam Maguire (2001), Sean Morley (2002), Kieran and Colin Byrne (2003), Gary Mangan (2003), Dave Gallagher (2004), Paul King (2004), Jason Loughnane (2004), Brian Mosnick (2005), Matthew O'Driscoll (2006), Shay O'Reilly (2006); Declan Woods, Kevin Gleeson and Kevin Higgins (2007).

St. Pat's was privileged to have had many great people over the years: John Molloy (R.I.P.) from Moycullen, Galway, and Erskine Avenue, Toronto; Monahan's Gerry McKenna and Enda McGuinness (President), who kept things going through the '80s and '90s; and none more than John Morley (Mayo), who has been active in the club for more than 30 years. He has weathered the decline of players coming from Ireland in the last 20 years and brought the club along with the introduction of Canadian-born lads, including his son Sean who was the youngest of their great Presidents. The club is going strong today and held its 40th anniversary on May 24th 2008 at the Strates Banquet Hall. Music was provided by Hugo Straney and St. Pat's hosted Nickey Brennan – President of the GAA and Sheamus Howlin – Chair of the Overseas Committee.

OTTAWA GAELS

Ottawa did not seem to attract the number of Irish immigrants that the other Canadian cities did, so Gaelic games had a spasmodic existence down through the years. Dick Bracken (Kildare) and Mike Kelly were some of the Ottawa Irish who would, on occasion, travel to compete with the Montreal hurling teams. As members of the Sons of Ireland, they and other pre and postwar immigrants were great supporters of Gaelic games. The Sons of Ireland was the main Irish organization from the early 1930s to the late 1950s. Unfortunately, travel was onerous for anyone wanting an opportunity for regular play of Irish games.

Kerry man Pat Scott, who arrived in 1957, was the first President of the Ottawa Irish Society. This Society was established to aid Irish immigrants over rough spots and to promote Irish culture. That year, Ottawa brought its members 120 miles to have a hurling match with the Montreal Shamrocks. Montreal lent a number of players to Ottawa and a fine exhibition of hurling was put on display. The Shamrocks won in the end. All those who traveled were fed, watered and entertained at a rented hall in Verdun. A great night ensued with music by box player Willie O'Neill (Galway).

The Ottawa Irish would continue to have informal training sessions, and from these sessions, an exhibition football match was scheduled against the Montreal Shamrocks in May 1965. At the time, an Australian Rules Football Team from Melbourne was visiting Montreal.

In the late '60s, Tom McCay (Tyrone) started a social club called *Tir Na nOg* (The Land of Eternal Youth), which eventually grew to over 3,000 members. Show bands were the rage and soon Molly Maguires, in the heart of the nation's capital, was born with grand support from the community.

The Founding

In the fall of 1974, in the back of Molly Maguire's Pub on Rideau St., Galway man Pat Kelly (who had been a stalwart of Toronto's St. Vincent's before he moved to the nation's capital), John Keenan, Don Kavanagh, Frankie Casey, Brendan Mulhall and a few other friends decided that they wanted to play a Gaelic Football match. From this meeting, the Ottawa Gaels Gaelic Football Club was born.

On Sunday November 3, 1974, in Montreal, history was made with a tight match that ended in a draw. Montreal's Paul Moran was the referee. The Montreal players were Paddy Dunne (R.I.P.), Sammy O'Connor, Pat Donnelly, Pat Leyne, Billy Coen, Des Mackie, Paul Loftus, Pat Short, Dennis Baker, Joe Kelly, Matt Dooley, Brendan Glennane, John Carroll, John O'Shea, Bro. Andrew Hobbin and Frank Nash.

The Ottawa team consisted of Noel Kenny, Chris Donnelly, Chris Carey, Brendan Mulhall, Pat Kelly, John Mulready, Tommy Boland, John Keenan, Richard Carey, Louis Comerton, John Riddell, Frankie Casey and Sean Kenny. The subs were Pat Scott, Tom Murtagh and Paul O'Kane.

The majority of the above-mentioned names were gleaned from the exceptional memory of John Keenan, a Meath man and ex-Montrealer who joined the Gaels team when he relocated to Ottawa. John had the distinction of winning the Toronto Junior Footballer of the Year when he was playing with the Montreal Shamrocks in 1974.

Galway's Paul Moran, who arrived in Canada in 1955, brought his Montreal team, weeks later, to play Ottawa at St. Joseph's High School. Another match took place at the Potvin Arena off Shefford Road. This intermingling established a great relationship between the Montreal and Ottawa football crowd, which has continued through the years.

From these games, a "bunch of Irish guys" became a committed team that was keen for some broader competition. A letter, dated December 2, 1974, was received by the Ottawa Gaels' Don Kavanagh from former Montreal Shamrocks' player John O'Brien (Cleveland), acknowledging the registration of the Gaels as a team with the American County Board. John O'Brien was the Secretary of the NACB as this time.

The Toronto League

In 1975, Ottawa played their matches within the Toronto League and the Eastern Canadian Divisional Board of the NACB. The executive committee for the season was Chairman Pat Kelly, Coach John Keenan, Don Kavanagh, Coach Pat Scott and Louis Comerton. The Captain and trainer was Richard Carey with Tom Boland serving as Vice-Captain.

Paddy Lynn from Ballina, Mayo arrived in Ottawa in 1927 and from then, up until his death in 1975, played a leading role in the affairs of the Irish community. The Patrick Lynn Memorial Cup was named after him by the Irish Society of Ottawa and was donated to the Toronto GAA for the winner of the Canadian Junior Gaelic Football Championships. Captain Richard Carey was awarded the trophy by the First Secretary of the Irish Embassy, Jim Flavin on September 6 when the Gaels won their first Championship.

The following day, on September 7, the Gaels played the Midwest champions Pittsburgh in Buffalo. A loss by ten points, 0-14 to 0-4, saw Noel Kenny, S. Henchin, F. Connelly, Brendan Mulhall, Chris Carey, Peter Sorrenti, Peter Brennan, Tom Boland, C. Toland, Robert Carey, P. Wright, Tom Murtagh, Frankie Casey, Chris Donnelly, Pat Kelly and John Mulready play that day.

A September 28 Junior Football League semifinal match against Clan Na nGael saw a close loss of 0-11 to 1-6. Outstanding for Ottawa was mid-fielder Tom Boland, who was chosen as the Toronto GAA Junior Footballer of the Year, and Rob Fletcher in goal. The Gaels played a total of ten games that season; winning five, drawing one and losing four. Of the ten games played by the Gaels, four were played in Toronto, one in Buffalo, one in Montreal and four in Ottawa. To fulfill these fixtures, the Gaels traveled over 3000 miles during the four month playing season.

The 1976 executive committee that were elected included John Keenan, Coach Pat Kelly, Brendan Mulhall, Mary Coffey, Louis Comerton, Don Kavanagh and Dave O'Donohoe. Peter Sorrenti was chosen as Captain, Tom Boland Vice-Captain and David Coffey as equipment manager.

The 1977 executive included Peter Brennan, Pat Kelly, Ann Coffey, Charlie Toland, Louis Comerton, Vice-Captain John Keenan, Noel Kenny and Captain Liam Peel. Sean Henchon was selected as Junior Footballer of the Year while Pat Kelly was runner-up as the Sportsman of the Year from the Toronto GAA. The first annual dinner-dance was organised for November 5 at the Commonwealth Ballroom North at the Holiday Inn on

Kent Street. By the end of the year, new committee members included Tom Murtagh, Roy Oxton, Mike Mellon (Tyrone), Bob Wilson and Charlie Deeney.

A player selection tool was developed by the Gaels in July 1977 with five categories:
Category 1 - Players who always turn out for training and are willing to travel
Category 2 - Players who sometimes turn out for training and are always willing to travel
Category 3 - Players who never turn out for training and who are always willing to travel
Category 4 - Players who never turn out for training and who are sometimes willing to travel and the dreaded Category 5 - Players who never turn out for training and who are never willing to travel!

Tour of Ireland

The team journeyed from Ottawa on September 21, 1978 and competed in the famous Kilmacud 7's tournament on September 23 in Ireland. Too tired, too inexperienced and totally outclassed in a tournament of Irish Senior County Champions, the Gaels fell to defeat at the hands of Antrim men – St. John's of Belfast, Galway men – Dunmore McHales and Meath men – Skyrne.

A week later, the young men of St. Jarlath's Tuam, who were the All-Ireland College's Champions, handed a severe beating to the Gaels. The team retreated to the home town of Pat Kelly (Ballygar) where they were showered with great hospitality before a good match was played and the Gaels lost by four points on October 1.

On October 4, the Gaels moved north to Strabane for the final game of the tour where, once again, tremendous hospitality was put on display. Defeat, at the hands of a strong Eoin Roe O'Neill's team came after a tough, yet enjoyable game. The Chairman of the Strabane Urban District Council presented the club with the town's Coat of Arms as a memento of the Gael's visit.

The 1979 committee for the Gaels included Tom McSwiggan, Robert Wilson, Ben Coffey, Mike Mellon, Pat Kelly, John Mulready, Tom Boland, Vivian Boland and Peter Brennan. Players included Tom Faith, Sean Egan, Joe Dalton, Tom McGrath, Noel Kenny, Sean Henchon, Jack Sadler, Vince Murray, Larry Motiur, Des McCann, Chris McCann, Dick Gainey, Chris Donnelly, Bob Kerr, Charles Deeney and Manus Brennan.

The '80s and '90s

The club continued to thrive and one truly unique family holds a historic spot in Canadian GAA history. Tom Daly, a great Montreal supporter and traveler in his playing days, was now a resident of Ottawa. He saw his four Canadian-born sons make history when they all played together on the Gaels team in the late '80s. Billy, Kevin, Mike and Steve were a sight to behold when all four of them took to the field.

On November 12, 1983, Montreal's legendary Paul Moran, along with seventeen players, traveled to Ottawa and lost in the nation's capital 3-11 to 2-7. However, Montreal won by the narrowest of margins at Central Park in Ville LaSalle on May 20, 1984. A remarkable fact is that through the long association between Montreal and Ottawa, rivalries have always been left behind on the playing field, and the convivial spirit of both the Gaels and Shamrocks dominated the post-game receptions.

The Ottawa Gaels of 1984 included L. Bradley, M. Connolly, J. Kennedy, C. Deeney, T. McSwiggan, V. Boland, I. Kiernan, K. Daly, S. Foran, T. Quinn, G. Bali, M. Daly, R. Gannon, P. Kelly, J. Keenan, C. McGrath, J. Lecombe, F. Berry, B. Wilson, B. Daly, B. Keating and C. Keating.

A men's team photo of 1987 included Social Director Graham Bali (Ottawa), Tom Boland, Viven Boland, Noel Brisson, President Mike Connolly (Antrim), Billy Daly, Captain Kevin Daly, Mike Daly, Jim Gunn (Montreal), Bruce Holmes, John Keenan, Vice-President Pat Kelly, John Lacombe, Tom Lucy, Jim Lucy, Dean Sayer and Neal Valois. Executive members that year also included Treasurer Joan Daly (Ottawa) and Secretary Breda Kelly (Galway).

1989 saw the following men participate with the Gaels: Graham Bali, Mike Connolly, Ross Carmody, Fernando Diniz, Kevin Daly, Mike Daly, Steve Daly, Billy Daly, Mark Donagher, Dave Gunn, Jim Gunn, Kevin Gregoire, Cal Gutman, Bruce Holmes, Tony Hodgins, Pat Kelly, John Keenan, John Lacombe, James Mahoney, Rich McFall, Dave McFall, Ian Martin, Dean Sayer, Jimmy Walker, Anthony Walsh, Darryl Demsey, Brian Ladden and Liam Green.

A men's team list of 1991 included Trevor Spencer, Gabriel Tracey, Jonathan O'Neill, Earl Cochrane, Alex Anderson, Peter Crossan, Kevin Dennehy, John Dooley, Meredith Egan, Jim Gunn, John Kennedy, Pat Murray, James Mahoney, A. O'Mahoney and Joe Tice.

The 1992 squad had players such as Kevin Carroll, Kevin Gregoire, Steve Harwood, Fintan Hennessy, Roddy McFall, John Walsh, Damien Curly, Paddy O'Donohoe, Sean Pendergrast, Dean Sayer, Sean Conlon (Powerscreen 7's MVP), Velquin De Silva, Richard Gagnon, Rory Keenan, Dave Rowntree, Kevin Frazer, Kevin Wolfe, Scott Wolfe and Jim Brennan.

The squad of 1994 saw Pat Kelly, Fergal Macken, Shawn Walsh, Dave Gunn, Graeme Bali, Steve Daly, Neil Greene, Jim Gunn, Steve Harwood, Stan MacLellan, Robbie Chiasson, Shawn Dickie, Michael O'Hagan, Greg Wilson, Kevin Carroll, Jeff Specht, Pat O'Donohoe, Brett Baigne, Ray McSwiggan, Mark Tracy, Shawn Logue, Connor Reid, Doug Assaly, Steve Smith, Karl Brunky, Scott Plunkett and Frank Quinn tog out that season.

Men's World Cup

In 2000, Doug O'Connor and Blair Anderson, along with David Lambert (Tipperary) were the club selections for the Canadian men's team that would attend the Gaelic

Football World Cup. The Gaels were proud to have four of their players,—Monaghan's Noel McGinnity, Dublin's Peter Connaughton, and Canadian-born Doug O'Connor and Liam McDonald—selected in 2002. Canada made it to the semifinals of this six-nation tournament. The Ottawa men that were selected onto the 2004 Toronto All-Stars were Doug O'Connor, Peter Connaughton and Ned Flynn.

More Recent Days

In 2005, the club celebrated its 30th anniversary and Dermot Guinnane won the Toronto GAA MVP. Since joining the Ottawa Gaels, Dermot has not only demonstrated his all-round superb ability in the game, but has been a leader both on and off the pitch. Dermot's displays on the field have been quality, and through his abilities and determination he has helped lift his teammates and challenged them to achieve greater heights. Dermot was also a repeat winner of the Ottawa Gaels Men's MVP and has collected a few Toronto GAA All-stars.

In 2006, Doug O'Connor organized a new sign for the field that welcomed people to Uplands Gaelic Park—the home of the Ottawa Gaels. The Senior Men's team looked back on many positive moments that season, but ultimately it proved to be an "almost" year. Things began brightly for the lads when Graeme Bali was appointed team coach. He put the guys through their paces in a challenging pre-season that began in early April. In an encouraging start to the season, the lads reached the final of the Montreal tournament, only to lose to a very strong St. Mike's team. After this promising beginning, the Men's team took a few steps backward in the opening league games. Two heavy defeats in a row set the alarm bells ringing, but a patient attitude from the coach and hard work from the lads saw them gradually improve. With the addition of a few Irish lads to the fold in June, the team began to get into a rhythm, generated some team spirit and gathered a little momentum. The remaining league games saw drastically improved performances and the beginnings of some positive teamwork.

When Championship time rolled around, it was clear that the lads were hitting their form. They dispatched Montreal in a clinical manner before meeting St. Vincent's in the semifinal. In a tight encounter, the Ottawa men showed great character to come from behind in the second half and win by 1-1.

A replay of the Montreal tournament decider beckoned for the final. Five minutes into the second half, things looked ominous for the Gaels as they trailed St. Mike's by six points. It was shaping up as many in Centennial Park had predicted—it would be a facile win for the Toronto "supremos"—but two Ottawa goals changed that view and set things up for a grandstand finish. However, their valiant fight wilted in the August sunshine and St. Mike's held on, with a late goal that put a gloss on the score line. It was a huge team effort to bring the Men's Championship back to the capital for the first time, but the Gaels' quest for the Holy Grail came up just short. Dermot Guinnane would be selected as the Toronto Player of the Year.

Ladies' Football

New life came into the club in 1988 when Breda Kelly (Galway) started up a women's Gaelic Football team. It would be in 1989 that the ladies were admitted into the Toronto ladies' league except all Ottawa matches were deemed as challenge matches by the Toronto GAA that year.

Ladies who lined out for the Gaels in 1991 included Lianne Allinott, Sue Brown, Meredith Ballie, Laura Coyle, Marion Connolly, Angela Connolly, Tracey Connolly, Michelle Connolly, Kathleen Chappelle, Connie Corrigan, Lorna Campbell, Sheena Cullen, Nancy Daly, Erin Daly, Veronica Kelly, Jennifer Lynch, Karen Larock, Angela McFall, Nancy McFall, Donna Moore, Karen Moore, Sharon O'Connell, Anne Pregent, Linda Reilly, Lynn Sabourin, Jane Sadler, Jennifer Saunders, Cathy Shirley, Anne Marie Sinisac, Wilma Te Plate, Suzanne Taylor, Anne Marie Taylor, Denise Yetman, Isabelle Carrier, Heather Finlayson, Kerry Allinott, Natalie Julien, Marie France La Belle, Breda Kelly and those who first name is only remembered – Marci, Wendy, Amelia, Stephanie, Beth and Tina.

New additions to the 1992 squad included Nicky Watts, Kathleen Chappelle, Maureen Whelton, Michelle Boyle, Mary Grehan, Mary Mullins, Nancy Fairburn and Caroline De Silva. Additions in 1993 were Ann Brady, Mandy Watkins, Jennifer Lync, Sue Wong, Jacy Duperreault, Rose Anne Filipow, Mich Gregoire, Paule Carrier and Annie Savage.

In 1994 the club won its first Toronto League trophy and the squad was on the cusp of championship form. Those who were leading the way were Monique Salajka, Ann Marie Etheridge, Jennifer Saunders, Michelle Wilde, Roseanne Filipow, Sheena Cullen, Karyn O'Flaherty, Pat Lawrence, Nancy McCall, Karen Moore, Nicky Watts, Wilma Te Plate, Paule Carrier, Michelle Boyle, Meredith Baillie, Anne Marie Taylor, Susanne Taylor, Jennifer Lynch, Veronica Kelly, Breda Kelly, Sheila Kraag, Shannon Draper, Jodi Draper, Erin Keating and Brid McDonald.

The 1996 Gaels team included Anne Brady, Julie Brown, Martine Courage, Jodi Draper, Shannon Draper, Anne Marie Etheridge, Mary Lou Foley, Suzanne Glass, Mary Green, Breda Kelly, Veronica Kelly, Lisa Langevin, Jennifer Lynch, Sabrena Mackenzie, Karen Moore, Karyn O'Flaherty, Tanya Pierunek, Monique Salajka, Jennifer Saunders, Wilma Te Plate, Maria Tracey, Cherie Usher, Amanda Wilcox and Kate Flood. Coaches were Brendan McKittrick and Pat Kelly with Scott Plunkett, Karl Brunke and Jeff Specht serving on the executive committee.

1998 would see many veterans and a few new faces tog out for the season: Daphne Ballard, Anthia Batchelor, Tracy Boehm, Breda Brosnan, Joanne Cairns, Fontina Carzille, Emma Chester, Martine Courage, Jodi Draper, Shannon Draper, Anne Marie Ethridge, Brenda Fleming, Megan Grier, Kerry Gunn, Paula Horsford, Breda Kelly, Lisa Langevin, Sue Lussier, Dana McCabe, Karen Moore, Fiona O'Carroll, Karyn O'Flaherty, Niamh Ruane, Monique Salakja, Jen Saunders, Tiffany Shirley, Andrea Stewart, Wilma Te Plate, Nicky Watts and Amanda Wilcox.

The first Toronto Championship for the Ottawa Gaels occurred in 1999 with a league victory in 2000. Powerscreen 7s MVP awards have included Breda Kelly in 1992, Jennifer Saunders in 1998 and Daphne Ballard. The club's first back to back doubles happened in 2001 and 2002 with more doubles in 2004 and 2006; today the women's team continues to dominate competition within the Toronto Divisional Board.

The ladies have played a significant role on the international teams over the years, with many of their numbers being a part of Team Canada. Members of the 2000 Canadian team included Karen Moore, Selector; Megan Greer, Sue Lussier, Tiffany Shirley, Breda Kelly, Willie Te Plate, Niamh Ruane, Daphne Ballard and Jodi Draper. The Ottawa women that were selected onto the 2004 Toronto All-Stars were Niamh Ruane, Breda Kelly and Lisa Connaughton.

During the 2002 International Ladies series, Ottawa Gaels' Jarlath Connaughton was a selector for the Canadian Ladies' team. In 2005, he was appointed team manager. This marked the first time a truly representative Canadian team of players, drawn from Vancouver, Calgary, Edmonton, Montreal, Ottawa and Toronto, competed and won the Shield Cup at the International Tournament in Dublin. Jarlath's willingness to travel across the country to help select the best players was critical to the team's success. The Ottawa Gaels members of the 2005 Shield Cup winning team were Daphne Ballard, Lisa Langevin and Sara McTaggart.

Five Cups in 2006

In 2006, the Ottawa Gaels won both the League and Championship of the Toronto Divisional Board, along with the Durham Emmets, Montreal Shamrocks and the International 7's Powerscreen tournaments, for a total of five cups.

Great credit was due to Coach Mark Lannin for guiding the ladies to such heights. His dedication, commitment and encouragement ensured that the team was focused, sporting and skilful in each game played. Always calm, cool and collected, Mark played a pivotal role in this phenomenal season.

A coach, however, doesn't win games—the superbly talented squad boasted great strength and depth; they took care of business. With the arrival of a number of Irish students for the summer, there was healthy competition for all positions. These visitors gave the club a great boost and had a very positive influence, whether it was upping the intensity at training or encouraging teammates in games. A French-Canadian quartet enlivened things at Uplands Gaelic Park. These four rookies brought oodles of enthusiasm and energy, as well as some bilingual pleasantries. Seasoned veterans included a number of former internationals, who all played key roles in 2006.

Ottawa Gaels retained the Toronto Ladies' Championship in 2007 after a hard-fought win over a determined Michael Cusacks' team. Although Ottawa ended up winning by eight points, a truer reflection of the game is in how many scores both teams managed. Both teams ended up with 12 scores each, Ottawa 5-7 vs. Michael Cusacks 1-11. The difference at the end of the game was Ottawa's ability to be more clinical when it came to goal chances.

In this regard, it was Ottawa full-forward Niamh Ruane who proved to be the catalyst for Ottawa's victory; she had a stunning first half hat-trick of goals. Niamh's ability to be out in front of her marker and her excellent positional sense was the key to Ottawa's attacking play. Ottawa's tactic of playing corner-forward Emily Carr as a third midfielder left lots of space in the forward line for Niamh to exploit her sharp, direct passes into the full-forwards, which caused the Cusacks' defence lots of problems.

At the other end of the field, veteran goalkeeper, Willie Te Plate, who played and won her eighth championship final, was equally important to Ottawa's victory. On a couple of occasions, just as it seemed that the Michael Cusacks would pull themselves right back into the game with a goal, Willie's bravery and experience denied the Cusacks' forwards several scoring opportunities.

The Michael Cusacks' exciting half-forward line was involved in most of their attacking play, and it was a testament to the concentration and determination of Ottawa's halfback line: Lisa Langevin, Megan Grier and Sara McTaggart that denied them the opportunity to have things all their own way. In the middle of the park, Erin Gallagher again showed why she is one of the top ladies' players in Canada, with another assured performance. However, matching up in the middle with Gallagher was Dawn Price, whose unselfish attitude and team play stopped the Cusacks midfield from dictating the play.

Second-half goals from Ottawa stalwart Daphne Ballard and half-forward Kathryn O'Hara put some daylight between the teams and gave the Ottawa girls a greater sense of belief, which carried them through to the final whistle. Lisa Langevin and Daphne Ballard collected the Championship trophy with Coach Mark Lannin.

The Ottawa Gael's team included Wille Te Plate, Lisa Wright, Lisa Connaughton, Emilie Montgrain, Sara McTaggart, Megan Grier, Lisa Langevin, Dawn Price, Daphne Ballard, Aoife O'Toole, Kate Hynes, Kathryn O'Hara, Karen Moore, Niamh Ruane, Emily Carr, and Caitlin Crooks. Other squad members included: Veronica Quinn, Angela Martin, Kate Dean, Tyrenny Anderson, Kerry Mortimer and Breda Kelly. The Gael's ladies team were selected as Ottawa's 'Team of the Year' at the community Sports Award dinner later that year.

Toronto's Lady Player of the Year Award

1994	Breda Kelly	1998	Breda Kelly
2000	Daphne Ballard	2002	Lisa Connaughton
2004	Dawn Price	2007	Daphne Ballard

Youth Development

The makeup of teams representing the Ottawa Gaels has changed dramatically, and the "Irish-born" are no longer the dominant force in the club. Much work has gone into developing local talent to play Gaelic Football.

Robbie Chaisson, who served as a Development Officer on the 2001 Toronto GAA Board, and who was an enthusiastic Gaelic footballer and teacher, introduced the games into his school and eventually to his Director of Physical Education—Bob Thomas. Thanks to Bob Thomas and the supporting efforts of Jarlath Connaughton, Joe Diffey, Noel McGinnity, Mark Lannin and Dermot Guinnane, Gaelic Football is now part of the Physical Education curriculum in the Ottawa-Carleton Catholic School Board. "It's a great sport that many of these kids haven't seen before. They love it, and it's new- it's something that they can call their own. They're really breaking new ground here in Canada in what is old hat for the Irish," said Chiasson after one successful tournament.

Five ready-to-go kits are available for schools to borrow when a teacher wishes to teach the game to students. In these kit bags are a number of footballs, video, pinnies, cones and an easy-to-use manual for the coach/teacher. More than two thousand children enjoy the sport in their schools each year.

On a day that started so foggy that players could not see across the pitch, grade 7 and 8 students from across the Ottawa-Carleton Catholic School Board made history with a tournament that brought together 17 teams – over 300 boys and girls aged 11 to 14 – at Twin Elm Rugby Park in Nepean, Ontario on October 26, 2000.

Tournament convenor Robbie Chiasson was thrilled with the tournament's success which saw boys and girls teams from seven Catholic schools: St. Pat's Intermediate, St. Paul's Intermediate, Lester B. Pearson, Frank Ryan, Holy Trinity, St. Mark's, Jean Vanier Intermediate and St. Joe's. The boy's final saw Holy Trinity facing off against Mother Theresa, while Mother Theresa's girls' faced Frank Ryan. In the end, Mother Theresa's teams swept the honours in both divisions.

In 2001, the Ottawa Gaels brought a U-14 youth team, to Tipperary and in 2002 to Carlow, to compete in Feile Peil Na nOg. The Canadians brought back silver medals. Members of the U-14 team in 2002 included Jon Sanchez, James Honshorst, Bryan Jaksic, Tony Gallo, Matt Valois, Andrew Legassick, Kevin McCleery, John Licari, Pawel Szulc, Rod Barillas, Sean Kerwin, Jason Thompson, Matt Picciano, Nick Scroggins, Emmond Bell, Kellen Walsh, Scott Cowie, Andrew Mather and Andrew Richardson. The team was managed by Pat Kelly, Joe Diffey, Tanya McClendon-Hustins, Wexford's Conor Power (a Gaelic Football tutor from Croke Park) and Jarlath Connaughton.

In October 2006, around 400 Ottawa-area students aged 11-14 took part in the annual Gaelic Football tournament; 14 schools participated. The Catholic School Board of Eastern Ontario sent teams to play in this tournament, which was hosted once again by the Ottawa-Carleton Catholic School Board. The winners were Frank Ryan (Boys) and St. Peter's (Girls).

Since 2004, Dublin's Jarlath Connaughton has served on the Steering Committee of the O'Neill's Continental Youth Championships (CYC). Ottawa has had representative teams compete in the championships in New York 2004 (U-16), San Francisco 2005, Boston 2006, Chicago 2007 and will, once more, in Philadelphia 2008.

At recent Ottawa Sports Award banquets, Gaelic Football was officially recognized in the local community. Dave McMurchy, Lisa Wright and Kate Dean (U-16), came through their schools and the club minor programme of the Ottawa Gaels, and they were recognized for their accomplishments in the sport. Kate, in particular, has been playing for five years and has made great progress. Although a high school student, Kate has represented the Ottawa Gaels' senior ladies' team and has displayed a growing maturity through her play. She has been rewarded with winner's medals in the league and championship, as well as for a Montreal tournament in 2006. Kate also represented the Ottawa Gaels at the Continental Youth Championships in New York, San Francisco and Boston. In 2007 the Gael's ladies team was selected as Ottawa's 'Team of the Year' at the community Sports Award dinner.

Pat Kelly

Peter Brennan wrote a short piece on the occasion of the 30th anniversary of the Gaels in 2005, when reflecting on the early days of the club, where he mentions names like Joe Dalton, Anto Dempsey, John O'Kelly, Paud Curran, the Kellys, McSwiggans, Careys, Keenans, Comertons and Bradleys. He writes: "Driven by a character called Kelly, possessed with a love and commitment for the GAA hitherto unknown, we shook up the GAA establishment in Canada. No longer were the boys from Toronto, Hamilton and Montreal going to have their own way. Such was our determination that wives were regularly abandoned early on a Sunday morning at the pleadings of Kelly knocking on the window door (breaking them down if need be) and saying 'Ah! Jaysus, come on, we really need you!' Those warriors who usually answered that call would find that when they got to the front door (or the bloody school bus) Kelly had only ten or eleven players and would then be off to annoy a few other wives/girlfriends."

On November 23, 2001, the Irish Hall of Fame inductees of the Irish Canadian Aid & Cultural Society Community Awards were Breda Kelly and her Uncle, Pat Kelly. The "Godfather" of the Ottawa Gaels, Pat, has been instrumental in keeping the games and culture ever present in Ottawa. From forming the club in 1974, to ensuring the storied Sam McGuire Cup visits to Ottawa in 1992, for the 2002 St. Patrick's Day parade, and in 2006.

Paul Moran of Montreal has said on numerous occasions that if there were a Gaelic Football on the other side of a wall, Pat Kelly would go through the wall than rather go around it! His determination and passion for the game is well-known. He has made many sacrifices of his time, and supported the game with his talent and treasure. Across the country, people have paid tribute to Pat's late dear wife, Ann (nee Dermody), who passed away on September 15, 2007. She was the rock from which Pat Kelly received the most support while building Ottawa's GAA and his beloved Irish community.

2008 and Beyond!

The Ottawa Gaels have a proud history, and with more and more Canadians taking up the game, the future looks increasingly bright. Ottawa leadership includes Lisa Langevin, Dermot Guinnane, Daphne Ballard, Jean-Francois Chapman, Noel McGinnity, Lisa Connaughton, Mark Lannin and Bill Wright who lead with their time and service.

GAA Person of the Year

1988	n/a	1989	Breda Kelly
1990	Dave Gunn	1991	Breda Kelly
1992	Pat Kelly	1993	Dave Gunn
1994	Breda Kelly	1995	Pat Kelly
1996	Brendan McKittrick	1997	David Forsyth
1998	Breda Kelly	1999	Doug O'Connor
2000	Robbie Chiasson	2001	Jarlath Connaughton
2002	Jarlath Connaughton	2003	Jarlath Connaughton
2004	Noel McGinnity	2005	Sarah McGinnity
2006	Mark Lannin	2007	Lisa Langevin and Dermot Guinnane

Sportspersons of the Year

1987 Jim Gunn and Mike Connolly
1988 Dave Gunn
1989 Steve Harwood and Breda Kelly
1990 Steve Harwood and Jennifer Saunders
1991 Steve Harwood, Dave Gunn and Nancy McCall
1992 Dave Gunn, Fintan Hennessy, Sheena Cullen and Karen Moore
1993 Greg Wilson, Michael O'Hagan and Michelle Boyle
1994 Shawn Dickie, Wilma Te Plate and Nancy McCall
1995 Chris Hulan, Jodi Draper and Monique Salajka
1996 Kevin Sheehan
1997 Gavin Duffy, John Stewart and Jodi Draper
1998 Jennifer Saunders and Wilma Te Plate
1999 Eoin Ruane and Wilma Te Plate
2000 Darragh Slowey and Niamh Ruane
2001 Ian Lazenby and Wilma Te Plate
2002 Liam McDonald, Wilma Te Plate and Kerri Beeching
2003 Daragh Slowey and Susan Lunn
2004 Doug O'Connor and Shauna Stewart
2005 Declan O'Sullivan, Doug O'Connor, Susan Lunn and Wilma Te Plate
2006 Barry Byrne and Shauna Stewart

2007 Jean-Francois Chapman, Karen Moore and Niamh Ruane

Rookies of the Year

1992 Nicky Watts
1993 Neil Greene and Jennifer Lynch
1994 Karl Brunke, Robbie Chiasson, Shannon Draper and Monique Salajka
1995 Kevin Sheehan and Joanna Hackett
1996 John Stewart and Michelle Dennehy
1997 Jeff Chamberlain, Eoin Ruane and Megan Grier
1998 Daphne Ballard
1999 Doug O'Connor and Maarit Heiskanen
2000 Peter Connaughton and Lisa Connaughton
2001 Steve Wilcox, Suzie Battaglia and Betty Miller
2002 Seamus Egan and Dawn Price
2003 Stewart Bremner, John Hoyle and Ginette Vizena
2004 Alex Munro and Lorraine Hodds
2005 Thomas Drevniok and Sarah McTaggart
2006 Chris Wynot and Emilie Montgrain
2007 Michael Kennefick and Caitlin Crooks

MVPs of the Year

1987 John Lacombe
1988 Billy Daly
1989 Fintan Hennessy and Breda Kelly
1990 Fintan Hennessy and Karen Moore
1991 Kevin Daly and Wilma Te Plate
1992 Sean Conlan and Breda Kelly
1993 Steve Daly and Breda Kelly
1994 Neil Greene and Breda Kelly
1995 Greg Whelan
1996 Brendan McKittrick and Breda Kelly
1997 Peter Talon and Breda Kelly
1998 Breda Kelly
1999 Doug O'Connor, Daphne Ballard and Jodi Draper
2000 Doug O'Connor and Daphne Ballard
2001 Doug O'Connor and Daphne Ballard
2002 Peter Connaughton and Beth Miller
2003 Peter Connaughton and Dawn Price
2004 Ned Flynn and Daphne Ballard
2005 Dermot Guinnane and Daphne Ballard
2006 Dermot Guinnane and Dawn Price
2007 Dermot Guinnane, Marke Clarke and Dawn Price

LE CHEILE and THE IRISH CANADIANS

In the summer of 1987, Petra Scott (Dublin) met Jackie Murray (Roscommon) and toyed with the 'notion' of forming a Ladies Gaelic Football Club. A meeting was scheduled on June 28, 1987 at the Irish Canadian Centre where the game was explained, plans for the future laid down and many strategies discussed with those who attended. Fionnuala Scott (Dublin) put forward the name Le Cheile (le Kay-la), meaning 'together' as a nod to the many ladies from different walks of life coming together to play and experience a bit of Irish heritage.

Almost immediately rigorous training began at Eglinton Memorial Park. The first ever trainers Sheree O'Connor, Pat Grant and Ross McDonald turned out religiously and put the team through their paces every week. Through their commitments and sacrificial efforts, the ladies learned the skills of Gaelic Football and what was once a 'notion' became a 'reality'.

The 1987 Le Cheile 'A' members were Marie Killeen, Geraldine Quinn, Maureen Looney, Geraldine Carney, Julie Morris (Most Valuable Player), Siobhan Kinahan, Ann Loughnane, Caroline O'Kane, Angela Finnegan, Petra Scott and Lyn Jones.

Le Cheile 'B' members were Ann Kinsella, Liz Neylon, Sally Elridge, Maura Ryan, Sandra McKnight, Angela Howley, Debbie Ferguson, Heather Wilson, Mary Neylon, Jackie Murray, Tonya Dempsey, Terri Reilly and Fionnula Scott.

Le Cheile went to Chicago, the "Windy" city, where the team was definitely 'blown away' by the talent of two long established teams. The club would decide to split to form a second club in 1988, the Irish Canadians. With the addition of the Michael Cusack's Club – the Toronto Ladies' League was born in 1989. Matches with the Ottawa Gaels were all challenge games that year.

Great support and encouragement for the Irish Canadians came from the 1987 Toronto GAA president, Paul Kennedy, and great service was provided by players like Mary Looney, Colleen Looney-Hussey, Fionnuala McGovern and Mary Neylon.

Success for the Irish Canadians came with 1988 and 1989 Toronto League victories over Le Cheile and Cusacks along with a 1991 Powerscreen 7-a-side championship. The ladies would continue as a club team until the end of the 1994 season when they called it a day.

From 1988 until 1996, Le Cheile was the Toronto Champion with five doubles as league winners. In total, nine championships and six league cups for Le Cheile. Kelly Bradford was active in the leadership of the club and in 1995 the Ladies Player of the Year was Margot Page. Page was involved with Canada's women's hockey team along with Le Cheile team mate Geraldine Heaney. Le Cheile would not take the field for the championship in 1997 and that would end a very powerful and historic ladies club of the Toronto GAA.

A significant highlight for all involved in Canadian ladies' football came during the 2002 Winter Olympics in Salt Lake City, Utah. Irish-born Geraldine Heaney (Antrim), a former Toronto Ladies' Footballer of the year, played with the Canadian Women's Hockey team as one of their star defensive players on the gold medal winning team. She was the only Canadian team member to play on all seven world championship gold medal winning teams. She received her Canadian citizenship requirements in 1990, just two days before the start of the first ever women's world hockey championships held in Ottawa. Geraldine's Canadian hometown was in Newmarket (just North of Toronto), but she has moved to Hamilton to settle down. She was recently inducted into the International Hockey Hall of Fame in 2007 as one of the first women ever.

IRISH CANADIANS

The history of Gaelic Football in Canada, and in the city of Toronto specifically, likely stretches back to the first large-scale introduction of Irish immigrants to Canada in the 19th century. For the better part of a century, however, the game in Canada was little more than a Sunday afternoon kick-around featuring made-up teams of men and boys from the old country.

The fully evolved version of the game—with clearly defined clubs and following formal rules—did not really begin to appear in Canada until the 1950s and '60s, when a new wave of postwar Irish immigrants landed on its shores. It was then that many of the clubs that exist today were first established in cities like Toronto, Montreal, Ottawa and Vancouver, along with their respective local GAA boards that governed play between the clubs (the Toronto GAA was founded in 1947). In the old days, though, these clubs were invariably populated with players from the old country, young men who had spent their formative years learning to play the ancient game in the fields of Kilkenny, Kerry and Cork, or on the streets and parks in Dublin, Galway, Belfast and Limerick.

Like most newcomers to Canada, the Irish immigrants who arrived in the '50s and '60s embraced their new country, but they maintained the culture and traditions of their homeland and passed those on to their own Canadian-born children. Those first-generation Irish Canadians grew up listening to Irish music; learning Irish dancing; going "home" to visit grandparents and relatives from time to time; and hearing the various accents of Ireland at parties for family and friends. At the same time, those children also grew up surrounded by the influences of Canada, their homeland: they played hockey and lacrosse; learned to skate and ski; and they developed a special love for Canada, familiar to those who lived through the shared experiences of Expo '67, Trudeau-mania, the '72 Summit Series and the '76 Montreal Olympics.

By the late 1970s, the boys born to that postwar wave of Irish immigrants were reaching their teen years and becoming very active in sports. Many of them had watched their fathers play Gaelic Football and hurling on Sunday afternoons in the summertime. After years of kicking the ball back and forth on the sidelines, or behind the goals, these young Canadians were eager to get into the game themselves. However, even the best of them found that breaking into the established Gaelic clubs was more difficult than it appeared.

The clubs that existed in Toronto were drawn clearly along regional lines, and even Irish players from the wrong areas were often directed to the "appropriate" club. Canadian-born players, regardless of lineage, had very little chance of getting a place.

By 1980, the problem of what to do with the growing number of young Canadian-born players in Toronto eager to get into the game was worsening. Several Irish-born members from the Toronto GAA decided the time had come to do something about it. A meeting was organized by several Irishmen who had Canadian-born sons who were directly affected by this invisible barrier—Danny Columb Sr., Jimmy Hayes, and the late Michael Holly Sr.—and some younger Irish immigrants—Sean Harte and Cormac O'Muiri—who were interested in growing the game in their new country. These men determined that a new Gaelic club specifically for Canadian-born players was needed. With the help of their Irish coaches, these players could train together and learn the game, and perhaps play exhibition games against existing clubs. With that, the Irish Canadian Gaelic Football Club was born. Cormac O'Muiri became the club's first president and along with Harte and Columb Sr., he led the first training session at Kingsmill School on Royal York Road in Toronto.

Initially, the Irish Canadians were somewhat of a barnstorming team that played exclusively outside of the Toronto GAA Senior League schedule. That meant "friendlies" against other Toronto clubs and exhibition matches against US-based clubs in places like Pittsburgh, Detroit, Boston and Cleveland. At a distinct disadvantage in terms of game experience when compared to Irish-born players, the Irish Canadians made up with determination what they may have lacked in skill. The sideline coaches, Danny Columb Sr. and Jimmy Hayes, made the most of the Canadian players' natural aptitude for hitting and defence, learned on the hockey rink and playing American football, and managed to hand the Irish-stacked US clubs some unexpected defeats.

Following the Irish Canadian's early success in the US, in 1983, club president Joe Walsh applied to the Toronto GAA for entry into the Senior Football League. At this time, the Irish Canadians were completely administered by native-born Canadians, making it a unique club in the Toronto GAA, and perhaps even in North America and the world. The bid was accepted, and the Irish Canadians debuted as a fully-fledged club in the Toronto Senior League that year.

Hockey Players

After joining the Senior League, the Irish Canadians wasted no time in making their presence felt both on the field and on the administrative side. The club won the McKenna Cup in 1984. That same year, seven members of the Toronto GAA Executive Board were from the Irish Canadians, including club member Pat Morrison as President. In 1989, the team claimed the Fay Cup. One year, the Irish Canadians even fielded two teams, but for the sake of club unity, they decided to go back to one team the next year.

The Irish Canadians entered the Senior League at a time when it was likely at its most competitive. The economic boom of the Emerald Tiger was still years away, and that meant there were plenty of talented Irish players more than willing to spend a summer working in Toronto and playing football for one of the established clubs. The talent pool for the Irish Canadians was not nearly as deep, but no team in the league played with more heart. Not only that, but the Irish clubs in Toronto soon discovered, just as the Irish-heavy American teams had in previous years, that Canadians know how to play contact sports, perhaps somewhat better than they did. The Irish Canadians were the equal of their opponents at two facets of the game: body contact and defensive coverage, and those aspects tended to dominate the team's approach to the game. As a result, more than a few county-level players from Ireland learned the hard way what it meant to "keep your head up and your stick on the ice."

The hard edge often displayed by the Irish Canadians on the pitch was not always appreciated by their usually more skilled and experienced opponents from the old country. However, in classic Canadian style, the Irish Canadians were not a team to back down from a challenge, and they maintained a determined attitude in every game and on every play. This sometimes sparked derisive calls of, "Hockey players," from the purists on the sidelines, but the competitive spirit they displayed playing a game they were not born to, earned them the respect of most Irish-born players in the league.

The Roster

Although the Irish Canadians may not have had as many flashy players as some of the other clubs, by the time the club entered the Senior League, there were a number of Canadian-born players on the roster, who were as good as almost any Irish-born player in the league. In 1984, in fact, the Irish Canadians sent four players—Pat Grant, Stuart Hunter, Michael Hayes and Pat Cummins—to Boston as part of the Toronto All-Star team in the North American Championships, and they sent four players to the Toronto side that played against the Tyrone club, Coalisland, in 1990.

It was often said that hurling, rather than football, suited the skills of the Irish Canadians better. This was probably true, in light of the fact that eleven nephews of Frank Cummins, winner of eleven All-Ireland Senior Hurling medals for Kilkenny, played for the Irish Canadians at one time or another. The Irish Canadians always competed well in fielding and defence, but failed to turn possession into scores because they lacked the basic scoring skills of the Irish players, who were reared in the "mists and glades" of Ireland.

The Irish Canadian roster, through its brief existence, included many family names familiar to members of the Toronto Irish community. The Cummins name, of course, was most prominent in terms of sheer numbers, and half-forward Pat Cummins claimed the league's inaugural Canadian Player of the Year award. Four Foran brothers played for the club at various times, and centre-back Sean G. Foran won the Footballer of the Year award. Other familiar Irish Canadian names include Grant, Sexton, Molloy, Tynan, Hughes, McMahon, Murphy, Columb and Condron, all first-generation Canadians. Several players, who did not come from an Irish background, also made key contributions to the club. These included Stuart Hunter, Richard "The Aussie" Smith (a transplanted Australian Rules player from Adelaide) and Klaus Oberparleiter.

A 1987 Irish Canadians men's team photo included John Malloy, Paul Cummins, John Hughes, Dave Cummins, Rob Cummins, Frank McKeown, Richard Smith, Frank Condron, Denis Grant, Danny Columb, President Pat Grant, Klaus Oberparleiter and Stewart Hunter. Other supporters of the club that year included Treasurer Steve Woodward and Secretary Karen Sexton.

Although the vast majority of players on the club were Canadian-born of Irish parents, several native-born Irishmen did line up for the team over the years. Along with the club's founders and original coaches, other prominent Irish contributors to the club included player/coach Paddy Morrison; player/coach Steven Rice; coach Paddy Cullan; and the O'Loughlin brothers, Don and J. J., whose family farm in Clare was the site of the home of Michael Cusack, founder of the Gaelic Athletic Association. Jimmy Kennedy came over to the club following a distinguished career with the St. Mike's team, and John McGlynn was one of the club's greatest supporters: he contributed funding and attended more Irish Canadian games than any player. Paul Connally, a tall full-forward from Dublin, was the longest-serving "Irish" Irish Canadian. Paul joined the club in 1989 as a recent immigrant to Canada, and the club became like a second family as he adapted to his new home. "I played purely for the pleasure and camaraderie of the unplanned, hilarious sessions that were sure to happen after the work on the training field, or a game at Centennial Park had transpired," remembers Paul. "I was lucky not to have transpired myself on a few occasions."

The 10th Anniversary banquet was held on November 3, 1990. Past Presidents that were honoured included Cormac O'Muiri, Pat Morrison, Mike Holly Jr., Tim Hayes, Rob Cummins, Pat Grant, Eugene Sweeney, Danny Columb Jr., Mike Tynan and John Hughes.

Club Spirit

In truth, winning was never really the focus of the Irish Canadians, often to the dismay of many a competitive player. It is fair to say that friendship and the spirit of competition, rather than results, inspired the club. And when it comes to measuring the club in terms of the overall atmosphere on the training field, in the clubhouse, and, equally as important, after the game, the Irish Canadians were second to none.

For club members, summers in the 1980s and early 1990s revolved around the team. First, there were the weekly training sessions in North York and the Sunday game at Centennial Park in Etobicoke; this was usually followed by dinner and pints at the Galway Arms. In addition to that, there were youth dances at the old Irish Centre, on Dupont Street, to look forward to, as well as the Caravan at the Irish pavilion, team house parties, barbecues and annual weekend road trips for games in Ottawa and Montreal. Special weekend road trips were also organized around friendly matches in places like Cleveland, Kitchener, and the Potato Festival in Lindsay.

The highlight of the summer, however, was always the annual barn party hosted by Gene Cummins and his family at their property just west of Toronto. The upper floor of the barn was decorated with streamers and lights, and one end of the massive room was transformed into a dance floor. Outside, Gene Cummins roasted corn in an iron pot suspended over a huge campfire. The entire Irish Canadian club was always in attendance, as were many players from other teams in the Senior League. Without a doubt, the event helped to connect young Irish Canadians with their culture and strengthened ties within the community. Today, echoes of the old Irish Canadian barn party can be heard at the Cummins' annual Irish picnic held at the same location.

St. Pat's Canadians

As the years and trips went by, players started to disappear from the teams around the Toronto Senior Football league. By the early 1990s, the Celtic Tiger had come to life in Ireland; this meant that the incentive no longer existed for young footballers to come to Canada looking for work in the summer. Through natural attrition, the Irish Canadians also found themselves struggling to field a team, and Toronto's St. Pat's Club was in a similar position. In late 1993, a meeting was held between representatives of both clubs, —Paul Connally and Steve Murphy from the Irish Canadians and Enda McGuinness of St. Pat's attended—at Jack Murphy's bar on Eglinton Avenue, to discuss the possibility of amalgamating the two clubs.

The clubs had done some indoor training together over the winter months and everyone seemed to get along. The decision was made to combine the clubs so they could field a more competitive team able to challenge the likes of Clan Na nGael and St. Mike's in the league. The deal was discussed among the members and voted on, and the new era of "St. Pat's Canadians" was born. About the same number of players from each club made up the roster. Enda McGuinness was voted the first President and Paul Connally was chosen as Vice President.

A new red and white strip was purchased to recognize the Canadian colours, but sadly, the era of the Irish Canadians was effectively over. Ironically, by joining forces with a club that had a large contingent of skilled Irish-born players, the Irish Canadians who remained went on to enjoy the most competitive and successful phase of their football careers. The new team quickly established itself as a new force in the Toronto Senior Football League. They were able to combine the toughness and defensive strength of the Canadian players with the ball handling and scoring touch of the Irish players. In 1995, the club made it all the way to the Championship Final, but they came up just short against the powerhouse St. Mike's club.

Remembering

The energy that drove the Irish Canadian Gaelic Football Club was quintessentially Canadian—open, welcoming, inclusive, determined and ever optimistic, even in the face of daunting opposition. In truth, a club like ours could really only have existed in a place like Canada, a country that allowed you to be both, as Canadian and as Irish as you wished to be, or any other nationality for that matter.

This country has an identity-less way of sneaking up on you, causing the best of the old and the best of the new to come together to create something unique and special. For those lucky enough to be a part of the Irish Canadians, those brief years will always be remembered as the best of times. Looking back, the characters that roamed the Irish Canadian dressing room were truly Shakespearean in their quality and distinctiveness—qualities that many players have found hard to duplicate since. Eventually, of course, boyfriends and girlfriends became husbands and wives, then fathers and mothers, and life took us all down our individual paths. Still, in spite of the time and distance that has passed between us, we have found that the bonds formed in the dressing room, on the pitch and in the pub are just as strong today, and we remain forever friends and teammates, in thought, if not in action.

Canada, if you let it, allows your identity to quietly, peacefully, emerge from your coat of many colours—and God knows that the Irish coat is colourful! What former Irish Canadians remember most about adding to *our* coat of many colours is the laughter, the laughter and the laughter.

Aussie Smith

Ironically, one of the driving forces of the Irish Canadian Gaelic Football Club was neither from Ireland, nor Canada. Just as the club was getting its feet wet in the Senior League in Toronto, a lanky Australian named Richard Smith showed up for a training session and, translating his Australian Rules Football skills to Gaelic, he went on to become one of the most dominant midfield players in the league in the 1980s. Lacking both an Irish background and a Canadian upbringing, Richard experienced both the club and the league from a unique vantage point:

In August 1983, I arrived in Toronto to study at the University of Toronto. I came from Adelaide, Australia, where I had grown up playing Australian Rules Football. As an Australian, I had vaguely heard of Gaelic Football and knew that is was similar in many ways to Australian rules. Because I wanted to keep active, I combed through the phone book looking for clues that might help me find people to phone for further information. I eventually found a helpful soul at the Irish Centre and she put me on to someone (long forgotten) from the Toronto GAA who said there was a struggling team in need of players called the "Jung Carnayjans." It turned out that this team was formally called the "Irish Canadians," as they were composed of first-generation Canadians and the sons of recent immigrants. Despite the formal name, the Irish community always called them the "Young Canadians," or with the appropriate accent "Jung Carnayjans."

I contacted someone from the club and was instantly made to feel welcome by the players—all similar in age to me. At the first training sessions, I was nicknamed the "Aussie," and the name stuck. We practiced at the back of a school near the

Fairview Mall and afterwards would usually end up at a pub on Yonge Street, staying until late in the night. Most of the time we did not have a coach, which was something that annoyed some players, as we were not playing to our complete potential, but that did not seem to perturb others.

Over my five-year association with the team, I guess we won as many games as we lost; had some more successful seasons; some less successful. The games were played at Centennial Park in Etobicoke in the field immediately north of the swimming centre. The football games often preceded or followed a hurling game. There was always something interesting going on at Centennial Park. Every now and then, a recent arrival from Ireland would turn up, and they were instantly recognizable by their "Milk-bottle legs," with skin as white as a ghost. The same player could be easily recognized the next week as well, with their skin sunburned as red as a lobster.

The real highlights of my seasons with the Irish Canadians were the out-of-town trips that the team made to Montreal, Ottawa and other locations. The whole team usually traveled together in a rental van. The Ottawa trips were the more frequent. At that time, the Ottawa Gaels played at Shefford Park, and after the game, the Ottawa team (made up mostly of Canadian-born players) always showed their hospitality by inviting us to dinner. One year, we were hosted at Pat Kelly's house overlooking the Gatineau River. There, we were served a 10-lb bag of potatoes roasted on the BBQ—true Ottawa-Irish hospitality.

Another year we traveled to Ohio to play a team from Cleveland. They were a crafty bunch, arranging the game for the Saturday. When we arrived at the field, there was initially nobody there. Eventually we found someone, but it seemed a team could not be raised until the next day, but it would have to be early because we had to return to Toronto. Because our club had nothing to do on the Saturday afternoon or evening, we adjourned to the nearest pub to discuss options. Somehow, this managed to keep us amused until the early hours of the next morning. Of course, the other team arrived fresh, bright and early the next morning and gave us a lesson in how to play the game (and live cleanly).

TORONTO GAELS

Former Cavan star and long standing Garryowen member, Tommy White (R.I.P.) was instrumental in forming a new team called "Erin Nua," The club soon transformed into a new club in 1987, the Toronto Gaels. Four long-standing Toronto GAA members—Joe Matthews (Antrim), Billy Gilroy (Antrim), Paddy Callan (Dundalk) and former Antrim football star Billy Millar—were among the founding members.

In their first year, the Gaels were finalists in the Powerscreen 7's, League Winners and Championship finalists. A team photo that year included President Joe Matthews, Treasurer G. Houston, Alan Sibbald, Liam Og McKee, John Neeson, Mickey McConnell, Secretary Hugo Straney, J. Buckley, Manager Billy Gilroy, Gerry Mullane, Brendan

Rossiter, Tommy White, Alan Henderson, Tom Holten, Colbert Clifford, Damien McCullough, Terry Devlin, Captain Billy Millar, Peter White, Niall O'Bracken, Mickey Doherty and Paddy Callan.

The Toronto Gaels success continued, winning the football league in 1988 and 1989. The year 1990 proved to be a prestigious one for the Gaels; they won the Men's Senior Football Championship for the first time.

The early years featured a number of very talented players: the Fitzsimonds brothers, Gerry Straney, Niall Cotter, Mark O'Brien, Peter White, David Rossiter and Captain Gerry Mullane, who played senior football for Limerick upon relocating to Ireland in 1991. The Gaels also had a strong hurling team in those days; many players played both codes on the same day for the club. One of the most prominent hurlers at that time was John O'Neill (R.I.P.), who unfortunately passed away suddenly before the age of 40.

The club was well supported in those days by a number of characters who would go on to contribute greatly to the club's success off the field and for the future. Brendan Rossiter, Alan Henderson in addition to the aforementioned White, Gilroy, Millar, Matthews and Callan would shape this club for longevity.

By far the most successful year for the club was 1994; they won the Men's Senior Football Championship and the League. They also had a memorable Powerscreen 7's victory, thanks to an outstanding scoring display in the final game from former St. John's of Belfast star Donal O'Hara, who scored 1-7 from play.

Billy Millar's "no nonsense" approach to training and management ensured a very fit and well-prepared team. The squad was captained by the pride of Abbeyleix, Mark "The Bull" O'Brien, and included club stalwarts such as Charlie Doorley, Gerry Caldwell, Decko Kiernan, Niall Cotter, Shane Carroll, Niall and Damien Donnelly, and Roger McGovern, to name but a few.

An Offaly senior county player, Charlie Doorley, was named the Toronto GAA's player of the year that season, a feat he repeated in 2002, becoming one of the few players to win the coveted award twice. Other Gaels to win this honour include Mark O'Brien and Frank Coshignano, widely regarded as the greatest-ever "Italian" Gaelic Footballer, and one of the few Canadian-born players to receive this award.

10th Anniversary

In 1997, the club celebrated its first 10 years with a two-week tour of Ireland. While there, they played games against St. John's (Belfast), Derrygonnelly Harps (Fermanagh), and Whitehall Colmcilles (Dublin). The event was in recognition of the contribution of Belfast men such as Billy Millar and Pat Donnelly; Fermanagh folks such as Roger McGovern, Eamonn and Phyllis Gallagher, and John "Compo" Wadsworth; and Dubs such as Brendan Rossiter, and Pádraig and Jacinta Cosgrove, who all contributed to the success of the club in its first decade.

The club has always played an active part in the management of the Toronto GAA with members such as Billy Millar, Pat Donnelly, Cormac Monaghan and Sinead Canavan, each serving as Toronto GAA President for more than one season. Canavan, Monaghan and Gerry Heuston have each been named as Toronto GAA's "Person of the Year" in recognition of their contributions over the years. Heuston was awarded the "Referee of the Year" award in 1995 too.

The New Millennium

The 2001 final was a real heartbreaker. Coached by Bernie Dullea from the western extremities of Cork—and captained on the field by Listowel man Seanie O'Connell—the Gaels lead by three points with five minutes to play, but they could not keep their old rivals at bay. St. Mike's gradually clawed back to level, with Kerryman Eanna O'Malley of St. Mike's equalizing with the last kick of regular time. The scores ebbed and flowed in extra time, and a controversial decision as to whether or not a Gaels' strike had crossed the St. Mike's goal line proved critical in the end.

St. Mike's gave good value for the two point victory, but the feeling in the Gaels' camp was that they had let one get away. The club licked their wounds over the winter, regrouped in the spring, and again reached the final in 2002. They were level at halftime, but an inexplicable second-half collapse by the Gaels saw several goals conceded, with St. Vincent's running out easy winners in the end.

While the club has yet to return to those "on field" heights in the years since 2002, they have continued to field solid teams and they have produced several fine players. The Toronto Gaels participated in, and won, a 7-a-side tournament that was hosted in Buffalo in 2004. Club MVP for every year that he played (2001–2005), Ciaran Shannon (former Wicklow and Sligo senior county player) is arguably one the greatest players ever to grace the Toronto GAA, and certainly one of the best to never win a Toronto championship.

Sinead Canavan and Friends of the Gaels

The Gaels were proud to have Sinead Canavan help coordinate 25 women from across Canada for the International Women's Tournament of 2005, in Naomh Mearnog, Dublin. Sinead has served in administration on both the club and board level for many years and she started her playing career with the Michael Cusacks. With the exception of two years (2002–2004) she has been a volunteer on the Toronto GAA executive since 1996 up until 2007.

There are many other individuals not mentioned, who have made huge contributions to the club over the years. Some of the more recent supporters include Past President Pat Murray, President Greg Callan, David and Stephen Millar, Chris Gaffney. Relative newcomers, such as Mike Donnelly, Anthony McGuire, Rory McNaboe, Eamon Gallagher, Paul Deeney and Steven Owens, are also playing a big role as the club moves into its third decade. The club has always been a very big part in the daily lives of its members and, with a bit of luck, will continue to do so. The Gaels has always enjoyed strong support from its sponsors—fortunately too many to name, but particular mention must be made of Kemptville Travel, Ross-Clair Construction, Tara Inn and Dunmurray Electric who have been long-time supporters of the team.

The club has been fortunate over the years to gain the services of visiting Irish students, most of whom have made a very positive contribution to the club's performances on and off the field. The club regards these, and indeed the many other former members who have since moved back to Ireland, as lifelong Gaels.

MICHAEL CUSACKS' LADIES

The Michael Cusacks' L.G.F.C. was founded in 1988 by two sisters, Noreen McCann and Terri Cassidy (nee Reilly). Members toyed with the notion of perhaps starting a men's team, but the Cusacks have always run their club as a ladies only. It is the only remaining independent (not affiliated with a men's club) Ladies' Football Club in the Toronto GAA of the original ladies' teams in Toronto, which included Le Cheile and the Irish Canadians.

The first sponsor, who was instrumental in helping the Cusacks off the ground in 1988, was the Hurley Brothers. Michael and Dick Hurley, (Clan Na nGael G.F.C.) of the Hurley Corporation, approached the ladies and volunteered to purchase the Cusacks very first team kits. Without their generosity, the Cusacks may not have come to be.

The Cusacks have always taken pride in being a very strong social club. The closeness of the team off the field has always stood out on the field. The Cusacks' strength, over the years, can be attributed to solid recruitment locally, which compensated for lack of immigration from Ireland. Christina Campanelli and Pauleen Conway were some of the players, along with Audrey Eccles who participated in the committee work of the Ontario team that toured Ireland in 1992. Despite best efforts and lots of talent during the first few years, the Cusacks failed to win any major competition. However, it was team spirit and their ability to socialize as a club that held them together.

Championship Form

In 1993, the Cusacks claimed their first League win. It would be seven years more before they had another League win in 2000, with Coach Michael Gordon (Garryowen). With much celebration, in 2003, the Cusacks won their first double of the Championship and League, led by coaches Ollie Walsh (Mayo) and Mick Burke (St. Pat's). In 2005, the Cusacks' Ladies repeated the double in an undefeated year; they were led by coaches John Paul Horgan (St. Vincent's) and Noreen O'Shea. The Cusacks' Ladies celebrated their win with a photo taken in Ottawa; it is displayed on their club website. Those listed included Roisin, Gissel, Mags, Anto, Erin Gallagher, Sarah Callan, Noreen O'Shea, Jeannine, Danielle Hurst, Yvonne G, Stella, Ollie, Fiona (Captain), Louise, Leanne, Lorraine Morley, Anne, Mick Burke, Yvonne M, Tanya, Edel, and Maureen Keane.

With a total of four League trophies and two Championships on the mantle, the team continues to thrive in attracting new players to the game. Down through the years, the Michael Cusacks have had many talented and experienced coaches including Gerry Mullane, Toronto Gaels; Peter White. Toronto Gaels; Paddy Burns, St. Vincent's; Charlie Doorley, Toronto Gaels; Mark O'Brien, Toronto Gaels, Mike Cassidy, St. Vincent's; and Ken Ray, St. Vincent's.

From the late 1990's to present, the Cusacks were led by the experience of Michael Gordon, Garryowen G.F.C; Pat Sheridan, St. Vincent's G.F.C.; Mick Burke, St. Pat's G.F.C.; Ollie Walsh, County Mayo; John Paul Horgan, St. Vincent's G.F.C.; Noreen O'Shea, Michael Cusacks L.G.F.C.; Ken Ray, St. Vincent's G.F.C.

Member Contributions

In addition to the Cusacks running their own club, many members have gone on to contribute to the Toronto GAA and the GAA in Ireland. Yvonne Morley was the corresponding secretary of the Toronto GAA from 1999–2003 and Youth Development officer in 2004; and in 2002 she won the Toronto GAA Person of the Year award. Yvonne Morley is now based in London as the Games Promotion Officer for the Provincial Council of Britain's GAA.

Lorraine Morley has been the corresponding secretary for the Toronto GAA since 2005, and in 2007 she won the Toronto GAA Person of the Year award. Sinead Canavan was a Corresponding Secretary, Recording Secretary and Public Relations Officer for the Toronto GAA. She has been the President of the GAA since 2006 and won the GAA Person of the Year award for 2005.

From the very first year in 1998 that Team Canada was represented at the World Cup Tournament in Dublin, the Cusacks have had an extremely strong presence. Michael Gordon, a former Michael Cusacks' coach, took Team Canada to the semifinals in 2000. Most recently in the 2005 tour, Cusacks' player Erin Gallagher (Toronto) was honoured with the well deserved title of Tournament MVP. Cusack members Maureen Keane and Canadian Captain Sarah Callanan also contributed to the team's success. The 2005 team had Sinead Canavan as team manager and the equipment manager was Lorraine Morley.

Over the years, several of the Cusacks Ladies have been honoured with the Toronto GAA Ladies Player of the Year award, namely: Anne McKee, 1997 (Antrim); Noreen Gordon, 2000 (Toronto); Fiona Latham, 2003 (Toronto); Erin Gallagher, 2002 (U-21) and 2005 (Toronto).

A memorable occasion on the field for the Cusacks' Ladies was in 1998 at the prestigious Powerscreen International 7's Tournament in Toronto. Led by Coach Michael Gordon, the Michael Cusacks were up against Durham in the final game to fight it out for the gold watches. The game was in double overtime, when Suzanne Tinney (Donegal) of the Cusacks scored a beautiful point, as a result of a free from the 50-yard line, in the last play of the game. It was a hard fought battle and one not to be forgotten.

The strength of the Michael Cusacks has increased substantially and they continue to stay strong by promoting the GAA outside of the Irish community. In 2008, the Cusacks will be celebrating their 20th anniversary under the leadership of Sinead Gordon as President, Orla Smith as Vice-President, Aisling Smith - Treasurer, Brenda Nugent - Secretary, Noreen Gordon, Sarah Callanan and Tiffany Carroll as Toronto delegates.

DURHAM ROBERT EMMETS G.F.C.

The Durham Region (enveloping such towns as Pickering, Ajax, Whitby and Oshawa) is found east of the greater Toronto area and is the home of the Durham Robert Emmets G.F.C. The club was initially founded in 1989 as a minor club of the new Toronto minor programme which included clubs in Brampton, Etobicoke and Scarborough. This was done to introduce an important part of Irish culture, Gaelic Football, to Canadian born kids. As immigration continued to ebb over the years, this program successfully provided players to supplement the clubs in Durham and Toronto in future years.

The club name, Robert Emmets, came from one of the founding members, Brian Farmer, whose home club in Armagh was named Clonmore Robert Emmets. The team colors of blue and white were selected by the founding members and were a replica of the jerseys worn by the men from Laois.

As is somewhat usual with a lot of "overseas" clubs, the founding meeting took place in the local Pub in Ajax known as the Harp and Thistle. This popular establishment was owned by Paddy and Alice Columb, who hail from Roscommon and Waterford respectively. Other members who were present included Eddie Mangan (Dublin), Florrie O'Donoghue (Kerry), Matt Healy (Kerry), Nishi Farmer (Armagh), Jim Kelly (Carlow), Sean Laverty (Down), Ronnie Coughlin (Dublin), Tony Walsh (Wicklow), Mike O'Hara (Antrim) and Paddy Columb (Roscommon) all of whom contributed financially to help get the club off the ground.

In 1990, Eddie Mangan became the club's first president and directed the entrance of a senior team which initially had home games played at Dennis O'Connor High School in Ajax. A lot was asked of older players who were coaxed out of retirement, to reload their boots from the closet (their names are a well kept secret!), and along with some of the promising minors helped launch the clubs arrival to the football scene in Toronto. The first challenge games was played out in Pickering against a vastly experienced Clan Na nGael team, and let's just say that they learned a thing or two that day.

Players that lined out included Paddy Mealiffe, Mike McWilliams, Eddie Mangan, Jake Cunningham, Matt O'Leary, Gary McConville, Diarmuid O'Connor, Doug Columb, John Byrne, Paddy Columb, Ray Kilty, Aidan Murphy, John Hughes, Peter O'Leary, Nishi Farmer, Benny Bentham, Owen Kiely and minors Mark Kerr, Brian Healy, Barry Farmer and John Joe O'Donoghue.

As with any new club, the first year was a learning experience with victories hard to come by, but what was more important was the fact that the team was starting to get established, creating a good base out in Durham and thoroughly enjoying their post mortems back in the "Harp" afterwards.

But Durham learned from their defeats and, with the infusion of a few players from Ireland, combined with the minor players, things began to change. In 1992, the first trophy won was the McKenna Cup over a gallant St Pat's team by a one point margin. It was a poignant moment at the medal presentations that player and top scorer Billy McManus dedicated the victory to his late father, Willie, who had tragically lost his life along with many others in a sectarian bombing in Belfast.

The year 1993 saw the emergence of Durham reach the next level. The club had its best year winning the Senior Championship, the Senior League, the League Cup, the Montreal Tournament and the Owen Nolan Tournament. Team members that did the club proud were Paul Brady, Diarmuid O'Connor, Stuart Nesbitt, Micky Holland, Sean O'Neill, Derek Plunkett, Aidan Kilpatrick, Jock O'Connor, Conor Lowe, Billy McManus, Nishi Farmer, Owen Dillon, John J. O'Donoghue, Oliver Laverty, Aidan Murphy, Doug Columb and George Curry. Coach and selectors were Brian Farmer, Matt Healy and Florrie O'Donoghue.

This exciting year was capped by the guest appearance at the victory banquet of the successful manager of the 1993 All Ireland Champion's Derry, Eamon Coleman (R.I.P.), a very sincere and congenial person who presented the team with their trophies and medals.

It would be another ten years before the club would get their next title, winning the Senior League in 2003 and then, two years later in 2005, winning the Senior Championship by defeating St Mike's by two points in a very entertaining final. The team was well coached by the man from West Cork, Bernie Dulea, and another interesting fact was that four of the "minors" who played on the 1993 championship team also made a major contribution in 2005: Brian Kelly, Barry Farmer, Mark Kerr and Brian Healy. Other members of the team included Damian Boylan, Darren Farmer, Kian Cleere, Austin Dennis, Colm Savage, Lawrence Ledwidge, Michael Hamill, Gerry Daly, Barry Hurley, Ollie Malone, John Creery, Neil Rogan, Sean Mangan, Alan Martina, Matt Healy, Fergal O'Reilly, Paul Morris, Maurice Byrne, Donnie Fogarty and Kevin Walsh.

Another league title came Durham's way in 2007. Despite having contested five finals in the Powerscreen 7's International Gold Watch Tournament, the club has yet to come up on the winning side, having to play runner up each time to the visiting teams from Ireland. On a brighter note the club did capture two "Gold Watch" victories in the junior section winning over the Cayman Islands in 1999 and St Mike's in 2004.

County players that have played senior football for Durham throughout the years include: Liam Belton (Longford), Danny Barr, Aidan Kilpatrick, Peter O' Kane, Conor Lowe (Tyrone), Nishi Farmer, Kevin O'Reilly (Armagh), Aidan Quinn, Colm Savage (Down), Enda Sheehy, Kian Cleere (Dublin), Owen Dillon (Offaly), Joe Sullivan (Kerry), Brendan O'Neill (Louth) and John Creery (Armagh).

Minor Football

The Durham minor team enjoyed a major share of success in its first year. In March 1991, 20 players attended the Skydome Games in Toronto where Mike Ensor, Aidan Laverty, Darren Farmer and Brendan O'Hara were selected as ball boys for this occasion. They capped off a great 1991 season by winning the minor championship.

Championship medals were presented to the minors at the victory banquet of May 1992 by none other than T.V presenter, newspaper columnist and footballer supreme, Kerry's Pat Spillane. It was a night to remember and a tremendous thrill for Gaels, both young and old.

The club managed to coax Pat Spillane to don the blue and white of Durham in playing a challenge game against St. Mikes the next day. Needless to say, the previous night celebrations had a lot to do with the final score but Spillane still showed he had a few good moves left in him. He also managed to squeeze in a coaching session with the minors of Toronto, which was very much appreciated.

In June 1991, at the invitation of Kerry's Michael Keane, (Chairman of the New York Minor Board and present day Steering Committee member of the Continental Youth Championships) the team participated in a tournament in the Catskill Mountains, New York against New York Celtic and Rockland Hibernians.

The team panel included Mark Kerr, Darren Farmer, Brian Healy (Captain), Brendan O'Hara, Martin McCarran, Stuart Nesbitt, Steve Collins, Rob Halpin, John O'Donoghue, Brian Kelly, T.J. Gallagher, Barry Farmer, Mike Doyle, Richard Tartt, Joe Curry, Mike Ensor and Oliver Laverty. They acquitted themselves (adequately) playing against much more experienced opposition but it was a brilliant weekend for the team and supporters alike. Needless to say there are some stories that remain untold!

In 1992 Brian Healy was awarded the minor player of the year for Toronto with Darren Farmer picking up honours in the U-14 category. Darren would keep on improving his game and in 1995 was rewarded with the minor player of the year award.

Several minors have represented Canada in International Tournaments in Ireland including Brian Healy, Darren Farmer, Barry Farmer, George Curry Jr., John O'Donoghue, Mark Kerr, Brian Kelly and Mike Ensor.

There is no doubt that the evolution from this successful minor program played and continues to play a major role in the success and backbone of the present day Durham Emmet's senior team. Players like Brian Healy, Brian Kelly, Mark Kerr, Barry Farmer and Darren Farmer still show the same determination even through the years may have taken their toll.

So learning from this, in 2002, the Emmets began to lay the seeds to re-introduce underage football into Durham after a long absence. The first dive into youth development began with the club working with some of the local high schools. Members went into gym classes to teach the fundamentals of Gaelic football. By the end of the 2004 school year the club had introduced the game to approximately 1200 children.

In 2005 the club introduced the next phase of their youth development program. Branching outside of the school structures, Durham opened up the experience to the general public and broadened the age groups: they accepted children as young as five to as old as 18. That spring saw the birth of the Durham GFC "Football 4 Kids" program, a five week camp that introduced the kids to the sport.

The Durham Robert Emmet's conducted an indoor youth league for the participants of the "Football 4 Kids" programme, which was the first minor league football played in the region since 1997. Elaine Mealiffe and Shannon Savage spearheaded this programme and Leanne Beagan and Jayne Martina (2007 Club Person of the Year) continued the good work with the newly named Durham Shamrocks. With the continued development of youth in the Durham region, the goal of having youth participating at future Continental Youth Championships in the U.S.A. remains present.

Men's MVP		**U-21 MVP**	
2007	Darren Farmer	2007	Craig Coulter
2006	Brendan O'Neill		
2005	Barry Farmer		
2004	John Creery	2004	Sean Mangan
2003	Colum Savage	2003	Luke Brown
2002	Laurence Ledwidge		
2001	Brian Kelly	2001	Laurence Ledwidge
2000	Mark Kerr		
1999	Ollie Malone	1999	Darren Farmer
1998	Ollie Malone	1998	Brian Healy
1997	Alan Martina	1997	Mauriceo Castenherio
1996	Mark Kerr		
1995	Sean O'Neill		
1994	Darren Farmer		
1993	Paul Brady		
1992	Billy McManus		
1991	Gary McConville		

Ladies' Football

In 1992 the club formed a ladies' team under the guidance of Nuala McNamara. Julie Hughes (Dublin) and Karen Lynch (Dublin) would be among many players who contributed to the team's success. The ladies were in fine form between 1997 and 2000; they won both league and championships. Except for the Montreal tournament, the ladies of Durham have won all available trophies in the league, championship, Powerscreen 7's and the George Curry Tournaments.

The club has made a big contribution to the international Canadian Ladies teams that have played in Ireland. Players include Erin Lynch, Kristen Lynch, Sarah Gowdy, Trish Shaw, Shannon Murdock, Stephanie Fitzpatrick, Ashley Visser, Julie Mroczkowski, Kristine LaMonday, Sam Williams, Deanna Adams, Tara Abblet and Manager, Elaine Mealiffe.

Ladies' MVP		U-21 MVP	
2007	Ally Fox	2007	Christine Danford
2006	Heather Woodard		
2005	Ashley Visser		
2004	Stef Fitzpatrick		
2003	Sarah Gowdy	2003	Abbie Visser
2002	Kristen Lynch	2002	Stef Fitzpatrick
2001	Erinn Lynch	2001	Sandra Ramsbottom
2000	Trish Shaw	2000	Emma Grennon
1999	Sarah Gowdy		
1998	Erinn Lynch		
1997	Kristine LaMonday		
1996	Ciara McNaughton		
1995	Pauline Gilsenan		
1994	Julie Hughes		
1993	Pauline Gilsenan, Monaghan		

George Curry Tournament

The George Curry Tournament was named after one of the club's elder statesman. George could be found sitting on the hill beside Centennial Park at any one of Durham's games. He never had a bad word to say about anyone, and the club felt that it should remember this man with a tournament played in his honour. On July 14, 2007, the first George Curry Tournament for kids was held. The Durham Shamrocks and Brampton Rebels participated in a day of football, friendship and fun. Skill competitions of the longest kick, penalty shots, target shooting and matches were played on the day. This great day was wrapped up with matches played for age levels, 5 to 7, 8 to 10, and 11 on up.

	Men	Ladies
2006	St. Mike's	Ottawa
2005	St. Vincent's	Michael Cusacks
2004	n/a	n/a
2003	St. Mike's	Durham
2002	St. Mike's	Durham

It's fair to say that the club is enjoying a healthy existence in 2008 with a young executive (chaired by Brendan O'Neill along with members John O'Donoghue, Mark Kerr, Jayne Martina, Lorraine White, Ollie Malone and Alan Martina) being the drawing force behind it. The future looks bright as Durham reaches out to Canadians through recruitment, and underage programme in both men and ladies football.

BRAMPTON ROGER CASEMENTS

Founded in 1989 as a minor team, it quickly flourished into a competitive team among the minor board teams of the early '90s. Founding members included Liam McKee (Antrim), Jim Clark (Tyrone), Billy McKnight (Antrim), Pat Donnelly (Antrim) and Dermot Sheridan (Tyrone) who all gave great service during these early years.

The first club game was a U-18 match in July 1989 against Durham Robert Emmets at the Carabram in Brampton. The GAA club was one of four organizations that teamed up with the Brampton Irish Cultural Society, the Brampton Harps Soccer and Social Club and the Rover's Club to organize Brampton's annual multicultural festival at the Irish pavilion at Carabram. In 1991 the team won an inaugural U-18 match in Montreal against Durham along with league and championship wins.

The club incorporated as a non-profit organisation in 1992 and then created a men's team for the "aging" minors. The club had nine players selected on a Toronto team that travelled to Kilkenny for a minor tournament. The squad lost to New York in the semi-final and the team then traveled onwards to be hosted in Galway (Corofin), Kerry (Ballinskilligs) and Dublin (St. Vincent's and Crave Kieran). The Toronto minors would lose a close match by two points to St. Vincent's of Dublin.

Other special moments were 1997 and 2005 when Casements won the junior men's championships at the Powerscreen 7's. A women's team was formed in the '90s with Brampton native Kathleen Keenan and Galway native Sharon Higgins helping Team Canada, at the International Women's Tournament in Dublin, win the Shield Cup in 2005.

The summer of 2005 saw a rebirth of youth activities. This carried through into the winter with indoor youth clinics which had more than 50 participants. The club formed the Brampton Rebels Minor Gaelic Football Club as a separate entity so as to appeal to young Canadians.

2006 saw the club's first summer league for children 8–13, with over 32 participants. Numbers have increased yearly and, in 2008, the Rebels can proudly boast that they have had more than 70 children playing a part of their programme.

Lar Na nGael, Brampton's 14-year-old Irish centre is in an industrial complex of units at Dixie Road and Steeles Avenue. It caters to Irish Canadians in the Greater Peel region of Ontario, which includes Brampton, Bramalea and Heart Lake. The Casements organization continues to be a driving force behind the continued success of the Irish Centre.

Those that are leading the club in 2008 include President: Liam McKee; Vice President: Billy McKnight; Secretary: Kathleen Keenan; Recording Secretary: Erin Higgins; Treasurer: Helen Higgins; Registrar: Jim Kehoe; PRO: Ben O'Connell and Youth Development Officer: Damian Higgins. Many look forward to the 20th anniversary celebrations that are slated for 2009.

Owen Nolan Sr. Tournament Men's

2002	St. Mike's	2001	St. Mike's
2000	St. Mike's	1999	St. Mike's
1998	St. Vincent's	1997	St. Mike's
1996	Durham	1995	St. Mike's
1994	St. Pat's	1993	Durham

MANITOBA

In May 1914, a Catholic newspaper, founded in 1885 and called the *Northwest Review*, wrote about young Irishmen in Winnipeg thinking of nothing else but hurling. In Winnipeg, Manitoba, on Citizens Day in 1914, at the Canadian Exhibition, the "Shamrock" hurling team crossed camans with a County Cork selection to decide the championship of Manitoba. This was arranged by the Provincial Council of the GAA. We are told that the scene was very colourful with lots of green flags all over the grounds and that the ice hockey and lacrosse fans looked forward to the match with great interest. Early in the second half, the Shamrocks took the lead and, displaying considerable accuracy and determination, they won by a comfortable margin. The official attendance was reported to be 63,670. It is hard to know if the figure is accurate, but it would have to have been an attendance record!

Thompson – A Northern GAA Outpost

In 1967, when Canada was celebrating its 100th birthday, the local Irish Canadian Club organized a 10-a-side Gaelic Football tournament in Thompson, Manitoba. Thompson is located 830 kilometres north of the international border, and 739 kilometres north of the provincial capital of Winnipeg. Some of the founding club members that promoted the playing of Gaelic games at this time included Larry Gallagher, Johnny Devereux (R.I.P.) and Chris Darby.

The competition winners were a Westmeath team captained by Billy Comaskey and that included Bernie Comaskey, Pat Connell, Jimmy McDonnell, John Ward, Micheal Cassidy, Pete Smith, Eamon Kelly, Nick Shaw, Philip Conroy and trainer Vincent Conroy.

Godfather of Hurling

Rob Mullin was born and raised in Winnipeg and grew up in the frozen prairies skating and playing pick-up hockey on neighbourhood outdoor rinks. Even though the Mullin family had moved to Quebec from Derry in the 1800s, Rob grew up with Irish culture around him because of his mother Linda.

Mullin moved to Penticton, British Columbia, in the early '90s and was introduced to the Society for Creative Anachronism, a worldwide medieval recreation group. After marrying in 1997 and moving to Seattle, Mullins was introduced to hurling in 2003 and he was immediately hooked on playing the game.

Upon visiting his mother for Canadian Thanksgiving in North Vancouver, Mullin read an article in Vancouver's *Celtic Connection* newspaper about a hurling match with Vancouver's Irish Sporting and Social Club. As a result, he decided that there was enough interest in the sport, and he started a competitive hurling club in Seattle.

In 2004, the Seattle Hurling Club affiliated with the North American County Board and competed at the Nationals. The year 2005 saw the creation of a Hurling league in Seattle and, in 2006, the team won the Junior C Division Hurling title of the NACB in Philadelphia.

Hurling in Seattle has gone from three players standing in a field to over 60 registered players, three inner-city league teams and a travel team, which competes nationally and internationally in Vancouver, B.C. All this, thanks in part to one extremely dedicated prairie boy from Winnipeg.

ALBERTA

EDMONTON WOLFE TONES

Before the Edmonton Wolfe Tones were founded in 1975, there had been a previous attempt to establish Gaelic Football in Alberta. In the mid-1950s, Jack Bell played senior football for Louth. He proudly wore the number two jersey for Louth in two All-Ireland semifinals and in the only National League contested by Louth. Bell immigrated to Edmonton a few months before Louth went on to win the All-Ireland in 1957.

Bell took on the role of a Gaelic Football missionary in Edmonton and formed a team, which folded after a few years due to lack of competition. At that time, a team would have to travel several thousand miles to compete. In 2000, Jack was presented with a Millennium Trophy at the Fairway Hotel in Dundalk by Terry Maher, Chairman of the Louth County Board to honour his selection on Louth's Team of the Millennium in the Right Fullback position.

In 2002, a trophy was designated that would go to the winner of Edmonton's internal 7-a-side season for men, in honour of Louth's Jack Bell.

Jack Bell Cup

2002	St. Albert	2003	St. Mary's
2004	Sherwood Pairc Gaels	2005	n/a
2006	Sherwood Pairc Gaels	2007	Shannon Rangers

Christy Whelehan

In 1975, Christy Whelehan, from Westmeath, was responsible for the second coming of Gaelic Football with the modern day Wolfe Tones. The team was named after the 18th-century Irish nationalist Theobald Wolfe Tone. Christy's stewardship guided the team through the good and not so good years. He still wears the team jersey with pride whenever the GAA is in session. Christy was recently honoured with a cup in his name for men's football.

Edmonton Irish Sports and Social Society

A group of Irish people held a meeting on Saturday April 18, 1958, in the Cloverdale Community Hall in Edmonton, Alberta. At that meeting Peter O'Donovan, Charlie Quinn and John P. Murphy were elected chairman, treasurer and secretary respectively, of the organization to be known as the Edmonton Gaels.

In February 1959, they met once more at the Y.M.C.A. and emerged calling themselves the Irish Sports and Social Club. At that meeting, they received the blessings of the old Irish Society and of the St. Patrick's Society as Edmonton's official Irish club. In the summer of 1962, the club applied for "society" status and was incorporated on November 28, 1962. The organization was now called the Edmonton Irish Sports and Social Society.

With no place of their own, for over 25 years the club held events such as St. Patrick's Day and New Year's Eve celebrations at various venues throughout the city. Other activities included picnics, curling, bowling, golf, soccer and Irish dance lessons. The first Feis was held in 1972, and the club was one of 11 ethno-cultural communities to participate in the first Edmonton Heritage Days Festival in 1976.

In 1985, the club purchased property, with a building that was previously a garage and an upholstery shop, at 12546-126th Street. After extensive renovations and many hours of volunteer labour, the first "pint" was drawn on Canada's greatest football day, the Grey Cup, November 30, 1986. The club officially opened on St. Patrick's Day in 1987, the atmosphere was vibrant and friendly.

In 1999, a dinner dance was held to celebrate the 40th anniversary of the Irish community with some special guests who celebrated their 80th birthdays. They were Rose McDonnell (Cavan), Denis Walsh R.I.P. (Kerry), Philip Doran (Dublin) and Doug Newel (Dublin).

The club has held 36 annual Feis competitions, participates in Heritage Days, supports Irish dancing and Gaelic Football, and in general promotes and nurtures Irish culture in Edmonton. Live presentations of the All-Ireland GAA games (football and hurling) are received by satellite on Saturday and Sunday mornings.

Since the first meeting back in the spring of 1958, the club has survived by the policy that any healthy organization that institutes new ideas will automatically acquire, rather than autocratically require, membership and participation. This kind of strategy is the lifeline of any group. The club is looking forward to celebrating its 50th anniversary with the early pioneers who set the foundation back in 1958.

The 20th anniversary of the club building was celebrated on October 21, 2006, and all past presidents were honoured for their leadership.

Edmonton Irish Sports and Social Society Presidents

1958–60   Peter O'Donovan   1960–61   Charlie Quinn

1961–62	Bryan Bundred	1962–63	Jack Bell and Peter Nolan
1963–64	Tom Cummins	1964–66	Herb Monteith
1966–69	Liam Fagan	1969–74	Pat Sheridan
1974–75	Tim Coghlan	1975–76	Bryan Gallaher
1976–78	Maurice Kearney	1978–79	Julianne O'Loughlin
1979–81	Maurice Kearney	1981–83	Honor Byrne
1983–84	Pat Donovan	1984–85	Tom Morris
1985–86	Tony Dowling	1986–87	Julianne O'Loughlin
1987–88	Tom Morris	1988–89	Honor Byrne
1989–91	Pat Donovan	1991–92	Tony Dowling
1992–95	Tom Morris	1995–96	Sean Armstrong
1996–99	Julianne O'Loughlin	1999–00	Tom Morris
2000–02	Seamus Donaghy	2002–04	Martin Doyle
2004–05	Sean Gay	2005–08	Bill Morris

Fort McMurray

Part of the reason for the vitality of the Wolfe Tones, in its early years, was the economic prosperity of Alberta. In 1975, a team was formed by Mick McKenna (Armagh) and Brendan Loughran in the boomtown of Fort McMurray. In a subarctic oil town like Fort McMurray, with a population of 64,000 (30,000 of whom are transient), the Gaelic Football team was never hesitant in making the drive or flight into the metropolis of Edmonton.

Easter 1975 saw the first of a number of challenge games, and in 1976 the Edmonton/Fort McMurray duel continued, with Fort McMurray winning the Alberta Championship after a four-game series. Fort McMurray's traveling ways even brought them to San Francisco to play some exhibition matches.

In 1977, Edmonton hosted six Alberta teams to a very memorable 9-a-side tournament. Players traveled, on the weekend of May 5–7, to San Francisco to take in the matches of the GAA All-Stars from Ireland. Gerry Guest was often in correspondence with many clubs outside of Alberta, inviting them to visit Edmonton for Gaelic games.

Seamus McElwain was one of six members of the Irish Ventures band that included Pete McDonald, Brendan Sherlock, Henry Keenan, Tommy Flack and Alan Heasty. All of them were from Monaghan. The band was popular in many towns in Alberta, B.C. and Saskatchewan. Seamus, along with Henry Keenan and Brendan Sherlock, played football with the Edmonton Wolfe Tones in many competitive weekend matches against Fort McMurray and Calgary.

In 1978, the Wolf Tones won the Alberta championship. In 1979, Fort McMurray was victorious over Edmonton and Calgary, and the trophy disappeared into the Northern Alberta parkland.

The 1980s

The competitive hurling years in Alberta were 1980 and 1981; Calgary played in a 13-a-side game against Edmonton in both years. The first year Edmonton won convincingly 7-15 to 2-4, but Calgary won the next year.

In 1983, the Wolfe Tones affiliated with the NACB. They competed regularly in football against teams from Seattle, Calgary, Vancouver, and Portland (1991–94) as part of the Northwest Divisional Board. The team traveled to Calgary on June 29-30 in 1984. They played against Vancouver, the first day, and had a two point loss 0-10 to 0-8. Next day they came back and beat Seattle, with a last minute goal; they won by a point.

On July 13, 1984 at Jericho Park in Vancouver, Edmonton found themselves down by 4 points in a game against Vancouver, after 10 minutes of play. The Wolfe Tones rallied and scored a goal and five points in succession. Vancouver narrowed the margin before halftime with Edmonton leading by a point, 1-5 to 0-7.

The second half resumed, at a fast and furious pace, with Edmonton's catch and kick style contrasting with Vancouver's short, crisp passing. The teams matched score for score until Edmonton opened up a three-point lead, with an opportunistic goal. They followed that quickly with a point to lead 2-9 to 0-11 with about five minutes to go. However, with their backs to the wall, Vancouver showed great determination and replied with a goal and a point to level the game, the final score was Vancouver 1-12 to Edmonton 2-9.

The following day, July 14, the Wolfe Tones faced Seattle. The game was closely contested with the scores level at four points each at halftime. Though the game would prove to be a classic example of good football, Seattle would win by two, 0-12 to Edmonton's 1-7.

The Championships of the '90s and Beyond

The early '90s saw some of Edmonton's strongest years. The men would win the Bailey's Cup in 1990 and come second in the Northwest Division to Calgary. In 1991, the Edmonton team was the Northwest Champions and they won the Bailey's Cup. The marathon flight home from the Northwest Championships, via Kelowna, Penticton, Calgary, and finally to Edmonton, gave the team many opportunities to celebrate loudly.

Some of the players and supporters from this time included Noel Reilly (Meath), Seamus Tracey (Cavan), Tommy Fitzmorris (winner of a minor All-Ireland for Tyrone), Billy Morris, Seamus Coyne, Sean Smith (Meath), John and Christy Whelehan, Mike and Ollie Coughlan (Meath), Mike Quirke (Kerry), Jack Whelehan, Pat O'Donovan, Peter Moore, Walter Leebody, Rick Murray (R.I.P.) (Down), Dessie Keenan (Monaghan), Brendan Brady, Pat Quinn, Kieran Kelly and Mike McGibbon.

Richard O'Donovan (R.I.P.), who had partnered with Larry Thompkins in midfield for Castlehaven, Cork, was a charming man, with a sense of humour that made him a joy to be around. He was an inspirational captain, a brilliant footballer, and a gentleman on and off the field.

Edmonton players are of many nationalities with Polish, French-Canadian, Guatemalan, Ukrainian and Asian backgrounds. Wolfe Tones' players who have given notable service include: Vincent Mannion, Jack Kennedy, Andrew Walker, Seamus Tracy, John O'Connor, Robert Murphy, Marvin Dentzien, Corey Bodnarek, David Gallagher, Sky Johnston, Ollie Corcorahan, Ultan Peters, and the first Canadian-born captain (1997) of the men's team, Richard Karsten.

In 1999, Edmonton had an opportunity to play a young Irish team from Saville Systems who were computer trainees working in the city. The Wolfe Tones won the game 7-12 to 5-8 in a highly competitive match.

Gerry Muldoon

Gerry Muldoon, from Tyrone, served the Wolfe Tones well as a player and coach throughout the '90s and early 2000s. The day Gerry arrived in Canada, in June 1993, a woman who had lived in his village in Ireland picked him up from the airport and then made an unexpected suggestion. She mentioned that there was a football match going on at that very moment in St. Albert. She thought that he might want to meet some of the team members. The next thing you know, boots were found and he was on the playing field the first day he arrived in Canada.

Edmonton Ladies' Football

It was not until 1997 that ladies' football in Edmonton began. The Wolfe Tones' team ended their first season with a remarkable win over their hosts in Vancouver. Leo Creedon from Cork coached the team with Captain Maggie Charlton, who was an Edmonton native. The team consisted mainly of University of Alberta students; they had very few Irish players.

J.J. Hyland, of Vancouver, presented the team a trophy to commemorate their memorable first year of competition. On his own initiative he also sent some training videos to the Edmonton Club that year. His good grace and selflessness will not be forgotten; J. J. passed away in early 1998.

From 2004 to 2006, the Wolfe Tones team fielded two strong women's teams. They had an unbeaten run within the Western Divisional Board, winning three Tom Gibbons Memorial Championship cups. Some of the players who gave great service included Janet Harvey, Danielle Bodnarek, Siobhan Whelehan, Kim Budd, Pam Mathieu, Andrea Mooney, Ashley Garrard, Nahida Teliani, Jodi Harding, Mary Bennett, Chandra McQuarrie, Dawn Krawchuk DeBoer, Alecia Baldwin, Sarah Baugh, Jaime Feddema, Tanya Cebuliak, Rania Burns and Kyna Kowalchuk-Adams.

The Wolfe Tones were proud to have three of their Canadian-born players, Carlin Acheson Johnston, Colleen Whelehan, and Ainsley Baldwin, help represent Canada at the International Women's Tournament of 2005 in Dublin. Karen Hansen was chosen as a Western Canadian All-Star in the lead-up to the naming of the Canadian team.

In the Ladies' Gaelic Football final, on the Canada Day weekend in 2005, for the Kevin McFadden Memorial Trophy in White Rock, B.C., the Seattle Gaels cruised to an easy victory over the Edmonton Wolf Tones 8-9 to 3-2. Seattle Gaels' Captain Rebecca Fox received the championship trophy and plaque from Helen McFadden. The tournament MVP, Carlin Acheson from Edmonton, received her award from Canada's International Team selector Jarlath Connaughton, who had traveled from Ottawa for the weekend.

In August 2006 during the World Handball Championships, the first GAA president to visit Edmonton paid a social call on the Edmonton Irish Sports and Social Centre. The Wolfe Tones were pleased to have their ladies' team and international players honoured with presentations of the Shield Cup and the Western Canada Divisional Board plaque by *An tUachtarán,* Nicholas Brennan.

Edmonton Memories

Edmonton has been organizing their own tournaments for years with various clubs, winning its share of the championships. The 2004 tournament was memorable because the two Edmonton teams that reached the final were ultimately unable to play, due to a sudden severe storm that flooded half the city. That year there was also a revival in Northern Alberta, as Ronan Deane formed the Fort McMurray Brian Dillons GFC for the Edmonton tournament.

The O'Byrne Cup is a year-end blitz and a social mixer. Players come together to ease any "tension" there may be and to have one last chance for a kick-around before welcoming the Alberta winter. The *craic* evolved into a complete mixer one year, with women and men playing side by side. Calgary was invited in 2002 and, though they could not warm up to the idea of playing with ladies, they did walk off with the Cup that year.

In recent years, the club has travelled to Montreal's tournament and Toronto's Powerscreen 7's. It is hoped that this east-west travel will continue in the future with teams from Eastern Canada travelling out West to compete.

The Edmonton Wolfe Tones GAA have a wealth of supporters, managers, coaches, wise old men, talented ladies and, most importantly, players with whom they can build further successes for the club and for Gaelic games in Alberta. Those who are leading the club into 2008 include Sky Johnston, Kim Budd, Brian Daly, Carlin Acheson, Jonathan DeBoer, Jessie McKitrick and Monique Arsenault.

Edmonton Tournament Champions

Ladies	Christy Whelehan Cup - Men's
2007 Vancouver Harps	Vancouver Harps
2006 Edmonton Wolfe Tones	Calgary Chieftains
2005 Edmonton Wolfe Tones	Vancouver Harps
2004 Edmonton Wolfe Tones	Edmonton Wolfe Tones
2003 Edmonton Wolfe Tones	Calgary Chieftains
2002 Edmonton Wolfe Tones	Edmonton Wolfe Tones
2001 Vancouver Harps	Edmonton Wolfe Tones
2000 n/a	n/a
1999 Edmonton Wolfe Tones	Edmonton Wolfe Tones
1998 Edmonton Wolfe Tones	Calgary Chieftains
1997 Vancouver Harps	Vancouver Harps

CALGARY CHIEFTAINS

In 1977, Mike Quirke, of Fylemore, Kerry, helped to start the Calgary Chieftains with a group of avid supporters. This was probably the strongest year ever for Gaelic Football in Alberta; Edmonton hosted a 9-a-side tournament that was contested by no fewer than six Alberta teams; two from Edmonton, two from Fort McMurray, the Calgary Chieftains and a team from Red Deer.

Two years of competitive hurling in Alberta saw Calgary playing 13-a-side matches. In 1980, Edmonton won convincingly 7-15 to 2-4 but Calgary would win the following year in similar fashion.

Northwest Division Champions and the '80s

It was 1983 when the Calgary Chieftains joined the Northwest Division of the NACB that consisted of teams from Vancouver, Edmonton and Seattle. The rookie team accomplished quite a splash that year, as they won the championship over Vancouver. Calgary did not need to play a qualifier quarterfinal match, as the NACB had suspended the Western California Board due to their decision not to travel to Canada. The Chieftains went on to Chicago to play St. Brendan's of Chicago in a junior semifinal. It was a losing cause, but Calgary gave a great effort with their determined play throughout the match.

Some of the Chieftain stalwarts in these years included Paddy Slater, Tom Casey, Sean Hayes, John Connolly, Eamonn McMahon, John Doyle, Joe Thornton, Tony Broderick, James Doherty, Fintan McGivern, Gerry Foley, Finian Leahy (R.I.P), Adrian O'Mahoney, Brendan McCaffrey, Dan Donohue and Micky Clark.

The Chieftains traveled to Seattle for the weekend of May 19–20, 1984, and suffered losses to Vancouver 3-12 to 0-8 and to Seattle 1-8 to 0-6. The club went on to host a Northwest Divisional tournament on June 29–30 that year and organized quality food and entertainment. The Chieftains played Seattle for 60 minutes of close football and the game ended in a draw, Calgary 2-4 to Seattle 1-7. Calgary played Vancouver in the final game of the weekend, and Vancouver got off to a quick start with a goal in the opening minutes from midfielder Davey Carroll. At halftime, Vancouver led 2-2 to 0-4 and, though the lead extended to six points in the second half, Calgary rallied back with a goal. However, two outstanding saves by Vancouver's Pat Burns meant a Chieftain loss by only three points (2-6 to 1-6).

In 1989 and 1990, the Chieftains would win the Northwest Division with outstanding play and team spirit. Great support in promoting Gaelic Football in Calgary came from Sean Murray, Kieron Garvan, Sean Kelly, Frank Campbell, John Connolly, Sean and Ray Kavanagh, Stephen Kane and John Doyle. Sean Darby (Down) served as a player coach in the mid '90s. He had played in Vancouver, Toronto and Edmonton during his football career and his fondest memory was being part of the 1985 Vancouver Championship team.

The Rebuilding Years

After a brief Gaelic Football recession in 2001, where the club was inactive, the Chieftains regained form and had extraordinary success in 2002 and 2003. Calgary leadership in the GAA scene included the likes of brothers Paddy and "Deno" McCallion (Tyrone), Dave Kiernan, and Ronan Deane, all of whom were instrumental in reviving the Chieftains.

Other Chieftain players of note include Noel Tuohy of Father Murphy's Pub; Simon Kelly, John McGrath, Wayne Kavanagh, Nigel McCarthy, Stephen Connolly, Chris Kelly, Brian Geoghegan, Kenneth Flynn, Mark Hoey, Mike West; and Phil Henderson, 2007 Poc Fada Champion. Calgary won Seattle's tournament in 2003; they had a convincing victory over the Seattle Gaels, and they beat them again in Edmonton at their home tournament later that summer.

Ronan Deane

Ronan Deane was born in Cork City and played both hurling and football in his early years. He was active in Western Australia in 2000 as a member of Southern Districts GFC and took part in the Australasian Championships in Adelaide that year. Ronan traveled to Canada where he became a member of the Vancouver Harps in 2001.

Following his work-related move, later that year to Calgary, he rose to the position of President of the club in 2003 and 2004. His charitable work was noted, as he worked raising funds for the benefit of community members. He also wrote a four-part series of articles promoting development of the games in Western Canada.

Ronan was also a founding member of the Fort McMurray Brian Dillons, who competed in a few tournaments in 2004. Fort McMurray is a remote outpost of humanity not far from the Arctic Circle, and any living thing that survives up there is made of strong stuff.

Thanks to a handful of Irishmen and women working in the oil industry there, Ronan handed out contact details to anyone who could walk during the St. Patrick's Day parade. A week later he had fifteen lads lined up for training.

He once said, "Basically you have to look at the positives rather than the negatives; you have to allow yourself to step away from all the GAA norms, and then you have to be absolutely focused."

Deane later went to Vancouver in 2005; there he was able to inject his enthusiasm into the GAA scene where his love for the Gaelic games continues to shine forth in his activities with the Western Canada Divisional Board and the Vancouver ISSC.

"All you really need is a field, a ball, and a strong focus. You've got to set a time and place for training. Be there ahead of time. Ask everyone you meet, will they play? Argue with them when they say they're not interested. Take phone numbers of people that you've convinced to play and call them back. Bully people from already-in-place teams to support your initiative. Go to the schools.", but the results of this type of initiative, as shown by Ronan Deane, speak for themselves; the approach works.

Paddy McCallion and Crew

Paddy McCallion immigrated to Toronto in 1992 and played Gaelic Football for the Brampton Roger Casements. In 1996, he moved to Calgary and played for Edmonton, but in 1997, he established himself as the Captain of the Calgary Chieftains. His leadership of the Chieftains soon had him coined as the "Christy Whelehan" of Calgary; the club had a turn of good fortune because of his efforts.

Tim Hamill, 2007 Poc Fada Canadian Champion, is the son of St. Mike's legend Mickey Hamill who played on the 1975 NACB Hurling Championship team. Other former Calgary players of note include Steven Kane who played with Toronto's Clan Na nGael (1973–77) and John Fitzgerald who was actively involved with the Clan Na nGael as Captain.

Western Canadian Championships

The men's team won the first Tommy Butler Western Canadian Divisional Board Championship in 2004. In the following two years, they combined forces with the Edmonton Wolfe Tones to participate as a junior team in the Powerscreen 7's in Toronto, Ontario. The "Chief-Tones" had much success in round-robin play, but close losses in the semifinals both years, prevented them from setting any of the gold watch prizes to "Rocky Mountain Time."

In Vancouver during the 2006 tournament, there was a classic "Battle of Alberta" championship final with the Calgary Chieftains squeaking by the Edmonton Wolfe Tones 12 to 10. The J. J. Hyland Memorial Trophy was awarded to the Chieftains, and the Most

Valuable Player trophy was awarded to County Tyrone's Connor McNally from the Wolfe Tones.

In 2007, the Chieftains doubled their club membership and won the Tommy Butler Western Canada Divisional Championship for the second time, despite not winning either of the two tournaments held in Edmonton and Vancouver that were part of league play. Still, the championship win proved that the talent was available for Calgary when it came to winning the matches that mattered in the standings.

Members of the Championship team included Will Henderson, corner forward; Tom McAroe, Gary McCafferty, goalie/full-forward; Ted Beales, midfield/forward; Brendan O'Hara, Dan Fagan, Sean Louge, Canadian cornerback; Micheal O'Donnel, half-forward and 2007 Calgary Tournament MVP; Captain Adrian Lagan, midfield/full-forward; Jeremy Klemkey, Chris Rodgers, half-forward; Liam Mailey, manager; Brendan Bakay, Sean Moriarty, Calum Bonnington, centre halfback; Tim Hamill, midfield; Ryan Bakay, fullback; Eamon Gormley, halfback; Barry Sinclair, fullback; Noel Tuohy, coach.

Irish and Aussie Adrian Lagan

The Chieftains developed a firm relationship with the Calgary Kangaroos Aussie Rules team, which first began to play Gaelic on June 21–22, 2003 at the Calgary Irish Rugby Club. That year, the first International Rules Series was played between the two teams with each team winning a game apiece. The Aussies had the bigger margin of victory, however, and so took home the bragging rights.

History was made August 5–6, 2006 when the Kangaroos, who are not affiliated with the GAA, but are part of AFL Canada, won the Calgary Cup with victories over Vancouver in the semifinals and Calgary in the finals. MVP Brad Flowers, of the Kangaroos, was gracious in receiving his award when he mentioned his father's connection to the sport of Gaelic Football. The Chieftains were delighted to win back the Calgary Cup in August 2007 with a dominating victory. Preliminary talks are on-going with the "Roos" to work out affiliation with the Western Canada Divisional Board.

One of the current playing stars and club leaders of the Calgary Chieftains is Adrian Lagan. He won a National League medal and a Dr. McKenna Cup medal with the Derry Seniors in Football. Adrian missed out, in Derry's one and only All-Ireland B medal for hurlers, when he suffered a broken jaw in a game against Antrim earlier that year. Trying to block a sliotar with your mouth is not advisable.

Adrian has been active in a variety of sports and also plays Aussie Rules Football. He played for Canada at the International Cup in Melbourne, and contributed to the team's success with a number of scores from play. Adrian's father, Michael, played for Toronto's Clan Na nGael in the mid-'60s, but transferred to St. Mike's when the club was gathering up players to form their club. Michael Lagan was well known for his gifted abilities and skill on the field.

Supporters of the Calgary GAA

The Irish Cultural Society of Calgary celebrated 20 years in 2006, and is located in Bowness where there are two separate areas available for GAA activities. The first is Bunratty Hall, which holds upward of 170 people and includes a full kitchen, bar and stage. The second area available is Rosie O'Grady's pub that seats 80 people in a comfortable atmosphere. Many entertaining evenings following GAA tournaments and games have occurred with guests from all over Canada commenting on the functionality of these premises. Special thanks are directed to John Doyle of the ICS for his promotion of the Calgary GAA over the years.

The Calgary Irish Rugby and Field Hockey club, at 4334-18th Street, NE, has served as the Calgary Chieftains home since 2004. The club has been training and playing there regularly. The Chieftains have developed a good friendship with past president Ron Oates and staff members such as Gary and Carolin Hewison, whose sons, Rhys and Dye, are learning the game. The Calgary Irish Rugby grounds provide excellent facilities with quality pitches, showers, gymnasium and the opportunity to watch live All-Ireland Championship games. The Chieftains are grateful to current President, Ron Lockhart, for his help and Catholine Butler of the *Celtic Connection* newspaper for her instrumental support of the Calgary GAA over the years.

Lady Chieftains

June 12, 1999, at the Viscount Bennett football field, proved to be a historic event because it introduced the first women's Gaelic Football team to represent the city of Calgary. The Lady Chieftains were up against a Vancouver women's team that was seeing action for the second time that day. Despite the roaring support from the sidelines for the home team girls, the opposition proved too much. The following day, the newly formed Calgary team played Edmonton, but the experienced opposition claimed a victory too.

Though there were challenges in maintaining a competitive team in the early years, June 2003 provided a Calgary 7's Tournament victory over Edmonton 11-3. Players that day included Sinead and Leigh Kavanagh, Jody Patrick, Caroline Ross and Mandy Tuohy.

The Lady Chieftains were proud to have two of their Alberta-born players (Mandy Tuohy and Kim Tulloch) help represent Canada at the International Women's Tournament of 2005 in Dublin. Cindy Chalmers was commended for being chosen a Western Canadian all-star in the lead up to the naming of the Canadian team. Other players that were noted by selectors were Maeve McKiernan, Amanda Stewart-Lagan, Jocelyn Obreiter and Orla McKiernan.

The 2007 squad saw dedication and commitment throughout the season from Anna Doyle (daughter of former Chieftain John Doyle), Erin Sinclair and Sinead Brady. John Fitzgerald, a former captain of Toronto's Clan Na nGael, capably served as the team's coach and manager.

30th Anniversary Celebrations

The Calgary Chieftains had a big night to celebrate their 30th Anniversary on November 10, 2007, at Father Murphy's Irish Pub. Under the chairmanship of Adrian Lagan, club members worked hard selling tickets prior to the event and decorated the bar with County jerseys from all parts of Ireland. The 120 guests were treated to a beautiful prime rib dinner and a healthy slice of anniversary cake that was donated by Father Murphy's.

Special guests that evening were J. Cameron Millikin, Honorary Consul General of the Government of Ireland to Alberta; Ron Lochart, President of the Calgary Irish Rugby and Field Hockey club; Don McAuley, President; and Colette Smithers, Communications Director of the Irish Cultural Society.

A new club crest was unveiled featuring downtown Calgary, St. Bridget's cross and two crossed over hurling sticks with an O'Neill's football underneath. This was a special moment for all in attendance as a lot of members had put forward their ideas all season toward this night.

Tim Hamill and Brendan Bakay were both masters of ceremony for the night and got down to business with the Club awards for 2007. Ladies Newcomer of the Year was presented, by Noel Tuohy, one of the owners of Father Murphy's, to Erin Sinclair who had a great year and always gave 100 percent in training and tournaments.

Men's Newcomer of the Year went to Micheal O'Donnell from Tipperary. Tipperary would not generally be associated with having great footballers, but Micheal must be an exception to the rule. He was a constant threat to all the opposing teams and contributed both defensively and offensively with some great goals. He was also very committed to training and one of the last players to leave the bar after a heavy night's training session.

Ladies' MVP went to, none other than, Mandy Tuohy. Mandy may have to look for a bigger trophy cabinet soon, as she has been the driving force of Calgary ladies' football for quite some time. Mandy suffered from a recurring knee injury in Vancouver this year, and after surgery she plans to be back playing in the red and white next season.

The Men's Most Valuable Player award was presented by Liam Mailey (Men's Coach) to Tim Hamill. When presenting the award to Tim, Liam explained that the decision was based on whom they would least like to take off the pitch in a game. Tim, who is son of St. Mike's legend Mickey Hamill, had another great year for the club in the middle sector of the pitch. His tireless work-rate up and down the pitch and solid tackles were keys to winning the Tommy Butler Western Canada Divisional Championship. Tim was also selected as a Western Canada Divisional All Star.

The final award of the night was for the Club Person of the Year. This was voted unanimously by the members of the club and went to the "Oak leaf" man from Derry, Liam Mailey. Liam was the club trainer and chief of fund-raising. There is no doubt that the club's success in 2007 was largely due to Liam's efforts.

Those that will lead the Chieftains into the future include Adrian Lagan, Liam Mailey, Erin Sinclair, Maeve McKiernan, Barry Sinclair, Tim Hamill, Orla McKiernan, Brendan O'Hara, William Henderson and Noel Tuohy.

Calgary Tournament Champions

	Ladies	Men
2007	n/a	Calgary Chieftains
2006	Edmonton Wolfe Tones	Calgary Kangaroos
2005	Edmonton Wolfe Tones	Calgary Chieftains
2004	Edmonton Wolfe Tones	Calgary Chieftains
2003	Calgary Chieftains	Calgary Chieftains 'A'
2002	Edmonton Wolfe Tones	Calgary Chieftains
2001	n/a	n/a
2000	Edmonton Wolfe Tones	Edmonton Wolfe Tones
1999	Vancouver Harps	Calgary Chieftains
1998	Vancouver Harps	Vancouver Harps

RED DEER EIRE OGS

Rory Lynch was born in Fort McMurray, Alberta, to Kevin (Down) and Josephine (Meath) Lynch. Kevin and Josephine were founding members of the Vancouver Irish Sporting and Social Club in 1975. They moved to Alberta in 1976. Blaine Lavery was born in Red Deer to Danny (Down) and Moya (Antrim) Lavery. Blaine had heard about Gaelic Football growing up, as his dad had played for the Down minors and in an All-Ireland final before immigrating to Canada. For a number of years, both Rory and Blaine spent a significant amount of time in Ireland as young men, where the love of the Gaelic games took a hold of them.

Back in Canada, Blaine was checking out some websites for Gaelic Football in the West. He stumbled upon the Calgary, Edmonton and Vancouver websites and thought it would be a good idea to set up a team in Red Deer that would be a part of the league play. Both Rory and Blaine were so keen on the matter that they made phone calls to their Irish and non-Irish friends. The lads sent out emails to the Calgary and Edmonton clubs to get the ball rolling. From Calgary, Adrian Lagan and, from Edmonton, Colin Baugh made contact with the founders.

The founders decided on the team name Eire Og, because the majority of the team's players were very young. Jerseys were sponsored by West Park Foods in Red Deer, and the club also received an equipment contribution from the Blarney Stone Pub. The Calgary Chieftains offered additional support and donated a couple of Gaelic balls; the young club was very appreciative and welcomed the support.

First Match

A game was played with the Calgary Chieftains in Red Deer in April 2007. It was a blowout for Red Deer, but expectations were always modest for the newest team in Canada. Red Deer attended tournaments in Calgary (May) and Edmonton (July); six team members travelled to Vancouver to hook up with the Wolfe Tones (August); and the last tournament was back in Calgary to wrap things up competitively for 2007.

Those who also contributed to the success of the Eire Ogs in 2007 included Fergus Lynch, Darren Lavery, Gaelan Lavery, Caolan Lavery, Mark Crossey, Braden Sacha, Jordan Unreiner, Mark Crossey, Mick O'Toole (Wicklow), Gary Murray (Dublin), Aidan Moran (Meath), Diarmuid Dalton (Meath), Greg Ducharme (Red Deer), John Dwyer (Red Deer), Brian Haines (Red Deer), Mike Veenstra (Red Deer), Ian Rattan (Red Deer), Phillip Harris (Red Deer) and Chris Weiss (Red Deer). Overall it was a good first year, with a few wins, a few losses and a few hammerings! Not bad for a team with only a few guys that had played before.

The club affiliated on January 22, 2008 with the Western Canada Divisional Board and looks forward to hosting their first Championship in 2010 with both mens and ladies teams representing Red Deer.

BRITISH COLUMBIA

VANCOUVER SONS OF ERIN

In 1922 four religious brothers—Lannon, Keane, Reid and Murtagh—of the Congregation of Christian Brothers, arrived from Ireland, to open and direct a Catholic school for boys (Vancouver College). The school holds the distinction of being the first to introduce, organize and promote the games of Ireland amongst its students. Dublin-born Bill Milne recalls seeing pictures in the main hallway of the school's hurling teams when his own sons attended Vancouver College in the early '70s.

Over the years, the Brothers have served the needs of Catholic education in the province through schools in Vancouver, Kamloops and Victoria. Their combination of solid Catholic education, firm discipline and rugged sportsmanship has attracted thousands of Irish Canadians for more than 85 years.

Gaelic Football had been played occasionally between the Irish communities of Vancouver, British Columbia and Seattle, Washington in the late 1950s. Pat Magee remembers playing a number of priests from Seattle's Irish American Club in 1958. The Vancouver Irish players only found out that they had been marking priests afterwards, when they were taking their post-game showers. It seems that only priests would take showers with boxer shorts on!

Jimmy Dunne (R.I.P.) remembers the priests being "as tough as nails" and Irene Fee remembers them being the "dirtiest ones" on the field. The Seattle teams, over the next few years, always comprised four or five priests, but once the Archbishop of Seattle got word of the priests' involvement with Gaelic Football in the early '60s, it brought an unfortunate end to their participation.

Gaelic Football took root with the Vancouver Sons of Erin Gaelic Football Club, whose marching song, "Roddy McCorley," was sung before each of their matches. A number of parishioners, who worked the bingo at St. Patrick's Church at 12th and Main, used to play broomball and floor hockey in the winter months on Friday nights. Trevor Carolan recalls being brought to the games a few times in the early '60s by his father John Carolan

(R.I.P.). For these games, the traditional straw, sweeping-broom bristles were cut quite short so the players could get a good blast close to the stitching and the wooden handle. John Carolan would also play Gaelic Football in goal and went on to referee matches at local GAA tournaments in the 1990's. His son Trevor recalls that there was a lot of thumping and banging when his father played his sports, and when he repaired for a cold beer afterward.

The Irish parishioners, with the encouragement of assistant Priest Father Neal Carrigan, introduced the game of Gaelic Football in the spring of 1961 and many joined to play this new sport. The Sons of Erin Club was formed with the Peter Fee (R.I.P.) as President, Joe Kelly as Treasurer and Terry Wheatley as Secretary. The Club conducted many dances, chartered two flights to Ireland and hosted various entertainers over the years. Local matches were played at John Hendry Park and Brockton Oval in Stanley Park.

Irish-born Sons of Erin footballers included Jimmy Dunne (R.I.P.), Pat Forrestal, Eddie Eviston, Matt Sheridan, Chris Morgan, Bob Jordan (R.I.P.), Nick Forrestal (R.I.P.), Mike Kelly (R.I.P.), Pat Flanagan (R.I.P.), Joe Tohill (R.I.P.), Mike Kiely (R.I.P.), Joe Kelly, Tom Doris, and Don McGuiness. Canadian-born players included Terry Wheatley, Al Favero, Tom Nellaney (R.I.P.), Jimmy Williamson, Chuck Krastel, Jack Cowie (R.I.P.), and Bill Stansfield. Well-known supporters of the club included Malachy and Peggy McKenna, Tom Butler and deceased members Tom Gibbons, Paddy and May MacDonald, Andy Anderson and Patrick McAreavey.

1962 Northwest Champions

Vancouver and Seattle, along with Portland, participated in the American County Board Northwest play downs in 1962. Seattle beat Portland in their qualifying match and the stage was set for the Irish American and Irish Canadian showdown. The Sons of Erin drew with Seattle in their first match. Eventually, the Sons went down in history as the first Northwest Champions when they beat Seattle 15-9 at Brockton Oval in Stanley Park on July 27, 1962.

Shortly thereafter, the Sons of Erin traveled to San Francisco for the West Coast Championships, where the Irish Community of San Francisco was very hospitable to the visitors. An excellent dinner/dance was provided and a good time was had by all, out on the streets of San Francisco. However, on the playing field, San Francisco's "Select" team promptly hammered the Sons of Erin; the referee put his pencil away at some point. As one former Sons of Erin player Terry Wheatley said, "The Vancouver substitutes came on, but we took no one off!" Albert Favero said, "They seemed to be so 'professional' in how they played."

The large number of inexperienced Canadians on the Sons of Erin team may have played a small part in the defeat. San Francisco had a much larger Irish community from which to draw its players. Still, this was an important event for a Vancouver team, and this match will be forever enshrined in the annals of Gaelic Games in Western Canada.

The following year, in 1963, the Seattle team won the Northwest playoff over the Sons of Erin. A select group, of five Sons of Erin players, was drafted onto the Seattle team in preparation for the visiting San Francisco team that was traveling north for the championship at West Seattle Stadium. Though Seattle would lose the match, the play of the Sons of Erin members was a welcome addition by the Seattle Irish Community.

To the onetime "Broomballers," the "new" game of Gaelic Football began to lose its lustre and place of importance due to the advancing age of some of the players and the ongoing responsibilities of family life. The Vancouver Sons of Erin Gaelic Football Club eventually gave way and became a soccer and social club. Peter Fee stepped down from the Presidency in 1967 and well-known local individuals who steered the club in its new direction included Tony and Gertie (R.I.P.) Leathem, the Macken brothers, and John Stewart, just to name a few.

VANCOUVER IRISH SPORTING AND SOCIAL CLUB

Bill Milne remembers one night in June 1973, when he got a phone call telling him that there was some hurling going on at Little Mountain Park in Vancouver. Bill grabbed his hurls, and he and sons Brian and Fergus, dashed over to the park to find Ned Walker and his son, Jim Cunningham, and his sons Joseph and James, and Tom O'Flynn Sr. with his sons John and Tom having a go.

A few years later, Bill solicited a donation of 10 hurls and two sliotars from a Dublin team called Eireann's Isle from the town of Finglas. Shortly afterward, he donated the hurls to the Vancouver Irish Sporting and Social Club member Liam Cadogan (Cork) for the club's use.

The formation of the Vancouver Irish Sporting and Social Club (ISSC) in 1974 and the Gaelic matches that were played by the ISSC against San Francisco were, in many ways, a replay of what had happened in previous years with the Vancouver Sons of Erin. Still, the ISSC was to take Ireland's games to a new level, never before seen by the earlier Vancouver Irish GAA pioneers.

The Founding

The Vancouver Irish people who gathered on December 1, 1974, decided that a name for the new club was needed. The choice of "The Irish Athletic Association" was considered but after Pat Donohue proposed "The Vancouver Irish Sporting and Social Club," it was unanimously accepted by all those present that night.

The first executive chosen were John Dooley (Armagh), Joe Heaney, Pat O'Connell, Joe McNally, Rene Dooley, J.J. Hyland and Ray Burns. Members who put their names forward to support the founding executive included John Smith, Pat McHugh, Kevin and Josephine Lynch, Pat O'Neill, Leonita Lively, Pearse Walsh, Maureen Rudden, Liam and Maureen Cadogan, Tony McDonagh, Paddy Hickey, Eamon Lane (R.I.P.), Noel Murphy, Maria Kelly, Michael Glavin, Pearse Ward, John Kelly, Maurice Ward, Pat Leathwood,

Anna Macrae, June Connolly, Tommy Roe, John Ryan, Sean Commins, Owen Farrelly and Malachy and Charlotte Swail.

Weeks later, the club chose as their credo, "Try and make a new friend at each function," for all future events. Those involved in the early newsletters were Editor Pearse Walsh; editorial staff Vickki Civitarese, Grace Gopaul and Donna Townsend.

In May 1975, John Dooley was re-elected President, with Joe Heaney, Pat O'Connell, Tony McDonagh, Joe McNally, Leonita Lively and Des Foley serving as the executive.

The following list denotes the executive members for each year, beginning with the president:

1976—Pat McKenna, J. J. Hyland, Eugene Hilbert, Maureen Cadogan, Des Foley, Leontia Lively, Marian McDaid, Paul T. Walsh, Pearse Walsh, Maria Kelly, Tony McDonagh, Maureen Rudden, Eugene Halferty, Liam Cadogan, Evelyn Doherty
Sub-Committee Members: Tom Monaghan, Joseph McNally, Sean Commins, Mick Mortell, Charlie McAleese, Mary Bowers, Sean Keogh

1977—J. J. Hyland, Leonita Lively, Maureen Cadogan, Eugene Halferty, Maureen Rudden, Pam Barnett, Kathy Walsh, Marian McDaid, Mary Hyland, Charlotte Swail, Pat O'Connell
Sub-Committee Members: Pearse Walsh, Charlie McAleese, Gerard McAleese, Rose McDermott, Frankie Kirby, Margaret Brown

1978—Pat O'Connell, Rob McHugh, Maureen Cadogan, Mairead McCabe, Danny Cuddy, Brendan Mulhall, Maureen Rudden, Pam Barnett
Sub Committee Member: Eamon O'Carroll

1979—Danny Cuddy, Kevin Dooley, Mary Fisher, Paddy Todd, Onagh Dooley, Margaret Shiel, Kevin Dunne, Maureen Rudden, Ken Fisher, Mavis Cuddy
Sub Committee Member: Pam Ferguson

1980—Charlotte Swail, Kevin Finnegan, Rob McHugh, Frankie Kirby, P. J. Ruddy, Peter Ferguson, Evelyn Doherty, Mavis Cuddy, Mary Fisher, Pam Ferguson, Yvonne McHugh
Sub Committee Member: Malachy McKenna

1981—Pam Ferguson, Maureen Gerrard, Eileen Finnegan, Mavis Cuddy, Sylvia Keye, Pat Burns, Jeannie Crawford, Yvonne McHugh, Trish Blowers, Kevin Finnegan, Maria Wong, Frankie Kirby

1982—Pat Burns, Jeannie Crawford, Onagh Dooley, Sylvia Keye, John O'Connell, Betty Forrestal, Tom O'Flynn

1983—Dan Jones, Tom O'Flynn, Anna Meagher, Pat O'Connell, Brendan Burns, Pearse Kelly, Frank Doherty, Mary Hyland, Donela Haynes

1984—Dan Jones (R.I.P.), Sean Commins, Donela Haynes, Brenda Johnston, John O'Flynn, Paraic Lally, Brendan Finnegan, Brendan Burns, Mary Hyland, Frank Doherty

1985—Sean Commins, Pat Burns, Katherine Fagan, Brenda Sloan, Deirdre Lane, Kevin Deevey, Maria Wong

1986—Sean Commins, Pat Burns, Katherine Fagan, Kathy Walsh, John O'Flynn, Kevin Deevey, Rose O'Connell, Brenda Sloan

1987—Sean Commins, Brendan Burns, Kathy Walsh, Kathy Burns, Kevin Deevey, Deidre Finnegan, John O'Flynn, Katherine Fagan

1988—Brendan Burns, John O'Flynn, Deidre Finnegan, Anne Dunne, Kevin Deevey, Katherine Fagan, Margaret Corrigan, Paul Stack

1989—John O'Flynn, Brendan Finnegan, Anne Dunne, Brendan O'Leary, Sean Fagan, James Kennedy, Kathy Stack, Michele O'Flynn

1990—James Kennedy, Brendan Finnegan, Anne Boyle, Brendan O'Leary, John O'Flynn, Sean Fagan, Kathy Stack, Deidre Finnegan, Brendan Lally

1991—James Kennedy, John O'Flynn, Tom Butler, Peggy McKenna, Mary Finn, Val Molloy

1992—J. J. Hyland, Brendan Burns, James Kennedy, John O'Flynn, Paul Stack, Danny Burns, Sadie O'Brien, Michelle O'Flynn, Roy Byrne, Kevin Molloy, Paul Walsh

1993—James Kennedy, Paul Stack, Liam Mackin, J. J. Hyland, Kevin Molloy, Tom O'Sullivan

1994—Declan Byrne, Jim Ritchie, Donny Considine (R.I.P.), Liam Mackin, Tom O'Sullivan

1995—Paul Stack, J.J. Hyland, Tom O'Sullivan, Bernard McKenna, Tomas Franklin, Mark Ford, Joe Burke, Christine Anderson, Sadie O'Brien, Richie Cannon

1996—Bernard McKenna, Karen McKenna, Karen Franklin, Tomas Franklin, Sean Minagh, Johnny Wilson, Richie Cannon, Kate McNamee

1997—J. J. Hyland, Susan Ditchfield, Arlene Bergsma, Grace McLeod, Richie Cannon, Tom Kristensen, Brendan O'Leary

1998—J. J. Hyland (R.I.P.), Sue Ditchfield, Arlene Bergsma, Paul Stack, Tom Kristensen, Erin Anderson, Michelle Boyle, Paul McGinley, Craig McAlee, Richie Cannon, Tom O'Sullivan

1999—Paul Stack, Tony Doyle, Bunny Vidotto, Jen Heal, Liam Mackin, Erin Anderson, Paul McGinley

2000—Tony O'Duffy Brennan, Tony Doyle, Kate McNamee, Colette Donnelly, Cathy Collins

2001—Tony O'Duffy Brennan, Paul Stack, Michelle Boyle, Nuala McLoughlin, Kate McNamee

2002—Mickey Hurley, Paul Stack, Kate McNamee, Nuala McLoughlin, Michelle Boyle, Stephanie Boggan

2003—Brendan O'Leary, Kate McNamee, James Kirk, Kami Bachana, Paul Stack

2004—James Kirk, John O'Flynn, Kami Bachana, Kate McNamee, Sean Quinn, Nuala Cyr, Paul Stack

2005—Gavan Connolly, John O'Flynn, Kami Bachana, Sean Quinn, Stephanie Boggan

2006—Gavan Connolly, Bernard Ward, Roicin Connolly, Katrina McAndrew

2007—Graham Hancock, Marcus Treacy, Katrina McAndrew, Roicin O'Connolly, Olivia O'Hara, Keith Clark, Erin McGinley, Ronan Deane, Ruairi Dolan

2008—Marcus Treacy (Kerry), Erin McGinley (Vancouver), Katrina McAndrew (Nottingham), Roicin O'Connolly (Cork), Kate Clark (Offaly), Ronan Deane (Cork), Tara Burns (Down), Ed Carbery (Donegal), Cian Lawlor (Waterford), Keith Clark (Toronto), Jerome O'Sullivan (Cork), Cathal O'Loughlin (Limerick), James Davoren (Galway)

Supporters of Gaelic Games

The ISSC has worked with and supported various groups, organizations and businesses over its 34 years in the Lower Mainland and British Columbia:

The *Celtic Connection* newspaper, Irish Heritage Society of Canada, Irish Women's Network, Irish Club of White Rock, Celtic Society of Canada, Celtic Fest Vancouver, Welsh Society of Vancouver, Tara Comhaltas Ceoltoiri Eireann-White Rock, Celtic Heritage Society of Canada, Rogue Folk Club, Club Ireland, Stage Eireann (Emerald Players), Irish Cultural Society of British Columbia, Belfast United, Vancouver Irish (1958-Glenavon and Eldorado/Glen-1982), Irish Canadian Celtic Association, Irish Canadian Club, Irish Society of British Columbia (Prior St.) 1981, Irish Heritage Society of B.C., Canadian Celtic Association (1976), Irish Canadian Business and Professional Association, Irish University Graduates' Association, Multicultural Society of B.C., Ireland Canada Chamber of Commerce, Vancouver Comhaltas Ceoltoiri Eireann,

W.I.S.E. Social and Athletic Club, Federation of Irish Associations and Societies of B.C., Van-Eire Traditional Dance Association, Vi Moore School of Dancing, Penk-O'Donnell School of Irish Dance, Claddagh Rince, MacDowell School of Dancing, Stewart School of Irish Dance, Comerford School of Dance, O'Connor Irish Dancers, Erin O'Daly School Of Irish Dancing, Scoil Rince de Dannan School of Dance, Folk Fest Society, Irish Canadian Cultural Society-Victoria, Friends of Ireland Club-Victoria, Vancouver Sons of Erin Gaelic Football Club, Vancouver St. Patrick's Day Parade Committee, Vancouver Irish Society, "Celtic Voices" Radio Show, "Celt in a Twist" Radio Show, "In the Claddagh Ring" Radio Show, Saoirse Eireann Radio Show-"Irish Sport and Social Report," Jam'r Productions, Irish Solidarity Committee, B.C. Catholic Newspaper, The BC Parkway-Irish Flag, Scribes Rugby RFC, Vancouver Cougars and Burnaby Eagles of the Australian Rules Football League.

The ISSC has hosted or supported various events including: Eamonn Coghlan's Run at Swanguard Stadium 1983; Irish Women's Field Hockey Team; Irish Ambassadors to Canada; Mayor and Councilors of Galway City; Folk Fest Open Houses; St. Patrick's Day Parades; Queen of Diamonds Boat Cruise-Coal Harbour; Grand Draw: Trip for two to Ireland and All-Ireland Football Tickets; President of Ireland - Mary Robinson; UBC Library Special Collections - Book of Kells; Gerry Adams MP Northern Ireland; Book Openings—"The History of the Irish in Canada"; Grosse-Ille Public Hearings—National Parks of Canada; "Emerald Ball"—Ireland Canada Chamber of Commerce; "Ragman's Ball"—Heritage Hall; "Blazing Saddles" Tour; John McKeachie "emcee" for Club event, Irish novelist—Brian Moore; live All-Ireland Hurling and Football Finals.

Business supporters of the ISSC include: The Spinning Wheel Pub, The Harp N' Heather Pub, Paddy's Cabaret, the Blarney Stone, the Medieval Inn, the Spaghetti House, the Celtic Shop, Irish Fancy Store, Celtic Creations, Pat Cleary Insurance Agencies, Uniglobe Travel, West Limerick Holdings Ltd., Liam's Irish Shop, William Kelly and Sons Plumbing Contractors Ltd, Donegal Developments Ltd., Penny Lane Pub, Liam and Germaine Gibbons, Celtic Connection, British Ex-Servicemen's Club, Scribes Rugby Club, the Irish Heather, O'Hare's Pub, Seagram's Canada, Oscar Books, Deli King, Austin Gourmet, Emerald Caterers, Cedar Cottage Pub, Shamrock Construction, Pro Coat Coatings, Doolins, Johnnie Fox's Irish Snug, Wolf & Hound, Clare Construction, Limerick Junction, The Black Frog and Emerald Heating and Plumbing.

Sporting Venues

The pitches for Hurling, Gaelic Football, softball, tennis, soccer, picnics, Sports Days (An Poc Fada / Long Kick Outs), walkathons and instructional workshops in Gaelic Games in Vancouver: Capilano Stadium, Jericho Park, Brockton Oval, Montgomery Park, Slocan Park, John Hendry Park (Trout Lake), Douglas Park, Locarno Park, Andy Livingston Park, David Lam Park, Rupert Park, Stanley Park, Clinton Park, Quilchena Park. In Burnaby: Burnaby Lake Park, Swanguard Stadium. In New Westminster: N.W. Senior Secondary, Douglas College. Surrey: South Surrey Athletic Fields, Peace Arch Park. In Richmond: Minoru Oval, RCA Forum Park. In Victoria: University of Victoria,

Braefoot Park. Kelowna: Rutland Secondary; and Harrison Hot Springs: Harrison Elementary School.

The sports of floor hockey, volleyball, handball, racquet ball, ladies' netball, indoor soccer, ice hockey and golf have occurred in various schools, community centres, rinks and courses such as: Sacred Heart School, South Hill School, Maquinna School, Cecil Rhodes School, Nelson Elementary School, St. Mary's Hall, St. Augustine's Hall, Blessed Sacrament Hall, Nootka School, Fleming School, Begbie School, McPherson Convention Centre, Dunbar Community Centre, Mt. Pleasant Community Centre, Richmond Sportsplex, Richmond Ice Rinks, Burnaby Four Rinks, UBC Thunderbird Rink, Britannia Ice Rink, McCleery's Golf Course, Tsawwassen Golf and Country Club and the Country Meadows Golf Course.

Venues for meetings, St. Patrick's Day dinner dances, dart tournaments, children's Christmas parties, Halloween costume balls, Valentines Day dances, discos, Gaelic Games broadcasts, hockey pools, table quizzes and other Irish cultural events of the ISSC: Lucas' Restaurant, Culpepper's Restaurant, Sheraton Landmark Hotel, the Blarney Stone Inn, Holiday Inn, Hotel Vancouver, Georgia Hotel, Bayshore Hotel, Penny Lane Pub, Cambrian Hall, Douglas Park Community Centre, Oakridge Auditorium, the Irish Centre (Prior St.) TB Vets Hall, Minoru Club House, Polish Community Centre, Multicultural Centre, Polish Veteran's Hall, Croatian Cultural Centre, Russian Community Centre, Irish Club (White Rock), St. Patrick's Gymnasium, British Ex-Serviceman's Club, W.I.S.E. Club, Scribes Rugby Club, Burnaby Lake Clubhouse, Legion Hall, Hellenic Community Centre, N.D.P. Hall, Hillcrest Hall, Hudson Manor, St. Mary's Ukrainian Centre, A.N.Z.A. Club, St. Augustine's School, St. Anthony's Church Hall, Blessed Sacrament Hall, Holy Rosary Hall, Carpenter's Hall, O'Hare's Pub, the Irish Heather, Burnaby Firefighters Union Building, Burnaby Lake Rugby Club, Elephant Walk, the Pump House, RCA Forum, Cedar Cottage Pub, Sports Town Tavern, Mt. Pleasant Community Centre, the Wolf & Hound, Doolins, the Foggy Dew, Astoria Hotel, Bel-Air Café, New West Carpenter's Hall, Dentry's Bar & Grill, the Limerick Junction, Wolf and Hound, Ceili's Irish Pub and Mahony & Sons.

The bands and music that have entertained over the years: John McGregor and the Merry Macs, Solid Gold, Tunisia, Mag'gty Butter, Three Row Barley, the Crofters, Limerick, Redivider, Short Notice, the Summer Time Pops, Irish Mist, Killarney, Comhaltas Ceoltoiri Eireann, Sons of Erin, Rogues n'Tinkers, Disco DJ's "Record Hop" Paddy Todd, Russell Hannibal, Danny Burns and the Ballad Band, the Sons of Terra Nova, Sheila Ryan and Sarsfield, Murphy's Lagh, Allan Carr, Rathlin Sound, the Rollicking Stone & Sea, Ballyhooley, Celtic Conspiracy, Blackthorn, Anchors Down, the Stoaters, the Quenchers, Tiocfaidh Ar La, Mark Downey's Jolly Rogers and Tara.

Honour Roll

Awards and trophies (won and lost!): Club Person of the Year; Nick Forrestall "Most Promising Young Athlete" Memorial Trophy; Darts Tournament "The Cuddy Trophy"; Senior Footballer of the Year; Minor Footballer of the Year; Ladies Award, JJ Hyland

Memorial Trophy; Finian Leahy Memorial Trophy; Bailey's Cup; Donny Considine Memorial Trophy; ISSC Scholarship (St. Patrick's Regional Secondary); St. Stephen's Day Challenge Cup; Michael O'Malley Memorial 7-a-side Trophy; Mackin Trophy; Jim O'Sullivan Memorial Trophy; Canadian Footballer of the Year Award; West Limerick Holdings Ltd. Hurling Challenge Plaque; Calgary Cup; the Christy Whelehan Cup; the Tom Gibbons Memorial Western Canada Divisional Ladies' Cup; the Tommy Butler Western Canada Divisional Men's Cup.

Pearse Walsh

Pearse Walsh (Mayo) originally arrived in Canada in the fall of 1971, after spending three years in Southern Ontario. While there, he played Gaelic Football with the Clan Na nGael Club in Toronto; he decided to "Go West" and arrived in Vancouver in 1974 at year's end. Prior to leaving Ontario, he had heard there was an effort under way to form a new Irish club in Vancouver.

Shortly after arriving, he found his way to one of the early meetings of the new ISSC at the downtown Holiday Inn. He recollects being very impressed with the young leaders, their extraordinary energy and their emphasis on wanting to create a very open, inclusive club that focused on sports and culture, but above all was a place of welcome and support for Irish people arriving and living in Vancouver. The timing for an Irish club was perfect as, at the time, there were a lot of young Irish coming to B.C. and migrating to Vancouver.

Moreover, it truly was a most welcoming environment. Being young also and having a continuing interest in Gaelic Football, it was not long before Pearse was making the Sunday afternoon trek to John Hendry Park. Initially there were 10 to 12 players who showed up, but before long the numbers grew to 25 to 30 players. Plans for a trip to San Francisco, to coincide with the Carroll's All Stars GAA visit to that city, began. The Dublin All-Ireland Football Champions and the Kilkenny All-Ireland Hurling Champions were scheduled to play the All-Stars in Balboa Park on April 6 and 13, 1975. On April 6, the All-Stars won 5-8 to Kilkenny's 3-10, and on April 13, Kilkenny came back to win 3-15 to 1-16 over the All-Stars.

Contacts with the club in San Francisco allowed for a curtain-raiser game against a minor Gaelic Football team that San Francisco was developing under the management of Danny Boyle. Enthusiasm and preparation for the trip kicked into high gear, and despite a number of set backs—a few drop-outs over visas and paperwork—they arrived in San Francisco for a memorable few days.

Nobody remembers the final score of the match—Vancouver was not victorious. Pearse was not sure if this was due to the speed, precise passing and goal scoring of the young, athletic San Francisco boys and the skills honed from playing basketball and soccer, or if it was Vancouver's late-night partying. No one cared—they were there to have fun and enjoy the moment, and they sure did that.

The club arranged a meeting with the senior officials of the GAA; they were seeking support for the fledgling club. Pearse recollects that the meeting resulted in many platitudes from the GAA, lauding their initiatives and some vague promises to consider some form of assistance in the future.

This was not consistent with the "can do now" way of making things happen, and at the Sunday night banquet, honouring the Carroll's All Stars, the ISSC presence was acknowledged and they were invited to say a few words. The club seized the opportunity, got up, and thanked the Secretary and Director General of the GAA (1954–1979), Sean O' Siochain, for his generous offer to donate the stack of backup hurling sticks they had on tour for the Vancouver team. That is how the ISSC reintroduced hurling to Vancouver with a 9-a-side hurling league, which they developed over a few summers.

Pearse left Vancouver in the summer of 1977 and returned to Ontario. When he looks back at those early days of the club, they were exciting, enjoyable, and above all, most rewarding. He hesitated to recognize the folks who were on the executive, partly because he would undoubtedly forget a name, but more so because the club's success was built on the combined efforts of all of the members. There were few passive members and there were so many who contributed in so many ways. However, Pearse does feel a debt of gratitude to John Dooley, the first president of the club, for his leadership, can-do attitude, his unwavering belief that the club was so important and his sense of humour, all of which contributed to the early success of the club. It must be said that Pearse himself was an important catalyst and spokesperson for the club in those early years with his impeccable written correspondence.

The '70s Unfold

The Secretary and Director General of the GAA, Sean O'Siochain, had some connections with Vancouver due to some correspondence with Vancouver's Liam Cadogan (Cork). In response to Cadogan's letter, on July 30, 1974, O'Siochain sent copies of the rules of hurling and football and passed on the news of special rates available through Aer Lingus to ship hurleys to Canada.

An ISSC letter dated June 21, 1975, was sent to the Toronto GAA's Mike O'Driscoll, informing him that the club had 35 footballers, 20 hurlers and 60 supporters. He was asked to forward copies of the letter to all of the clubs and societies in Toronto, Hamilton, Ottawa and Montreal. Of course, the club included 10 copies of this letter to make things easier for him.

On July 5-6, 1975, the San Francisco GFC, under the chairmanship of Jarlath O'Connor, made a visit to Vancouver. There is no doubt that they still talk today about that wonderful weekend and the hospitality of ISSC club members. The club played one game of football at Brockton Oval in Stanley Park and a game of hurling and football at Swanguard Stadium. Members billeted players and their families, and they partied all weekend—again Pearse does not remember the final score of the games, but he did recollect they were close matches that included a hurling victory for Vancouver.

A trophy presentation dinner and dance, with the Crofters band providing entertainment, was organized at Rudy Viktora's Blarney Stone Inn. Des Kennedy from San Francisco was named the "Outstanding Hurler." Vancouver won the Donegal Development Perpetual Trophy for hurling, and the Blarney Stone Perpetual Trophy for football went to San Francisco. Added sponsorship came from Ray Carlin's Harp n'Heather and the Spinning Wheel during the tournament.

Vancouver Island and "Down Under"

An exhibition of Gaelic games, including Camogie, was hosted in Victoria by the Irish Canadian Cultural Society on August 30, 1975. Those who traveled by Pacific Stage Lines bus had a grand time. People who played a significant role in the promotion of the Gaelic games on Vancouver Island in the '70s included Jim and Breda O'Sullivan, John and Maura Clancy, Brian Gillen, Paul Larkin and Kevin McFadden (R.I.P.)

In a letter, dated August 22, 1975, to President Jim O'Sullivan of the Irish Canadian Cultural Society in Victoria from Pearse Walsh of the ISSC, the following were listed as participants: Liam and Maureen Cadogan, Alex Carey (Westmeath), Sean Young, John Dooley, Seamus McGuinness (Armagh), Kevin Doran (Armagh), Pat Donohue, Frank Dooley (Armagh), Tom Cahalan, Tom Halferty (Derry), John Ryan (Tipperary), Pat O'Neill (Cavan), Sean Farrelly (Dublin), Des Kennedy (Tipperary), Eugene Tansey, (Sligo), Pearse Walsh (Mayo), Eamon Ward (Antrim), Paul Walsh (Waterford), Tony McDonagh (Galway), Eoin Farrelly (Dublin), Vivian Plunkett (Mayo), Frankie Kirby (Portsmouth), Margaret McGee (Down), Marie Donnelly, Marie Kelly (Down), Leonitia Lively (Down), Maureen Rudden, Mary Burns (Down), Joe McNally (Down), Pat and Rose O'Connell (Mayo) and Tom Monaghan.

An ISSC letter, of January 21, 1976, to the Secretary of the American Board, Peter Donnelly in Pittsburgh, provided an overview of the club. The letter outlined the Vancouver league of four teams, in each sport, which played twelve games over the season. Information about affiliation was asked for, along with the standard inquiry into the availability of All-Ireland Final tickets.

From May 1976 to June, a 7-a-side football league of three teams was organized. The three captains were Pat McHugh (Mayo), J. J. Hyland and Eugene Halferty; Joe McNally oversaw the competitions. In a match played in Victoria, Jim O'Sullivan, of the Irish Canadian Cultural Society, led his local team to a loss. The media was in attendance and Vancouver's Bill Milne provided a running commentary for the local television station.

Later that year, first contact with football played "Down Under" was made with a local Australian Rules football team that was managed by Nick Tarasiuk. A mixed Gaelic and Aussie rules match was played for the first time. The Irish were victorious on October 10th at Montgomery Park in Vancouver.

St. Patrick's Day Parade

The 1976 Vancouver St. Patrick's Day Parade organized by Tom Byrne and Terri Turner (R.I.P.) saw Maureen (nee Rudden) Gerrard as the Chief Grand Marshall and the following members represent the ISSC: Mary Bowers, Vickki Civitaresse, Evelyn Doherty, Maria Kelly, Frankie Kirby, Charlotte Swail, Audrey Troelstra, Donna Townsend, Nick Forrestal, Paddy Hickey, Noel Hickey, Emmot Hickey, Tony McDonagh, Eamon O'Connoll, Jimmy Speiran, Malachy Swail and Pearse Walsh. The ladies were dressed in green shorts and shirts with Irish flags on them, while the men dressed in white shorts and green/gold football sweaters.

On March 14, 1976, at Brockton Oval, a football match was played with Malachy Swail, Pearse Walsh, Dave Pitham, Tony McDonagh, Eamon O'Carroll (Dublin) and Dennis Neenan (Kildare) losing to Jim Fitzgerald, Eoin Farrelly, Eamon Lane, Bernie Ward, Joe McNally and John Smith. Tommy O'Boyle served as referee.

A hurling match was played between the Fir Bolgs and the Guinness Exiles. The experience of the 'Bolgs' saw some tenacious play from Eoin Farrelly, Max Corkhill, Kevin Dunne and Eamon Lane as they led at half-time 3-5 to 1-3. The opening of the second was marked by a 'Guinness' resurgence from Eugene Halferty, Tom Monaghan, Ed McGrath (Galway) and Liam Cadogan. The "Bolgs" carried the day by 6-9 to 3-6 with P.J. O'Donnell providing the colour commentary.

San Francisco Revisited

Another trip to San Francisco occurred on the first weekend in May 1977. Participants took in the US Tour of the Dublin Football and Cork Hurling teams versus the All Star football team led by Dr. Jim Brosnan (Kerry), and the All Star hurling team led by Jim Berry of Wexford. Cork would beat the All-Stars 2-17 to 1-15 on May 8.

Included among these games were local matches organized by Vancouver with two San Francisco teams and Sacramento. Club members met Father Patrick Leslie who was Chair of the Sacramento GFC, which had a number of Irish priests on the team, and President of the GAA in San Francisco, Louis Roche.

Vancouver beat Sacramento by three points, but lost to the two San Francisco teams in football. A hurling match took place and the visitors lost to a San Francisco team. Among those that traveled from British Columbia were Eugene Halferty, Tommy O'Boyle, Pat McHugh, Joe Heaney, Paul Walsh, John Smith, Pearse and Audrey Walsh, Liam and Maureen Cadogan, Sean and Moira Keogh, Charlie and Gerard McAleese, Tony McDonagh and Terry Vellinoweth, Maureen Rudden, Pam Barnett, Patty Wildgen, Karen Brundage, Joanne Corkrill, Pirette Dufas, Mairead McCabe, Kevin Dunne, Nick Forrestal, P.J. O'Donnell, Matt Cremin, Paul Larkin, Fred Barry, Barry Tenneyson, Brian Gillen, Jim Tubman, Eamonn O'Carroll, Tom Martin, Charlie O'Sullivan, Jimmy Speiran, Tom Barrett, Dan McCarthy, Kevin McFadden and Joe McAleese.

Later that year, Secretary John O'Brien invited Vancouver to send motions and delegates to the American County Board convention in Boston. The ISSC did not followed up with the letter, dated November 3, 1977, as the club was not committed to affiliation at that time.

The 1980s

An August 16, 1981, starting lineup for Coach Peter Ferguson's Vancouver ISSC team, which competed against the Tacoma Evergreen Irish, included Sean Rafferty, Ed Butler, Joe Kenny, Don Cayer, Brendan Burns, Peter Ferguson, Vincent Donegan, Seamus Storan, Colm O'Brien, Eugene Halferty, John Campbell, John O'Connell, Jim Ryan and Pat Burns.

The football team went to Seattle for a "fun" game in 1982. The squad was beaten badly at football but won the drinking contest at Murphy's Pub. Donal Boyle sang a rendition of "Paddy McGinty's Goat" that apparently brought the house down. The 1982 Footballer of the Year was Seamus Frain.

The Nick Forrestal Memorial Trophy was established in 1983 for the "Most Promising Young Athlete," in memory of Nick's untimely death on November 10, 1982. His love of, and involvement in, Gaelic games was remembered by Canadian winners that included Sean Rafferty, '82; John O'Flynn, '83 and '84; Sean Forrestal, '85; Joe Dalsin '87; Liam Gibbons, '90; and Liam Segarty, '91.

Northwest 1984 Finian Leahy Divisional Championship

1984 saw a record number of 250 members. The football season started April 1, with a challenge game by Seattle in Vancouver. The ISSC won this game. On April 29 in Seattle, Vancouver trailed at halftime 0-4 to 0-7, but a second half comeback saw a victory of 3-10 to 1-7. Seattle put on a great feed afterwards and some of the Vancouver players did not make it back until 4:00 a.m. on Monday.

In a May 19 match versus Calgary, held in Seattle, there was good all-round display and a win of 3-12 to 0-8 for Vancouver. A May 24, 7-a-side football tournament in Vancouver featured five teams that included Seattle, the Antrim Selects, John O'Connell's Blarney Stone, Joe Thornton's Kitsilano Gaels and the St. Margaret Street Slashers.

On June 29 in Calgary, Vancouver faced Edmonton for the first time. The Wolfe Tones got off to a very fast start and led 0-5 to 0-0 after 15 minutes. Vancouver settled down somewhat and at halftime they trailed 0-7 to 0-3. In the second half, Vancouver fought back mainly due to a tremendous display from Aidan Colleran and Eugene Halferty, who were outstanding. Vancouver drew level with a great free kick from Billy Moyles (Kerry), from almost 60 yards with five minutes to go, and then scored twice to win by 0-10 to 0-8.

At the games of July 13-15, 1984, held at Jericho Park in Vancouver, a crowning match was played on the Sunday versus the Seattle Gaels. A spirited Vancouver team took an early lead and maintained it throughout the game. It was their best team performance of the year; they were able to run out winners by four points 2-7 to 2-3.

The ISSC men's team's win in the Northwest Divisional Championship of the North American County Board of the Gaelic Athletic Association in 1984 was a memorable and significant achievement. Coach Peter Ferguson, from Garrison, Fermanagh, played an important role in the team's successes. ISSC Presidents Sean Commins and Dan Jones (R.I.P.) also provided outstanding leadership. Brendan and Pat Burns (Down) were instrumental in providing support both in the boardrooms and on the playing field in the years previous and many years thereafter. Notably, Paraic Lally was awarded the MVP that year, because he attended training regularly, was sportsmanlike, and was a hard working and dedicated person.

Vancouver traveled to Seattle to vie for the West Coast Regional Championship against the Southwest California Champions, San Diego's Clan Na nGael. After a close first half 2-6 to 1-5 for Vancouver, the game went totally in Vancouver's favour with a final score of 3-11 to 1-6. It was the widest margin of victory for Vancouver that season, but San Diego deserved immense credit for the heart they put into the game throughout.

The team traveled to Boston to compete, in a junior semifinal on August 31, against a heavily favoured Philadelphia team. Vancouver looked like they would cause an upset as the teams were tied at halftime, and Vancouver would have the aid of the wind for the second half. But Philadelphia showed great skill and determination and overcame a tired Vancouver team to run out as the winners by six points. The eventual champions, Philadelphia Tyrone, won the final the next day by a very wide margin.

Northwest 1985 Finian Leahy Divisional Championship

In 1985, the ISSC repeated as the Northwest Divisional Champions, and Mick Hurley (Derry) was selected as the club's MVP that year. The club traveled to Chicago where they hammered Chicago's John McBride's in a quarterfinal match. Those who traveled included Sean Commins, Brendan Burns, John O'Malley, Sean Forrestall, Paraic Lally, Mick Hurley, Plunkett Mallon, Des Deevey, Peter Ferguson, Chris Boyle, Seamus Frain, Declan Corrigan, Pat Burns, John O'Flynn and Brendan Finnegan. Once again, however, Vancouver could not get by the junior champions, Philadelphia Tyrone, in the semifinal.

After the team's experience in Chicago, club members had a sour taste in their mouths following decisions made in the boardroom of the North American County Board. Financial penalties to the club were judged as unfair and punitive. There is no doubt that the expected funds from the County Board that were never provided to the ISSC signalled the end of Vancouver's and, indeed, Canada's future affiliation with the NACB. The Canadian County Board was formed towards the end of 1987 with the Western Canadian clubs represented by John O'Flynn at the founding.

ISSC's 10th Anniversary

In 1986 the club had its 10th anniversary, and the men's team included Peter Ferguson, Mick Hurley, Declan Corrigan (Captain), Sean Forrestal (Vancouver), Joe Dalsin (Vancouver), Steve Nasholm, Kevin Deevey (Cavan), John and Tom O'Flynn Jr., Pat Burns (Down), Paul Stack (Clare), Brendan Finnegan (Monaghan), Plunkett Mallon (Dublin), Malachy Swail, Brendan Burns (Down), John O'Toole (Vancouver) and Seamus Frain (Roscommon).

A challenge match held in Vancouver on May 11, 1986, was close; Vancouver won 0-9 to 0-7 over Seattle. Only eight players traveled to Seattle for the return match on May 25. Five Seattle players, who made up the back line, complemented the team. They played very well until the last few minutes, and then Seattle scored three goals to win 3-9 to 1-8.

On June 1, 1986, the first league match was held in Seattle. Even though Seattle often had possession of the ball, the game was still close. Seattle had a narrow victory of 1-8 to 0-8. Players of note were Brendan Finnegan in the backs, Joe Dalsin who scored two points and player/coach Peter Ferguson, who caused havoc in the full-forward position. The ISSC placed third in the league to Calgary and Seattle that year.

In 1988, the first exhibition game in Seattle proved to be a humbling experience; the very fit Seattle team gave ISSC a hammering. The score was 3-7 to 0-0 at halftime. Some respectability was brought to the final score due to a goal and a few points from Vancouver's Brendan Burns and a goal from John O'Flynn. Pat Forrestal played with passion, and Sean Fagan and Tom Gibbons were commended for their willingness to travel and give support from the sidelines.

A Gaelic Football match was played in Victoria on July 16, 1988, against Seattle for the inaugural Jim O'Sullivan Memorial Trophy. Jim was the founder of the Irish Canadian Cultural Society, which sponsored the trophy. The event was managed ably by members Garth Hurrell, Frank and Sheila Ryan and a host of others. Vancouver, missing a number of regular players, lost quite easily to Seattle, 2-6 to 1-3. Seattle's Tom Jordan and Martin O'Donnell played very well, and the O'Flynn brothers provided the bulk of the scoring for Vancouver.

Plunkett Mallon (Dublin) recalls his experience of the visit to Victoria: "It was a friendly weekend in Victoria. I had cycled from Burnaby to Horseshoe Bay, took the ferry to Nanaimo and on to Victoria to play. I got lost in Mill Bay and had a long, tiring detour on a very hot August weekend. Arriving fashionably late at the pitch in Victoria I was raring to go and was disappointed to find a team of unfamiliar foot soldiers with the exception of John O'Flynn and Kevin Molloy. I ran all over the field in search of a pass. There was a serious lack of quality ball delivered. The 60 minutes were up and the game was remarkable for its lack of excitement and good football. What was absent on the pitch was found at the post game reception. Warm communication and entertainment served up with the usual tea and sandwiches and copious amounts of after dinner drinks and deserts. We experienced a very joyful Irish gathering of story telling and song, one of the best."

The 1990s

The Vancouver players who traveled to Calgary for a football tournament in June 1990 included Colm O'Brien, Paul Stack, Frank Reid, James Kennedy, Joe Dalsin, Liam Gibbons, John O'Flynn (MVP 1990), Brendan Lally, Sean Fagan and trainer Tom Butler. The team suffered defeats to both Albertan teams. Vancouver's only victory that season was a 1-9 to 0-8 over the Seattle Gaels at Slocan Park on July 1, 1990.

In August, a grand weekend was had by all who traveled to Seattle for the final Gaelic Football tournament of the Pacific Northwest. Vancouver supporters and players included Ian Adams, Fergus and Sean Fagan, Kevin and Val Molloy, Paul and Kathy Stack, Tom Butler, Colm and Sadie O'Brien, John and Tom O'Flynn Sr., Frank Reid, Plunkett Mallon, Danny (R.I.P.) and Bridie Burns, Tom (R.I.P.) and Liam Gibbons, James Kennedy, Jim Dunne (R.I.P), James Carbin (Monaghan), Connor Corduff, Mike Hurley, Seamus O'Gorman, Ian Kiernan, and Bernie and Cormac Ward.

The team traveled by a propane-powered bus, which was loaned to the club by St. Patrick's Parish for the weekend. Drivers Paul Stack and Michael Hurley carried the great burden of wondering whether they would find a gas station that served propane in the States on the way down. Their prayers were answered as they pulled into a station on fumes.

Some of the Vancouver footballers in the 1990s included Gavin Murphy, John O'Toole, Brendan O'Leary, David Moyles, Brendan Mulhall, Siggy Maddai, Danny Crawford, Gerry Nicholson, Koenraad Verbruggen, Richard Healy, Arnie McFadden, Donald Considine (R.I.P.), Sean Stack (Clare hurling All-Star), Tom O'Sullivan, Tom Christiansen, Declan Byrne, Jim Ritchie, Ed Eviston Jr., Frank O'Connor, Richie Cannon, Marty McCann, Johnny Eilson, John Comerford, Tim O'Brien, Brian Begley, John Messenger, Declan Corrigan (MVP 1987), Jim McCann, Roy Byrne (Wicklow), Connor Corduff, Liam Siegerson and Liam Mackin.

A 1992 Vancouver squad that traveled for the first time to Portland, Oregon, saw Kevin Molloy, Frank Reid, James Kennedy, Goalie Danny Burns (R.I.P.), Harry Perron, Sean and Steven Burns, Micky Hurley (MVP 1989), Colm O'Brien (MVP 1988), Quentin O'Brien, Paul Stack, Liam Mackin, Paul O'Donoghue, Craig Edwards and Declan Byrne contribute toward two wins over Portland and Calgary. They had one loss to Edmonton by five points.

As early as March 15, 1987, and again in 1992, Richmond's Club Ireland St. Patrick's Day festivities meant an exhibition match of hurling to coincide with festivities. "Long Poc" and "Side Cut Swing" competitions were organized along with friendly matches. March 16, 1997, saw another hurling demonstration at John Hendry Park for the public to view.

A 1993 squad photo included Jerry Nickelson, Tommy Franklin, Arnie McFadden, Mark Korn, Liam Gibbons, Richie Cannon, Ian Kiernan, Bernard McKenna, Liam Feely, Pat

Forrestal, Sean Kenney, Michael Williams, John Bermingham, Donny Considine (R.I.P.), Vincent Osborne (Louth) and Johnny Wilson.

In 1995, a member of the 1956 Galway All-Ireland Football Championship team, Jack Mahon, visited the home of supporters Martin and Kathy King in White Rock. A number of individuals had an opportunity to meet with the legend during his stay.

In addition to the long-serving stalwarts of 1995, some Vancouver footballers were making their presence known on the field: Joe Burke, Tim O'Brien, Sean O'Connell, Andrew Kirvan, David Moyles, Tom Christiansen, Myles Queally, John Fitzgibbon and Roderick Murphy.

In a 1997 letter dispatched from San Francisco via the *Celtic Connection*, former ISSC members Pat McHugh, John Smith and P.J. O'Donnell send a St. Patrick's Day greeting to the Vancouver community. Gestures like this are indicative of the long-term connections former members keep with Vancouver. In July 2007, P. J. O'Donnell was in attendance at the Gaelic games played in Redmond, Washington; Vancouver's ISSC competed in ladies football and men's hurling—whilst Pat McHugh and John Smith met up with Vancouver's John O'Flynn at the O'Neill's Continental Youth Championships in Chicago the same month. A small world indeed!

The Millennium ISSC

An Australian rules men's team, called the Vancouver Cougars, have played the Gaelic code on a number of occasions in St. Patrick's Day challenges and tournaments with the ISSC. Their first match of Gaelic occurred on June 22, 2002, at John Hendry Park. In 2007 the Australians were the winners of the annual St. Patrick's Day match over the Irish, 8-12 to 6-12.

In May 2001, the Vancouver Harps won the Michael O'Malley Memorial 7's Trophy in Seattle. Ronan Deane, Marty McCann, John O'Flynn, Tony Doyle, Eamonn and Paul McGinley, John Reddy, James Kirk and Paul Stack all contributed points and goals to the victory.

The Vancouver line out in August 2001 at the Edmonton tournament was Paul Stack, Tom O'Sullivan, Emmett Fitzgerald, Ronan Deane, Craig Edwards, Chris Cyr, Caley Boggan, Paul McGinley, Jim McCann, Eamonn McGinley, Sean Quinn, John Stocking, John Wilson, Marty McCann, Liam Mackin, Steven Burns, Tony Doyle, Shane Donnelly, Paul Kelly, Tom Christiansen and Sean Minagh.

In 2003, Vancouver did not plan a tournament and instead supported the Seattle Gaels tourney. Individual members, such as Chris Cyr and John O'Flynn, played with the Edmonton men's team. Vancouver ladies helped form an all-Canadian squad with their Albertan counterparts that included Nuala Cyr. Calgary men won the tournament over Seattle, while the Canadian ladies lost out in a semifinal match to eventual champions Fog City Harps of San Francisco.

A 2003 squad that traveled to Edmonton's tournament later that summer included Brendan Flynn, Coach Sean Quinn, Fergus O'Leary, Shane Stack, Steven Devlin, James Kirk, Brian Darcy, Anthony O'Grady, Sean Minagh, Colm Brennan, Willie McNamee, Paul Stack, Gavan Connolly, Liam Gibbons and John O'Flynn in goal.

Hurling Awakes!

In 2003, the ISSC purchased two full sets of hurls and sliotars from Gary Parsons, who had bought them in Ireland 10 years earlier, but had let them languish in a basement unused due to a lack of interest. A teaching colleague of John O'Flynn mentioned their availability and the ISSC acted quickly to purchase them at the bargain-basement price of $450. Club President at the time, Brendan O'Leary, applied linseed oil and sanded them down so they would be ready for their first test, which would prove to be memorable.

On August 1, 2004, the "Clash of the Ash" resonated loudly in White Rock, B.C., as a Western Canadian Select team of Irish- and Canadian-born players from Calgary, Edmonton and Vancouver played the newly formed Seattle Gaels Hurling club of the North American County Board. This was the first competitive hurling match played in 28 years between an Irish American and an Irish Canadian team. The West Limerick Holdings Ltd. Challenge Plaque, donated by Thomas O'Flynn of Limerick, was the prize for the winners.

The referee was Martin King of Galway, who played on Montreal's 1961 American County Board Senior Hurling Championship team. ISSC members who played on the Irish Canadian team included: goalkeeper, Bernard Ward; fullbacks, Sean Quinn and Jim Fitzgerald; midfielders, John O'Flynn and Paul Stack; full-forwards, Gavan Connolly and Richie Gough. These men all contributed to the 4-13 to 2-5 victory over Seattle. The Seattle team was a remarkable sight for the many spectators, as their protective headgear gave them the amazing similarity to a group of beekeepers.

One of the Canadian players, Ronan Deane, originally from Cork, proudly wore a shower cap in the first half. He did this in order to provide a visual target for his teammates. It was loudly noted by one local, Jack Maloney (Charleville, Cork), that overall the players seemed to spend a lot of time, "plowing the ground…as if they were going to sow a few potatoes." Only one hurl was broken that day; Jim Fitzgerald was delighted it was an ISSC hurl and not his own. He had wisely put his hurl away just before the match.

The Western Canadian Hurling All-Stars—Captained by Vancouver's Ronan Deane— and the Seattle Gaels Hurling team provided an outstanding match for the numerous spectators in attendance on Sunday July 3, 2005. A hard-fought match resulted in a tight victory of 5-16 for the Irish Canadians and 6-11 for the Irish Americans. Thomas O'Flynn of West Limerick Holdings Limited presented a commemorative plaque to the Seattle Gaels team. The Most Valuable Player award went to Seattle's captain, Rob Mullin.

Many enjoyed the "Clash of the Ash" in 2006, when Seattle won the competition for the first time. Seattle continued to demonstrate its championship form in 2007 with another victory. Hurling has a promising future for the Vancouver Irish community with the strength of the game being played in Seattle. It is a certainty that the ISSC, with capable instructors and willing volunteers, will draw continued interest in the playing of this ancient game.

West Limerick Holdings Limited Hurling Challenge Plaque

2007	Seattle Gaels
2006	Seattle Gaels
2005	Western Canada
2004	Western Canada

30th Anniversary

On Saturday November 13, 2004, the club celebrated its 30th Anniversary. Over 150 people attended the Cambrian Hall for a dinner/dance. Special guests at the dinner included: former Sons of Erin Gaelic Footballers Jimmy Dunne (R.I.P.), Terry Wheately and Eddie Eviston (Kerry). Others attending were John Dooley, first president of the ISSC; the Mayor of Nelson B.C.; Phil and Mary Shields from Sandspit, B.C. in the Queen Charlotte Islands; and Pearse Walsh from Kelowna, BC. A special anniversary supplement was published in the *Celtic Connection* and was distributed to thousands of readers in the Pacific Northwest.

Prior to the celebrations, a memorial mass was held at historic St. Patrick's Church in Vancouver, to remember members of the ISSC and the larger Irish community. Those who were remembered included Tom Gibbons, Fr. Joe Cuddy, Dan Jones, J. J. Hyland, Nick Forrestall, Mathias and Bridget O'Toole, Eamon Lane, Frank Dunne, William O'Malley Forbes, Donny Considine, Betty O'Flynn, Danny Burns, Betty O'Duffy-Brennan, Aoife McHugh, Rudy Viktora, Kevin McFadden, Paul Singh, Eugene Tansey, Sean O'Neill, David Finnerty, Paddy Kane, Teresa Butler, James (Jim) Kelly, Patrick Nugent, and Art and Flora O'Neill.

Championship Form Returns

In the 2005, at the Gaelic Football final for the J. J. Hyland Memorial Trophy in White Rock, the Vancouver Irish Sporting and Social Club's "Harps" dominated the Calgary Chieftains with a score of 3-21 to 2-4. Long-time Seattle GAA men, John Keane and Finian Rowland, presented the championship plaque to Vancouver Captain James Kirk. The Men's MVP, selected by Ottawa's Jarlath Connaughton, was Neil O'Connor from the Edmonton Wolf Tones. The Vancouver Cougars of the Australian Rules Football League was given special mention for their gamesmanship and skill throughout the tournament weekend. Tony Cooper and Stu Grills led the Cougars to their fine showing.

The Harps men won their own tournament, the Edmonton tournament and the Tommy Butler Western Canadian Divisional Board Championship in 2005; Manager Sean Quinn and President Gavan Connolly were commended for keeping the Harps finely tuned throughout the season and for setting the standard for championship form in the years ahead.

In 2006, the Vancouver Harps won the Western Canada Divisional Board Tommy Butler Championship again. They accomplished this without winning either of the two tournaments that were part of league play. In Vancouver, there was a classic "Battle of Alberta" championship final. The Calgary Chieftains squeaked by the Edmonton Wolfe Tones 1-9 to 2-4. The J. J. Hyland Trophy was awarded to the Chieftains, and the Most Valuable Player was awarded to County Tyrone's Connor McNally of the Wolfe Tones. Still, for the Western Canada championship, Vancouver proved that the talent was available when it came to winning the matches that mattered in the standings.

Members of the Harps 2006 winning team included Paddy Butler, Marcus Treacy, Gavan Connolly, Ronan Deane, Pádraig Leavy, Cian Lawlor, Graham Hancock, Colm O'Connell, Peter Mullally, Nick Chow, Kevin Murray, Patrick Ryan, Martin Brennan, Ronan Geoghegan, Jimmy Culliford, Eddie Dooley, Gareth Moore, Anthony Murphy, Stephen Egan O'Neill, Dorian Foley, D. W. Holmes and John Crimmins.

Frank Evers

West Vancouver resident Frank Evers was a notable referee for the Vancouver tournament played in White Rock, B.C., in 2005. From 1953 to 1962, Frank Evers was a household name in Ireland. The Menlough, Galway, native won every possible medal and trophy playing Gaelic Football. Frank played on the senior Galway football team, which won the All-Ireland Football Championship in 1956 and the National League in 1957. He traveled to the United States to play at the Polo Grounds against New York, and to England where Galway played Derry at Wembley Stadium in London.

In 1999, Evers turned all his medals and trophies over to the GAA museum in Croke Park. It gave him great pride to see all his medals alongside some of Ireland's greatest athletes, such as Christy Ring and former Taoiseach Jack Lynch.

Youth Development

ISSC member John O'Flynn, from West Vancouver's Mulgrave School, and Club Ireland's Stephen Burns, from South Delta Secondary, presented a workshop called "Gaelic Football and a Wee Bit of Hurling" to eight teachers from public and independent schools at New Westminster Secondary School in late October 2004.

Stephen and John welcomed long-time Irish community members Thomas Scanlon, Thomas Butler, Thomas O'Flynn and I.S.S.C. president Brendan O'Leary, who assisted with the workshop activities. The teachers were delighted to receive a comprehensive teaching handout for Gaelic Football that they will be able to make use of in their

Physical Education courses. Participants had the opportunity to use the hurling sticks that the ISSC had recently purchased. Practicing hurling on the school's field was a fun highlight for all. The weather was perfect and everyone was dressed for activity.

Since 2005, the ISSC has provided sponsorship of the Leslie Wilson's Scoil Rince De Danann Ceili Camp. This camp features week-long workshops in Irish music, language, dance and sport at Harrison Hot Springs in B.C. Introductory games of hurling and Gaelic Football are also part of the camp, and John O'Flynn and other members of the Vancouver Irish Sporting and Social Club provide support.

2007

On Saturday June 16, 2007, at John Hendry Park, approximately 80 players from both the Seattle Gaels (30) and the Vancouver Harps (50) played in a very successful Gaelic Games Day fund-raising event for the Harps.

All registered players names went into a hat, from which teams were selected. The teams played and each individual scored points based on their results and performance. Once a game was done, names went back into the hat and then players were selected to new teams.

The format worked great, and five ladies' football, four men's and two hurling matches were played over the course of the day. If all that activity wasn't enough, the ladies of the ISSC also prepared bag lunches to feed the masses. The football winners were Jackie Carr, Seattle; Kevin Murray, Vancouver; Denis O'Sullivan, of Vancouver, won for hurling.

Later that month, 20 men and 13 ladies, of the ISSC, traveled to Alberta and won the "double" in Edmonton. This was the first time in Western Canada that a traveling team won both titles in a host city. Justin Kenny—son of Joe Kenny who played hurling with St. Mike's of Toronto in the 1970s and Vancouver in the '80s—Ed Carbery, Peter Markey, Jerry Murphy, Peter Agnew (MVP), Gavan Connolly, Connie McMahon, Keith Clark, Peter Brennan, Jerome O'Sullivan, Denis O'Sullivan, Cian Lawlor, Mike O'Dell, Marcus Treacy, Derek Healy, Fintan Neville, Kieran, Eoin Nolan, and Clinton and Ashley Steier formed the winning men's team.

At a Gaelic Games Day, held in Seattle in July, the Vancouver men played their second sport of hurling and impressed their hosts. Vancouver beat the Seattle selection playing competitively for 40 minutes. Later, they fell to the wayside against an imposing Na Fianna outfit from San Francisco.

A surprise in the day was a very competitive and open men's football game that saw Na Fianna shade it over the Vancouver Harps by a mere point in a game that looked as though neither side wanted to win (at least, if hitting the target is a fair measure of that). Big hits and strong running football was played by both sides and were highlights throughout.

The August 2007 Vancouver Tournament was a day of emotion and skill. A combined Alberta and British Columbia team played two games of hurling against the Seattle Gaels hurlers. Some fine play was seen in the two closely contested matches. Aidan O'Callaghan of the Seattle Gaels picked up the West Limerick Holdings North West Challenge Cup, which was donated by Thomas O'Flynn. Competing for spectators' attention that day, the Leslie Wilson's De Danaan Irish Dancers also put on an incredible performance in the Burnaby Lake Clubhouse.

The Calgary Chieftains men's team was unable to contain a revitalized Edmonton Wolfe Tones, and was dumped in the semifinal. The tournament final was a game that Vancouver simply wanted more. The men made up for earlier shortcomings in the Western Canada championships and acquired their second tournament title of the year. Derek Healy and Cathal Lockey led from the half-forward line. Brian Daly of Edmonton and the Tournament MVP could not lift his team over the determined Harps. Captain Kevin Murray from the Harps collected the ISSC's J. J. Hyland Memorial Trophy.

St. Patrick's Day Mixed 7's Tournaments

Vancouver has seen the development of the mixed 7's league leading up to St. Patrick's Day each February and March in 2007 and 2008. Teams that have formed and participated on the artificial turf under the lights at Andy Livingstone Park include Team Munster, Kevin's Dream, UBC Students, The Burnaby Eagles, The Freckles, The Vancouver Cougars, The Moose Heads (Stu Grills), The S-Club Seven's (Peter Agnew), The Cherry Pickers (Richie Hannon), The 7's Deadly Sins (Keith Clark), St. Mary's Donegal (Brad Jorgensen) and the Squamish Rednecks (Ronan Deane).

Among the many male players that have participated: Marcus Treacy, Kevin Murray, Ian Twomey, Dave Tonge, Tony Doyle, Padraig McGinn, Andy Cunningham, Anthony Kimberly, Pat Lowney, Mike Lancaster, Richard Collins, Tadhg Rohan, Owen Hynes, Colin Coughlin, Cathal O'Loughlin, Colin Bakker, Jerry McCarthy, Tony Cooper, Dave Johnston, Frank Murphy, Ed Carbery, Duncan McDougall, Jerome O'Sullivan, Peter Sherwood, Ben Scott, Ashley Steier, Ryan Martin, Peter Campion, Matt Harrison, Gavan Connolly, Dave Wilson, Chris Harrison, Wayne Murray and Paul Stack.

The ladies in the tournaments included Liz Twomey, Stephanie Hann, Angela Dobson, Eimear Geoghan, Kate Bohan, Katrina McAndrew, Aimee Mangher, Erin McGinley, Tracy Clausen, Kate Clark, Tanya St. John, Susanne Cousineau, Barb Dworak, Ciara McLoughlin and Keara Stack.

Reflections

Over the last thirty five years the ISSC men's Gaelic Football teams have competed against clubs from Victoria, B.C.; Seattle and Tacoma, WA; Calgary and Edmonton, AB; San Diego, San Jose, Sacramento, and San Francisco, CA; Portland, OR; Philadelphia,

PA; Chicago, IL; Denver, CO; a Dublin Civil Service team (1982) and an Aer Lingus Select team (1992).

The ISSC had its members attend various GAA events, including the establishment of the North West Divisional Board of the NACB in 1981, the founding of the Canadian County Board in 1987, the Canadian County Board twinning meeting with the Ulster Provincial Council and the Toronto GAA Annual General Meeting in 2004, the founding of the Western Canadian Divisional Board in Edmonton and a referee's clinic in San Francisco in 2004.

Gaelic Football workshop presentations occurred at Physical Education and Coaches Conferences in Vancouver, Victoria, New Westminster and Kelowna. Members have also participated with officiating minor matches at the NACB Championships in 2004 (Boulder, Colorado) and at the San Francisco (2005) and Chicago (2007) O'Neill's Continental Youth Championships.

Jimmy and Maureen Speiran

14 Nollaig 2007

Jimmy agus Maureen,

I would like to take this opportunity to express my thanks, and those of the Association to you for all you have done for your Association in Vancouver and indeed the GAA in general over the course of your lifetime involvement with Cumann Lúthchleas Gael.

The GAA owes its strength to the parish and regional loyalties of its members. The often unseen dedication and commitment of our volunteers at local level is the blood which courses through the veins of Cumann Lúthchleas Gael. It cannot survive without the enthusiasm, perseverance and devotion of those who serve it. In short, it cannot survive without the likes of your selves.

I want to commend you for your outstanding efforts on behalf of the Association. I believe your contribution over such a long period of time significantly enhanced the profile and enjoyment of our games for many people in the Vancouver area. I am reliably informed that you have personified excellence throughout your involvement with the GAA and I have no doubt that you will continue to serve as role models for others to emulate.

Go raibh maith agat as ucht do chuid oibre.

Nioclás Ó Braonáin,
Uachtarán, CLG

Vancouver Tournament Champions

Kevin McFadden Memorial Trophy	J. J. Hyland Memorial Trophy
Ladies'	**Men's**

	Ladies'	Men's
2007	Seattle Gaels	Vancouver Harps
2006	Seattle Gaels	Calgary Chieftains
2005	Seattle Gaels	Vancouver Harps
2004	Seattle Gaels	Calgary Chieftains
2003	n/a	n/a
2002	Seattle Gaels	Calgary Chieftains
2001	San Diego	Vancouver Harps
2000	Vancouver	Harps Seattle Gaels
1999	Seattle Gaels	Vancouver Harps
1998	Vancouver Harps	Vancouver Harps
1997	Edmonton Wolfe Tones	Pearse Ogs, Seattle

Vancouver Ladies' Gaelic Football

When Michelle Boyle rolled into town in 1997, she was determined to keep her love of Gaelic Football alive. Having played for the Ottawa Gaels ladies' football team in the Toronto GAA for four seasons, she was not going to let her move to Vancouver deprive her of enjoying the game she had grown to love. "When I lived in Ottawa, after finishing university, I played soccer with an Irish girl, Rita Kelly, who got me onto the idea of joining the ladies' Gaelic Football team," explained Michelle. "Of course growing up in a small town called Antigonish (pop. 7,000) in Nova Scotia, I had never even heard of such a game. But once I started playing, I just loved it."

After finding the Irish community here in Vancouver through Catholine Butler and the *Celtic Connection* newspaper, Michelle discovered the Vancouver Harps Gaelic Football team. The fact that there was no ladies' football team in the club was no deterrent for this committed athlete. President at the time, J. J. Hyland (R.I.P.) was at first amused, but very impressed by Michelle's enthusiasm. He welcomed her like a breath of fresh air to the Irish Sporting and Social Club. Michelle was indeed a breath of fresh air (not hot air!) and, in no time, she had rounded up an impressive group of teammates from the Meraloma Club ladies' rugby team, as well as some other friends. She convinced them all to come out and play this great game. With the full support of the club and Michelle's enthusiasm, the Vancouver Harps ladies' team arrived in full force.

Tom O'Sullivan had been involved in playing with and coaching the men's team for a few years prior, and was impressed at how quickly all of this happened. Growing up in County Kerry, the home of Gaelic Football in Ireland, the idea of ladies' football was a novelty, a sideshow at best. O'Sullivan did not take Michelle Boyle and her squad very seriously, thinking at the time that it was just a fad. However, the squad was growing fast—they even had bona fide Gaelic Footballers, such as Nuala McLaughlin from County Offaly, joining up. The team was serious enough to require a coach.

When Michelle and her newly formed squad asked Tom to act as coach, he found himself in a quandary. The women were serious about playing the game and did not seem willing to accept any lame excuses. Tom wondered how he was he going to coach a bunch of lady footballers? He had grown up thinking this was a man's game. He grew up playing the game practically from the cradle. How was he going to explain the skills that he was born with, to a group who would be learning from scratch? He reluctantly said yes, and feared the worst. He felt it would be nothing but trouble; he anticipated lots of complaining and substandard football. He believed it would all fall apart after a few weeks.

Was he ever wrong! After the second training session, he tentatively asked, "Is everybody OK with the drills?" They answered, "Why? Are you afraid to ask us to run harder or practice more skills?" These women meant business. And so this was the beginning of the first of many successful ladies' Gaelic Football sessions.

Off the field, Michelle made contact with the Seattle Gaels ladies' team and this led to a strong rivalry that still continues. The very first game was a big test for the team. Seattle boasted an impressive number of Irish-born experienced players, but despite their strength, the Vancouver Harps played superbly. They pushed their rivals to the limit in that and every encounter that season. Players such as Erin Anderson, Sue Ditchfield, Bunny Vidotto, Sue Vaneenoo and Linda Louie contributed to the team's score lines.

As always, old and new members of the Irish community would come out and watch the Gaelic Football tournaments in Vancouver, Edmonton, Calgary or Seattle. The team has also competed against clubs from San Diego, San Jose, and San Francisco, California. The arrival of Ladies Football generated a buzz and an excitement that hadn't been witnessed in many years. Great rivalries as well as even greater camaraderie grew between the teams on and off the field. The ladies players are often the most reliable and active members of the ISSC.

A Testimony to the ISSC

On June 24, 2004, five Irish girls—Caitriona Carty, Niamh Hogan, Brid Leahy, Martha Mackey and Brid Ni Chonchuir—arrived in Vancouver with no jobs, nowhere to live and not knowing a soul. Three months later, without a doubt, they had had the summer of a lifetime, thanks largely to the Vancouver Irish Sporting and Social Club.

Originally the women were attracted to Vancouver by the lure of the Pacific Ocean, sun and surfers. However, they discovered that all great plans don't necessarily materialize; surfing was replaced by soloing, the board was swapped for a ball, and John Hendry Park became their Pacific Ocean!

Following a few phone calls, and a wander around Trout Lake, they located the ISSC gang. Tuesday and Friday nights were booked for Gaelic training, and their social scene was set for the summer. After arriving for their first training session laden with air mattresses and beach chairs, sympathy was evoked, and as a result, donations of pots and pans came pouring in.

The girl's football skills were called upon for the 2004 White Rock tournament, which proved to be one of the highlights of their visit. The ladies' competition consisted of four well-matched teams making for a tough path to the challenging final. Although no silverware was brought home by the Vancouver Harps, much more than that was achieved. A group who had known each other for just a few weeks, some taking up the sport for the first time, played as a team, and the bonds of friendship were strengthened. In addition, the intensity and passion shown on the pitch were equalled by the antics displayed during the post-match festivities!

Despite the empty threats that all help would be cut off once their football services had been rendered at the tournament, the kindness continued. The countless taxi services, furniture removal, roofs over their heads and, most of all, the *craic* and the friendship extended by all ISSC members made the summer one that will forever remain in their memories.

Championship Form and Style

Over the years, the ladies' teams have been coached by Tom O'Sullivan, Liam Mackin (Armagh), former Derry star Mickey Hurley; Canadian-born Chris Cyr, Kerry's Marcus Treacy and Kate Clark (Offaly). These individuals enjoyed success with their teams. At the 1998 and 2000 Bailey's Cup Tournaments held in Vancouver, the Harps won the Cup on both occasions. Michelle Boyle was the Vancouver Captain in 1998 and 1999; the ladies won the Calgary Cup for both those years. Karen Davies was honoured by being selected MVP in 2000 by the club.

Over the many years that the ISSC has existed, there are many success stories to recall. The addition of the ladies team ranks right up there with the greatest of the club's accomplishments. The excellent standard of play by these ladies is truly amazing and is complimented by their volunteer work with the club off the field.

The ISSC was lucky to have a great sportsperson like Michelle Drysdale (nee Boyle) initiate and bring to fruition the great expansion of the club for ladies of all ages, backgrounds and talents. The club also remembers our sadly missed former president, J. J. Hyland who instantly recognized the opportunity this addition offered the club to be energized by new members. He enthusiastically threw his full support behind the ladies' team when it needed recognition. His name is remembered every year with the J. J. Hyland Memorial Tournament. As well, the Kevin McFadden Memorial Trophy, donated by the Irish Club of White Rock, commemorates Kevin, who played a significant role in promoting and supporting the Gaelic games on Vancouver Island in Victoria and Vancouver.

Contributing players in the 2004 season included Linda Louie, Collette Donnelly, Michelle Drysdale, Catherine Flynn, Erin McGinley, Katrina McAndrew, Kate McNamee and Nuala Cyr.

The Harps are proud to have had two of their players, from Surrey, B.C., Tara Phillips and Cathy Jackson, help Canada significantly at the International Women's Tournament of 2005 in Dublin. Vancouver-born Erin McGinley is to be commended for being chosen a Western Canadian All-Star in the lead-up to the naming of the Canadian team. Other players that contributed in 2005 included Sue Cannon, Maire Kenny, Kamal Bachana, Nuala Cyr, Katrina McAndrew, Kate (McNamee) Clark and Coach Chris Cyr.

In 2006, the Seattle Gaels won the Kevin McFadden Memorial Trophy over the Vancouver Harps with a convincing 8-6 to 2-4 win. Seattle's Amber Talbot was selected the Most Valuable Player of the weekend for her inspirational play. The Harp's squad that year consisted of Coach Chris Cyr and players Kate Clark, Rita Burke, Maire Kenny, Tracey Borralho, Michelle Quinn, Tara Philips, Catherine Flynn, Erin McGinley, Cathy Jackson, Katrina McAndrew, Nuala Cyr, Therese Deane, and Deirdre Finneran.

Tracey Clausen, Stephanie Hahn (MVP), Kate Clark, Angela Dobson, Katrina McAndrew, Sandra Perriera, Liz O'Sullivan, Tanya St. John, Tara Philips, Cathy Jackson, Rene McGloin, Erin McGinley and Elan Park formed the victorious ladies' team that won the Edmonton Cup in June 2007. In 1997, 10 years previous, a Vancouver ladies' team won a tournament in Edmonton and it was the first time ever that the ISSC would do the "double" when the men's team was victorious in Edmonton, too.

The Seattle Gaels hosted a Gaelic Games Day in July 2007; it involved Gaelic Football teams from Seattle, Vancouver and San Francisco. The hosts put on a couple of excellent days of activities that were complimented by a high standard of play in all the games that Saturday.

The San Francisco's Fog City Harps, the Seattle Gaels (two teams) and the Vancouver Harps played that weekend. The standard of football was exceptional, and though they were tested by all, the Fog City Harps rounded out the day unbeaten to take the honours. The Vancouver ladies played four games. They had two wins, one loss, and one tie to close out an impressive day's work. ISSC's John O'Flynn spent the day refereeing all of the ladies' matches. He saw this as a way to test his fitness and sanity.

Western Canada Champions

The ladies made history by winning the Tom Gibbons Memorial Western Canadian Divisional Championship Cup for the first time at the Vancouver tournament in August 2007. All that remained was for the ladies to win the Kevin McFadden Memorial Trophy for the first time in seven years.

Allowing the Seattle team to combine, the Harps borrowed three Alberta players and played out an enthralling game against the Gaels. It was end-to-end stuff played at a frenetic pace. The Harps controlled much of the first half, but somehow the Gaels managed to stay in touch. Katrina McAndrew (Harps) and January Chay (Gaels and MVP) were relentless in their pursuit of each other, the ball and anyone else that thought they were coming through the middle of the park. There was an early Seattle flurry of scoring in the second half, and though they rallied, the Harps could not claw back from the deficit. Meg Starbird collected the Kevin McFadden Memorial Cup from the White Rock Irish on behalf of Seattle for the fourth year running.

As its name suggests, the Irish Sporting and Social Club encompasses both sporting and social activities. The fact that individuals meet and become couples through the club is testimony to its success as a social entity. Couples such as Nuala McLaughlin and Chris Cyr, Mark Ford and Christine Robidoux, Mickey Hurley and Jen Heal, Liam Mackin and Arlene Bergsma, Catholine Egan and Tom Butler, Keith Clark and Kate McNamee show that Gaelic Football is not just good for your health…it is also good for your heart!

PACIFIC NORTHWEST BOARD

John Keane— A Founder and Father of the Northwest

There is no doubt that none of the teams in Western Canada would have affiliated with the GAA when they did, if it weren't for the Seattle Gaels' John Keane (Westmeath). He pushed and pulled to organize games and convinced clubs to affiliate with the North American County Board.

Keane organized the annual conference calls for the Division; he got the clubs on the phone together to agree on schedules, etc. This was back in the days before anyone knew what a conference call was, but John was able to do it because he worked for a phone company.

In June 1979, John Keane's Seattle Gaels traveled to meet the Vancouver Irish Sporting and Social Club and they played an exhibition match that saw a friendly, yet competitive rivalry grow between the two clubs. May 4, 1980, P. J. Ruddy's Vancouver ISSC traveled to Seattle for the return exhibition match. Seattle's Danny Quinn provided much assistance to the success of the event.

The Seattle Gaels made a decision to affiliate with the NACB in 1980. They were the sole Northwest representative and they would play a senior qualifying playoff match in San Francisco that year.

John Keane attended a Vancouver ISSC meeting on November 16, 1980, in order to encourage Vancouver's affiliation for 1981. On January 6, 1981, Vancouver decided to seek affiliation due to Keane's good efforts. A meeting was held in Seattle to organize the Northwest division later that month. Keane remembers tracking down a very dubious

Mike Quirke (Kerry), who lived in Fort McMurray; he tried to convince Quirke that the Alberta teams should affiliate too.

Tacoma Evergreen Irish

Tipperary man Tom Quinlan and Waterford's John Duggan (R.I.P.) established the Tacoma Evergreen Irish. They affiliated with the NACB due to Keane's efforts. Thus a three-team Northwest Senior division was established.

Tacoma won the 1981 Championship. With the aid of players from Seattle and Vancouver, they took on a strong San Francisco team that traveled to Tacoma for a qualifying playoff match. The 1982 season was the last of competitive play for the Tacoma Evergreen Irish, but the entry of two more Canadian teams from Edmonton and Calgary in 1983 brought further vitality to the Northwest.

Mick O'Malley

Mayo's Michael O' Malley (R.I. P.) may not have been an off-the-field organizer in Seattle, but he was a huge supporter financially and otherwise. Michael was the backbone for the Seattle club; he helped to provide jobs for young footballers who came to town, and pushed and encouraged those, like John Keane, who did the legwork. He was greatly admired by all of his Canadian friends for his warm welcoming ways to all GAA members.

The 1980s

The North American County Board suspended the Western Divisional Board of California in 1983. This was done because they did not have a winner, by the scheduled date, to play a quarterfinal match against the Calgary Chieftains, who had won the Northwest. A $1,000 fine was handed down by the NACB, but later rescinded because immigration controls at the border were later viewed as a barrier for traveling teams.

The annual convention for the NACB was held in Seattle that year with representatives from Vancouver attending: Brendan and Pat Burns (Down), Dan Jones (R.I.P.), Tom O'Flynn (Limerick), John O'Flynn (Vancouver) and Peter Ferguson (Fermanagh).

In 1984, the Northwest created a junior division. Canadian teams maintained affiliation with the NACB up until 1986. High affiliation costs for the Western Canadian clubs with the American Board and the possibility of a Canadian County Board left Seattle as the only affiliated club with the NACB in 1987.

Still, the spirit of play that had been established within the division continued to see champions crowned. Though, there would be years where one or two of the Alberta clubs would be absent from West Coast tournaments.

The 1990s

At the final tournament held in 1990 hosted by the Seattle Gaels, the Wolfe Tones handily beat the Gaels 1-8 to 0-6. In the following game, Vancouver played a strong first half, leading 1-6 to 0-1 over the Chieftains, but Calgary dominated the second half and came from behind for a draw with Vancouver 1-8 to 1-8.

On the Saturday night, the Seattle Gaels provided dinner and entertainment for the teams. That night four GAA medals, donated by Vancouver's Thomas O'Flynn Sr., were given out as recognition awards to Mike O'Malley (R.I.P.), Christy Whelehan of Edmonton, John Connolly of Calgary and Tom Gibbons (R.I.P.) of Vancouver. Tom Gibbons also received two crystal glasses from the Divisional Board as a token of appreciation for his work as a referee that weekend.

On Sunday, the first game featured a hard-fought game between Vancouver and Edmonton. Goalkeeper Bernard Ward, of Vancouver, stopped many chances and Mike Hurley and Plunkett Mallon combined for a truly beautiful goal. However, the better team that day was Edmonton, as they won 1-9 to 1-4. In the final game, a great come-from-behind win occurred when Calgary scored two goals in the final minutes to win 4-3 to 3-5 over the Gaels. The final standings of the 1990 Northwest Division were

	W	L	T	PTS
Calgary Chieftains	4	1	1	9
Edmonton Wolfe Tones	4	2	0	8
Seattle Gaels	2	4	0	4
Vancouver ISSC	1	4	1	3

Vancouver's only victory that season was a 1-9 to 0-8 over the Seattle Gaels at Slocan Park on July 1, 1990. This was after the club had been hammered by the Alberta teams, June 23–24, in Calgary. The Vancouver players who traveled to Calgary included Colm O'Brien, Paul Stack, Frank Reid, James Kennedy, Joe Dalsin, Liam Gibbons, John O'Flynn, Brendan Lally, Sean Fagan and trainer Tom Butler.

Portland Kells of Oregon

There was an addition to the division in 1991: Gerard McAleese's Portland Kells of Oregon affiliated with the NACB and made it a five-team league, until the club folded in 1994. The McAleese family (Antrim) arrived in Vancouver in 1976 and brothers Charlie and Gerard were active on the committee of the Irish Sporting and Social Club in the late '70s. When the family moved to the United States in 1980, to establish the Kells Irish Restaurant and Pub chain on the West Coast, the sons involved themselves with the established Seattle Gaels.

Within Seattle, an inter-city rivalry developed in the mid-90s. Brothers Charlie McAleese and Patrick Pearse McAleese took an active role in the Pearse Ogs' club. Though the Pearse Ogs affiliated with the NACB for one year, they created a competitive spirit in

Seattle and enlivened tournaments with a classic 7-a-side championship in Vancouver in 1997.

Hugh Duggan

Hugh Duggan (Armagh) was an All-Ireland Gaelic Football Final referee, who sent off Paudi O'Se (Kerry) in the second half during Kerry's eventual championship win over Dublin. Duggan refereed a 1993 North West divisional match in Seattle and returned for another tournament in 2000. Hugh is presently living in San Francisco and remembers well his first visit to Vancouver in 1994.

Transition

It was during the 1997 football campaign that the wheels fell off the bus. Bold actions on the field caused boardroom disagreements. This, along with some short-term thinking, brought the season to an inconclusive end. The fact that the clubs of Vancouver, Calgary and Edmonton were not affiliated to the same governing County Board as Seattle meant mechanisms were not in place to deal with discipline issues, and thus resolution was impossible.

The clubs would remain on their side of the international border until new blood coursed through local GAA veins. With the rise of ladies' football, the international bonds would take root once again in the Northwest.

The Finian Leahy Memorial Trophy was created in honour of the former Calgary Chieftain and Toronto St. Pat's player who had passed away tragically in a car accident in 1983. The trophy had been held in trust by members of the Seattle Gaels in hopes of an anniversary reunion of all those connected with the Northwest GAA in the near future.

Finian Leahy Memorial North West Championships

1979	*Seattle/Vancouver*	1988	Vancouver ISSC
1980	*Seattle Gaels*	1989	Calgary Chieftains
1981	Tacoma Evergreen Irish	1990	Calgary Chieftains
1982	Seattle Gaels	1991	Edmonton Wolfe Tones
1983	Calgary Chieftains	1992	Seattle Gaels
1984	Vancouver ISSC	1993	Seattle Gaels
1985	Vancouver ISSC	1994	Seattle Gaels
1986	Seattle Gaels	1995	Seattle Gaels
1987	Vancouver ISSC	1996	Seattle Gaels

The Bailey's Cup

The year 1990 was significant. The All-Ireland finals were brought in live for the first time ever in the Vancouver area. Kevin Molloy (Armagh) and Catholine Egan (County of Gatineau, Quebec) were the organizers of this historic event. The hurling final—Cork vs.

Galway—was shown on September 2 at the Carpenter's Union Hall in New Westminster and the football final—Cork vs. Meath—was shown at St. Augustine's School in Vancouver on September 16.

A Northwest divisional tournament was scheduled for the weekend of the All-Ireland Football Final. Edmonton won the inaugural Bailey's Cup trophy over Seattle and Vancouver. In 1991, Edmonton and Calgary played for the Cup in Edmonton, Alberta. An amusing highlight followed, when the Cup was "rescued," by Catholine Butler, from the trophy shelf of the Edmonton Irish Centre in 1992. Christy Whelehan of Edmonton was convinced that it had been stolen, until it was eventually explained that the trophy was meant to be competed for annually.

All of the Bailey's Cup tournaments were coordinated by Catholine Butler (Egan). The cup was played for in Vancouver most years. Vancouver and Seattle competed in 1990, 1995, 1997, 1998 and 2000. The 1995 victory by Vancouver over Seattle was followed up by entertainment at the Legion Hall, on Kingsway at Joyce, in Vancouver.

Some of the Bailey MVPs over the years were: Martin Fitzsimons (Calgary) (1991), Vancouver's Sean Minagh (Cavan) (1995 and 2000), Jim McCann (Belfast) (1998) and Tom O'Sullivan (Kerry) (1997).

Vancouver Island

The Irish Canadian Cultural Association in Victoria was the gracious host of the Bailey's Cup in 1993–94 and 1996. There was much support from Victoria's Frank and Sheila Ryan in the coordination of these matches.

At the 1993 game between Seattle and Vancouver, at Braefoot and Mackenzie Park, there was a lot of media attention before the match. Mark Korn and John O'Flynn were guests on the C-FAX morning radio show. They explained the fundamentals, culture and excitement of the game. Roy Byrne and Vincent Osbourne participated in a television interview with CHEK-TV news. Jim Turnbull of Gilbey's, distributors of Bailey's Irish Cream, attended the match and presented the Cup to Vancouver's Captain Liam Mackin.

In 1994, the two teams met again. Don Adams, the Chairman of the Sports Council for Northern Ireland, who was with the Northern Ireland team that was competing in the Commonwealth Games at that time, was an interested spectator. Two sets of jerseys were donated by Bailey's that year; these were used each time the Cup was played for. A few went missing and according to unconfirmed reports, these jerseys remain "Sleepless in Seattle."

Much like the Finian Leahy Memorial Cup, the Bailey's Cup has remained in Seattle since 2000 and has yet to be brought back to Canada for an anniversary reunion with the organizer of these games, Catholine Butler.

Bailey's Cup Winners

1990	Edmonton Wolfe Tones	1996	Vancouver Harps
1991	Edmonton Wolfe Tones	1997	Vancouver Harps
1992	n/a	1998	Vancouver Harps/ Lady Harps
1993	Vancouver Harps	1999	n/a
1994	Vancouver Harps	2000	Seattle Gaels / Lady Harps
1995	Vancouver Harps		

WESTERN CANADA DIVISIONAL BOARD

The WCDB is dedicated to improving the standard of competition and to providing as many games as possible for its member clubs. In British Columbia, there is one club—the Vancouver Harps (Vancouver Irish Sporting and Social Club, ISSC).

In Alberta there are three clubs, the Calgary Chieftains, Red Deer Eire Ogs and Edmonton Wolfe Tones. The WCDB is evenly made up of representatives from each of the member clubs. The seven-person board consists of a Chairman, Secretary, Treasurer and four Members at Large.

Other clubs are invited to, and attend, club tournaments, even though they are not affiliated with the Western Canadian Division (Seattle Gaels and Fort McMurray) or are affiliated with the Australian Football League (Vancouver Cougars, Burnaby Eagles and Calgary Kangaroos).

Each year member teams play in the Western Canadian Championships. This is a league format where each team plays each other team twice, over two tournaments. The venues are rotated, which requires that each team cross the Rockies only once a year. The Championship is played out in such a way that it does not undermine the spirit or competition of the host cities' individual Gaelic Football tournaments.

Executive members that have served on the Western Canada Divisional Board include:

2004 **Chair**: John O'Flynn (Vancouver); **Secretary**: Ronan Deane (Vancouver); **Treasurer**: Danielle Bodnarek (Edmonton); **Members at Large**: Adrian Lagan (Calgary), Kim Tulloch (Calgary) and John O'Connor (Edmonton).

2005 **Chair**: John O'Flynn (Vancouver); **Secretary**: Ronan Deane (Vancouver); **Treasurer**: Danielle Bodnarek (Edmonton); **Members at Large**: Noel Tuohy (Calgary), Kim Tulloch (Calgary) and John O'Connor (Edmonton).

2006: **Chair**: John O'Flynn (Vancouver); **Secretary**: Ronan Deane (Vancouver); **Treasurer**: Danielle Bodnarek (Edmonton); **Members at Large**: Adrian Lagan (Calgary), Kim Tulloch (Calgary) and John O'Connor (Edmonton).

<u>2007</u>: **Chair**: Ronan Deane (Vancouver); **Secretary**: Calum Bonnington (Calgary); **Treasurer**: Danielle Bodnarek (Edmonton); **Members at Large**: Laura Olson (Calgary); Erin McGinley (Vancouver) and Sky Johnston (Edmonton).

<u>2008</u>: **Chair**: Ronan Deane (Vancouver); **Secretary**: Kim Budd (Edmonton); **Treasurer**: Sky Johnston (Edmonton); **Members at Large**: Fergus Lynch (Red Deer); Calum Bonnington (Calgary); Kate Clark (Vancouver) and Gary McCaffrey (Calgary).

Irish and Australian Codes

The Gaelic Football teams in Western Canada have great friends in the Australian Rules football teams. For years now, the Aussies have been fielding teams at Gaelic Football tournaments in both Calgary and Vancouver. They have become a fixture and seem to relish the chance to compete in our games. So much so, that the Calgary Kangaroos deservedly won the Calgary Chieftains' tournament in 2006. The Aussies defeated the Western Canadian Champions, Vancouver, and the tournament hosts on the same day.

To date, the Irish had taken advantage of the Australian desire for competition, but they had never repaid the favour. On Saturday June 2nd, 2007, that changed. The Vancouver Harps sent a team to the Australian Rules Tournament in Kelowna, B.C., and competed admirably in their first serious effort at this brand of football. The Calgary Bears, Calgary Kangaroos, Burnaby Eagles, Red Deer Magpies and Vancouver Cougars were the other teams involved in a great day's footie played out in the sweltering heat—32 degrees Celsius—of the Okanagan.

The Harps played two games. They lost to the experienced Calgary Canadians, but they beat a tough Magpies outfit. Mike O'Dell played a great ruckman's role and Kevin Murray was his usual dependable self around the halfback line. The Australians were impressed to see how competitive the Irish were, and several of the Vancouver team members were snapped up to play more games than their original schedule offered.

The Australians hope, now that the first step has been taken, that they will see other Gaelic Football teams follow suit and compete in Aussie Rules Tournaments in the coming years.

The Tom Gibbons Memorial Cup—Ladies' Football

Tom Gibbons (Thomastown, Kilkenny) came to Vancouver in 1957, where he met Agnes Morrison (Belfast). They married that year at St. Augustine's Church on October 23 and were later blessed with four children, Teresa, Thomas, Liam and Kieron.

With Tom's love for the Gaelic games, he supported the Vancouver Sons of Erin Gaelic Football club in the early '60s. In the 1970s up until the late 1990s, he contributed to the Vancouver Irish Sporting and Social Club. He cheered from the sidelines; volunteered to officiate; lined the fields of play; and often took beaten-up old hurls and gave them the attention needed to extend their playing life, as only a true hurling man from Kilkenny could do. At halftime, in any Gaelic Football match, Tom would lead the charge of hurling enthusiasts and gave a mighty exhibition of skill at John Hendry Park.

Tom was delighted that his sons took an interest in the Gaelic games. A proud moment for him was when his son, Liam, was awarded the Nick Forrestal Memorial Trophy in 1990 as the "Most Promising Young Canadian." That same year, at a Seattle tournament, Tom was awarded a senior medal of merit and two crystal glasses as a token of appreciation for his work as a referee.

The All-Ireland Football finals were brought in "live" for the first time in Vancouver in 1990 at St. Augustine's School. Tom was the custodian at the school and was well known for the standard of his "Shaggin" work.

In July 1998, Tom was presented with a Lifetime Achievement Award for his dedication to the Gaelic games at the Bailey's Cup and J. J. Hyland Memorial Tournament. It also gave him great satisfaction to see both the men and lady footballers of Vancouver win all the trophies that year.

On the day of his death, December 10, 1998, Gaels from around the Pacific Northwest traveled to salute Tom, to give thanks for his efforts for the Irish community and to offer their condolences to Agnes and his family. Each time Tom's trophy is lifted by a ladies' championship team in the years to come, we will remember him.

> The road did rise to meet you
> The wind has been always at your back
> The sun shines warm upon your face,
> The rains fall soft in Thomastown, Kilkenny
> And until we meet again,
> May God hold you in the hollow of His hand.

The Tommy Butler Cup—Men's Football

In 1951, Tom Butler and his wife Teresa (nee Ryan), who had been childhood neighbours in their hometown of Kilmaine in County Mayo, arrived in Vancouver to begin a new life in Canada along with their children, Mary Ann and Kevin. In the years that followed their arrival, almost every new Irish immigrant to Vancouver became aware of Tom and Teresa's address and phone number. There was always a warm welcome and many a party was hosted at their home.

So in 1957, Tom was not surprised to receive a call from another new immigrant named Tom Gibbons. Gibbons asked Tom to meet with him downtown. Butler asked where he would like to meet and Gibbons replied, "Under the shagging sun!" Butler was bewildered: "Under the shagging sun?" It turned out that Gibbons was referring to the old Sun Building on West Broadway in Vancouver. They met up and the two became good friends.

Tom Butler was a supporter of the GAA's first club, called the Vancouver Sons of Erin, which was formed in 1961. When the Sons of Erin wound down, Tom turned his GAA support to the Vancouver Irish Sporting and Social Club that was established in 1974. As their trainer, Tom traveled with the Vancouver team to Calgary in June 1990. In 1991 Tom served on the ISSC executive. During his tenure, Tom traveled to all of the tournament cities, at one time or another, in the Pacific Northwest.

A few years later, Tom lost his dear wife, Teresa. Many still recall the late Danny Burns, who sang his signature ballad song, "Grace," as a tribute.

In 1994, it was good to see Catholine Egan, of the *Celtic Connection* newspaper, and Tom Butler meet and eventually hook up—two mad lovers who married that same year. There is no doubt that the coverage of Gaelic games in Western Canada thrived because of this "love connection" between the *Celtic Connection* and the GAA.

Western Canada's Honour Roll

Tommy Butler Cup - Men	Tom Gibbons Memorial Cup - Ladies
2007 Calgary Chieftains	Vancouver Harps
2006 Vancouver Harps	Edmonton Wolfe Tones
2005 Vancouver Harps	Edmonton Wolfe Tones
2004 Calgary Chieftains	Edmonton Wolfe Tones

2004 WESTERN CANADIAN CHAMPIONSHIP RESULTS

Round	Venue	Game	LADIES	MENS
1	Calgary	1	**Calgary Chieftains 5-5 (20)** Vancouver Harps 0-0 (0)	**Calgary Chieftains 0-9 (9)** Vancouver Harps 1-1 (4)
1	Calgary	2	Vancouver Harps 0-0 (0) **Edmonton Wolfe Tones 5-5 (20)**	Edmonton Wolfe Tones 2-9 (15) Calgary Chieftains 1-12 (15) **Draw**
1	Calgary	3	**Edmonton Wolfe Tones 9-7 (34)** Calgary Chieftains 2-0 (6)	Vancouver Harps 2-1 (7) **Edmonton Wolfe Tones 1-7 (10)**

			LADIES	MENS
2	Vancouver	1	Vancouver Harps 1-2 (5) **Edmonton Wolfe Tones 3-5 (14)**	**Vancouver Harps 1-7 (10)** Edmonton Wolfe Tones 1-3 (6)
2	Vancouver	2	Calgary Chieftains 0-1 (1) **Vancouver Harps 1-5 (8)**	Edmonton Wolfe Tones 4-7 (19) Calgary Chieftains 4-7 (19) **Draw**
2	Vancouver	3	**Edmonton Wolfe Tones 9-6 (33)** Calgary Chieftains 0-3 (3)	**Calgary Chieftains 1-8 (11)** Vancouver Harps 2-2 (8)

2006 WESTERN CANADIAN CHAMPIONSHIP RESULTS

Round	Venue	Game	LADIES	MENS
1	Vancouver	1	Calgary Chieftains 2-3 (9) **Vancouver Harps 4-6 (18)**	Calgary Chieftains 3-3 (12) **Vancouver Harps 4-3 (15)**
1	Vancouver	2	**Vancouver Harps 2-4 (10)** Edmonton Wolfe Tones 2-0 (6)	Edmonton Wolfe Tones 0-4 (4) **Calgary Chieftains 1-8 (11)**
1	Vancouver	3	**Edmonton Wolfe Tones 4-13 (25)** Calgary Chieftains 1-2 (5)	Vancouver Harps 2-8 (14) **Edmonton Wolfe Tones 3-6 (15)**
2	Calgary	1	Vancouver Harps 0-3 (3) **Edmonton Wolfe Tones 5-3 (18)**	**Calgary Chieftains 1-4 (7)** Vancouver Harps 0-6 (6)
2	Calgary	2	**Calgary Chieftains 3-7 (16)** Vancouver Harps 3-1 (10)	**Edmonton Wolfe Tones 1-9 (12)** Calgary Chieftains 1-7 (10)
2	Calgary	3	**Edmonton Wolfe Tones 3-5 (14)** Calgary Chieftains 1-3 (6)	**Vancouver Harps 3-7 (16)** Edmonton Wolfe Tones 1-4 (7)

The 2006 manager for the Edmonton Wolfe Tones men's team was Tyrone's Colin Baugh. Edmonton came tantalizingly close to winning the Championship as each team recorded two wins and two losses. So the Championship was decided on a points differential, which came out in Vancouver's favour. This was the second year in a row that Vancouver would win the Championship this way.

The Ladies' Championship continued to be dominated by the powerful Edmonton Wolfe Tones, proving that their club spirit and commitment to practice paid dividends in all of their matches.

2007 WESTERN CANADIAN CHAMPIONSHIP RESULTS

Round	Venue	Game	LADIES	MENS
1	Edmonton	1	Calgary Chieftains 0-0 (0) **Vancouver Harps 4-13 (25)**	**Calgary Chieftains 1-10 (13)** Vancouver Harps 0-6 (6)
1	Edmonton	2	Vancouver Harps 4-4 (16) **Edmonton Wolfe Tones 5-2 (17)**	Edmonton Wolfe Tones 1-5 (8) **Calgary Chieftains 3-6 (15)**
1	Edmonton	3	**Edmonton Wolfe Tones 1-9 (12)** Calgary Chieftains 0-1 (1)	Vancouver Harps 0-9 (9) Edmonton Wolfe Tones 0-9 (9) **Draw**
2	Vancouver	1	**Vancouver Harps 5-5 (20)** Edmonton Wolfe Tones 0-0 (0)	Calgary Chieftains 0-6 (6) **Vancouver Harps 1-9 (12)**
2	Vancouver	2	Calgary Chieftains 0-0 (0) **Vancouver Harps 5-5 (20)**	Edmonton Wolfe Tones 0-6 (6) **Calgary Chieftains 2-3 (9)**
2	Vancouver	3	Edmonton Wolfe Tones 0-0 (0) Calgary Chieftains 0-0 (0)	**Vancouver Harps 0-12 (12)** Edmonton Wolfe Tones 1-6 (9)

Ledcor, one of the largest construction companies in North America and a large employer in Western Canada, was delighted that their first year of sponsorship of the Western Canada Division proved such an interesting one in 2007.

At the final tournament, held in August and hosted by the Vancouver ISSC, the Western Canadian teams were joined by a strong showing from the Seattle Gaels, which sent two ladies' teams and a men's hurling team. Vancouver fielded four teams: the Shamrock Rovers and Harps, which played men's Gaelic Football; the Harps ladies football team and the men's hurling selection.

Arriving in town knowing they could afford one loss, the Calgary Chieftains had their backs up, with no intention of having the men's football Championship pried away from them. However, the Harps made them sweat a little, when they recorded a relatively comfortable win to give themselves a chance. It was a chance only if Edmonton were able to do business. Alas for the Harps, the Chieftains knuckled down, and a fine display, from Brendan O' Hara and Tim Hamill in the middle of the park, sent the Championship back to Calgary for the first time since 2004.

The Ladies' Championship fizzled out in the Vancouver sun. Because the ladies from Edmonton and Calgary had difficulty in making the trip, they combined to form an Alberta team. In doing so, they forfeited their games; yet this in no way took away from the efforts of the Harps. Witnesses to Saturday's and Sunday's play felt safe in the knowledge that the best team had won the Championship. Rene McGloin and Tara Philips played a type of football that the West would be proud of.

Ledcor's Western Canada Division Ladies' All-Stars 2007

Alecia Baldwin (Edmonton) was goalkeeper; Dawn Krawchuk (Edmonton) and Stephanie Hahn (Vancouver), fullbacks; Mandy Tuohy (Calgary) and Rae Deen (Red Deer), halfbacks; Cathy Jackson (Vancouver) and Rene McGloin (Vancouver), midfielders; Carlin Acheson Johnston (Edmonton) and Katrina McAndrew (Vancouver), half-forwards; Ainsley Baldwin (Edmonton) and Tara Philips (Vancouver), full-forwards.

Notable mentions were Kate Bohan, Tanya St. John, Elan Park, Sandra Parriere (Vancouver); Kim Budd and Pam Mathieu (Edmonton); and Maeve McKiernan (Calgary).

Ledcor's Western Canada Division Men's All-Stars 2007

Gary McCaffrey (Calgary) was goalkeeper; Jerry Murphy (Vancouver) and Mick O'Toole (Red Deer), fullbacks; Tom McRae (Calgary) and Peter Agnew (Vancouver), halfbacks; Tim Hamill (Calgary) and Brian Daly (Edmonton), midfielders; Rory Lynch (Red Deer) and Colin Baugh (Edmonton), half-forwards; Adrian Lagan (Calgary) and Derek Healy (Vancouver), full-forwards.

Notable mentions were Brendan O'Hara (Calgary), Peter Markey (Vancouver), Brian Byrne (Edmonton) and Blaine Lavery (Red Deer).

GAELIC GAMES

HANDBALL

The origin of handball is shrouded in antiquity and defies all attempts to identify either a location or a period where it all started. It is safe to say that from the time walls were constructed, they were seen as a backdrop for games that involved throwing an object or projecting it by hitting it with a hand.

Whatever the ancient origins, there is ample proof that the modern game of handball, as we know it, evolved in Ireland. The game was played extensively in the small towns and villages of Ireland for hundreds of years, with no uniform rules, and it was frequently played for money. This is based on historical writings and Irish literature over many centuries.

The first known depiction, however, did not appear until 1785 in a painting by John Nixon, called *Castle Blaney*. It shows two individuals playing handball against one of the walls of the castle ruins, and a third individual with arms crossed in the pose of a spectator or referee. It was over 100 years later, in 1886, which the Gaelic Athletic Association laid down the first set of rules for handball.

The modern game is played on a court that has one, three or four walls, with two, three or four players, or two teams of two participating. The four-wall game is the most popular today. The ball is struck with gloved hands and must strike the front wall of the court during each volley. Returns are made to make it difficult for the opponent to return the ball to the front wall. A game is won when one player or team scores 21 points. Points are only scored when serving.

Christian Brother J. B. Darcy mentioned handball in his book *Fire upon the Earth*, which explores the life of Irish-born Michael Anthony Fleming, the Bishop of St. John's, Newfoundland. Fleming bought a house in August 1843 that had previously served as a handball alley from an Irishman named James McCabe. The Bishop turned this sporting house into a convent for some Presentation sisters, who arrived from Ireland.

In 1863, the press in Victoria, British Columbia, and Saint John, New Brunswick, were reporting handball matches to their readers. In 1916, the first organized national championships for Canada were held. These championships have been held annually in all parts of Canada ever since.

The St. Albert Irish Society of Alberta, established in 1985, contributed not only to Gaelic Football activities, but also sponsored a team of local Olympic handball players who qualified for the National Championships in 1994.

Canada hosted the second World Handball Championships in Toronto, Ontario, in 1967; the fifth Worlds in Kelowna, B.C., in 1986; the ninth World Championships in Winnipeg, Manitoba, in 1997; and the twelfth World Championships in Edmonton, Alberta, in 2006.

An tUachtarán of the GAA, Nicholas Brennan, attended the 2006 games to support the 300-strong Irish participants and to acknowledge the place of handball within the Association. The President also visited the Edmonton Wolfe Tones GAA clubhouse, where he presented members of the Tones' Ladies' Western Canada Divisional winners and individual Canadian international team members with their winning trophies.

Wexford born Pat Brennan arrived in Canada in 1958 and has lived in Edmonton since 1971. Pat resumed playing handball in the 1980s and is still an active player. His administrative experience led to his becoming club President, and later a Provincial and National President of the Canadian Handball Association. After being Secretary and Treasurer for six years, Pat has just completed his first term as Vice President of the World Handball Council. He is in line to become President in 2009.

Joey Maher, (Drogheda, Louth) won the All-Ireland Open Singles Championships in 1963 and 1964. He came to Toronto and was a member of the Toronto Police Service from 1965 to 1967. During this period of his life, he won the Open event at the Canadian Nationals in 1966. Upon his return to Ireland, he won the Irish Championships from 1968–70 and again in 1973. Not only was he one of the greatest players ever, he was also one of the real characters of the game.

Another person of note is Pat Kirby, of Clare, who won a world championship representing Canada in 1970. In 1975 St. Mike's played Garryowen in a hurling match. Pat Kirby had come in from New York to play for Garryowen that day, but was marked out of the game by St. Mike's Larry Carroll. Upon Kirby's return to his native Ireland, he would be the Irish handballer of the year between 1975 and 1977.

ROUNDERS

Rounders is one of the four original games of the GAA and its rules were included in the first official guide in 1884. It is a bat and ball game that develops hand-eye coordination for young and old alike.

Irish claims are strong that Rounders, as played in Ireland, was the original game that developed into baseball. It is also clear that the ball used in softball is almost identical—in size, but without seams—to those used in hurling at the time that the game of softball was "invented."

Rounders is very much the "Cinderella" department of the GAA, but rather interestingly, after almost fifty years since its revival, the Association seems to be much more interested in promoting the game and has become more pro-active in doing so.

In 1994, the Secretary-General of the GAA's Rounders Council, Peadar Ó Túatain, had a government (Irish) cheque in his hand to help fund a trip for rounders players to come to Canada to play against the Cree First Nation. The Cree are wonderful people, but they seem to beat the Irish at being laid back, and correspondence did not develop at the Canadian end, despite a visit by Peadar Ó Túatain to the James Bay offices in Place Ville-Marie, Montreal, in 1993.

Success occurred for the sport in July 2001 when a U-18 rounders squad from England flew to Toronto. The purpose of the trip was to introduce rounders to a third continent and thus improve the game's chance of entry into the Commonwealth or the Olympic Games. The squad flew in full kit and attracted a great deal of attention at the airport. This gave them the opportunity to discuss rounders with many people and to raise the profile of the game. The squad arranged to play three different softball teams, each within an hour's drive of Toronto.

The first match was against the Markham Tigers, who were surprised at the sight of the little bats and balls. The second match was against the Pickering Heat, who could not believe that rounders was played without any protective gear. The final match was against the Markham Lynx. Rounders equipment was left with each team to enable them to continue playing the game and so they could also teach others to play.

A baseball historian in the USA has proposed an International Friendship Rounders Tournament. It has been suggested that all of the various codes gather to play; however, there has been no mention as to how the variations of playing rules would be reconciled!

CANADIAN FOOTBALLER PROFILES

Goalie
Must have "great goalmouth presence"; this is a secret code for being fat enough to have gravitational pull. Always in the 42–52 age bracket, this is a gent that will almost convince you that he played minor for his County in goal, even though the last time he got his knees dirty diving was at Vancouver's St. Patrick's Day Dinner Dance where his version of the "Walls of Limerick" went out of control causing numerous casualties.

Right Cornerback
The quiet man in the lineup; he seems to escape the jokes in the dressing room before a match. Often no one has ever seen him angry and some are afraid of his hidden depths.

He is usually unmarried with severe emotional baggage. Contact with a woman consists of a handshake at mass. He often works in Northern Alberta.

Centre Fullback
First started playing football shortly after the St. Patrick's Day Games at the Skydome in Toronto. He will get a nosebleed if he passes beyond his own 50-yard line. Utterly, utterly useless and yet is a great hit with the supporters of St. Vincent's. Quite likes the smell of blood…not his own, mind you.

Left Cornerback
Has all the football skills of a piece of cheese, and yet has been known to disappear up corner-forward's arses for days on end. An absolute cast-iron guarantee that he will be asked to mark the other team's young, absurdly fast superstar from the minor programme in Brampton.

Right Halfback
This boyo hasn't missed a training session ever, in Ottawa. His selection is basically the manager's way of proving he "doesn't give a damn who you are, if you're not down training, we're not going to give you a game."

Centre Halfback
Disgruntled Michael Cusacks' lady, who has tried to remove various officials off the Canadian, Toronto and Western Divisional boards. Never trains and is still absolutely guaranteed her spot on a team.

Left Halfback
Young Canadian-born player, for Toronto's St. Pat's, who is about 5'4.'' He is told to get under the kick-outs and "take the game to the opposition": secret code for don't pass it to anyone unless your life is in serious danger.

Midfielder
Chronic alcoholic who last scored a point a few seasons back and yet reckons he is justified in having a go for a point from anywhere inside the opposition's half. Well-liked character because he always gets his round in at the post-match drink-up in Montreal.

Midfielder
The fullback's older brother, who sports a rather strange looking bandage on his knee, probably hiding teeth marks or something. Prone to making strange guttural noises every time he strains himself at Centennial Park when playing for St. Mike's. Eats five dinners a day and is a prime suspect for a coronary.

Right Half-forward
Quiet spoken and drives a flashy sports car around the West end of Calgary. Lads don't know what to make of him, "but he was an awful annoying bollox in elementary school."

Centre Forward

He is third in the set of brothers that play the fullback and midfielder positions. Is the target of all the brothers' clearances…all of them.

Left Half-forward
Utterly useless Canadian from Edmonton, who, by some fluke of nature, happens to be a deadly accurate free-taker. Tries to avoid open play altogether, as he is far too important to the team to get injured, and can often be a team's only source of points.

Right Corner Forward
Happily married Toronto Gaels' man, who hasn't played football since the inaugural Powerscreen 7's tournament, but who has decided to take up the game again. His beer belly completely and utterly overshadows natural talent, but he is guaranteed to bag a goal or two.

Full-forward
Rarely scores but is Captain of the team and an all-out nut case from Red Deer. The line commonly quoted to excuse his complete inability to find the target is, "He's a good man to bust up the play." He will no doubt be marked by a similar figure playing for the opposition. Only at this level will the full-forward and fullback play the game the exact same way. They could even switch positions with no effect on how the team plays whatsoever.

Left Corner Forward
Invariably sports an earring and a seriously dodgy haircut from Durham. He will be involved with the referee within five minutes of the throw-in. Plays Aussie Rules and is hence viewed with suspicion by all. He is guaranteed to bag a goal or two.

CANADIAN-IRISH PHRASES

Phrase	Definition	Use
Hames	A right sh*te	"Sean Souths' keeper made hames of that clearance…"
Lamp	A good thump	"I swung for the sliotar, missed by three feet and lamped Garryowen's goalie…"
A Crowd	A gathering of people that watch a match and hope for random acts of violence	"That crowd from Eire Ogs' is a right shower of sh*tes…"
Schkelp	To remove living tissue in the absence of surgical procedures	"That sh*te from Hamilton took a schkelp out of my leg…"

Bullin'	Angry	"The Clan Na nGael halfback was bullin' after I lamped him…"
Joult	A push	"'I gave that Le Cheile player a joult and she may have to wear a neck brace for two weeks…"
A hang sangwidge	Consumed with tea on the side of the road after a tournament	Usually contains half a pound of butter.
Namajaysus	What was that for, referee?	Commonly heard in B.C.
Ya-bollix-ya	Formal recognition of a score by an opponent	Commonly heard in Alberta
Leh-it-in-ta-f*ck-would-ya	A full-forward's appeal to a midfielder for a more timely delivery of a pass	Commonly heard in Ontario
Mullocker	An untidy or awkward opponent	Commonly seen in Quebec

BIBLIOGRAPHY

Brady, F. (2005). *A Century of Leitrim Football in New York, 1904–2004*. New York.

Byrne, C. (1984). *Gentlemen-Bishops and Faction Fighters: The Letters of Bishops O'Donel, Lambert, Scallan and Other Irish Missionaries*. Jesperson Press, St. John's, NL.

Comaskey, B. (2006). *If Ever a Man Suffered*. Mullingar, Ireland: Deel Publications.

Corry, E. (2006). *An Illustrated History of the GAA*. Dublin: Gill & Macmillan Ltd.

Darcy, J.B. (2003). *Fire upon the Earth*. St. John's, NL: Creative Publishers.

Egan, S. (1990). *Celts: Psyche, Games and Pastimes*. Draft Essay.

Farrell, A. (1899). *Hockey: Canada's Royal Winter Game*.

Grace, R.J. (1993). *The Irish in Quebec*. Quebec, Institute Québecois.

Humphries, T. (1996). *Green Fields*. London, U.K.: Orion Publishing Group.

King, S. (1998). *The Clash of the Ash in Foreign Fields: Hurling Abroad*. Tipperary, Ireland: Seamus J. King Publishing.

Lyons, S. (2000). *A Century of Boston GAA*. Boston, MA: Woburn Printing Ltd.

O'Driscoll, R. (1988). *The Untold Story: The Irish in Canada*. Toronto: Celtic Arts of Canada.

O'Longaigh, D. (1998). *We Irish in Oregon*. Portland, Oregon: All-Ireland Cultural Society of Oregon.

Stanway, P. (2006). *Birth of a Nation: Canada in the 20th Century*. Edmonton, AB: CanMedia Inc.

Ward, A. (1994). *Our Story Reviewed, 1884-1993.* Philadelphia, PA: North American County Board Gaelic Athletic Association.

Articles

Basu, A. (2002). *"Irish eyes are smilin': Montreal pair headed to Dublin with Team Canada."* The Montreal Gazette.

Bodnarek, D. (2004) *"Update from the Edmonton Wolfe Tones GFC."* The Celtic Connection.

Booth, M. (2005). *"Tara Phillips and Cathy Jackson suit up for Canada."* The Now.

Buckley, S. (1994). *"Hard Work and Vision Gave Calgary Irish a Home."* The Celtic Connection.

Budd, K. (2007). *"The Modern and Postmodern Aspects of Gaelic Football in Western Canada."* Athabasca University MAIS 601 Paper.

Butler, C. (2008). *"Gaelic Football Makes a Mark in Red Deer, Alberta."* The Celtic Connection.

Butler, C. (2007). *"The Edmonton Wolfe Tones Anticipating a Great Year."* The Celtic Connection.

Butler, C. (2007). *"Calgary Chieftains Look Forward to 2008 Gaelic Season."* The Celtic Connection.

Butler, C. (2006). *"Players from the GAA Tournament Welcomed at Limerick Junction."* The Celtic Connection.

Butler, C. (2006). *"A New Generation of Hurlers Now Training in Seattle."* The Celtic Connection.

Butler, C. (2006). *"Gaelic Football in Alberta: Gearing Up for the 2006 Season."* The Celtic Connection.

Butler, C. (2006). *"Edmonton Irish Club All Set for Live Gaelic Games – Robert Murphy."* The Celtic Connection.

Butler, C. (2005). *"In Fort McMurray, Everything is Big...Even the Mosquitos."* The Celtic Connection.

Butler, C. (2005). *"An Exciting Year Upcoming for Vancouver Cougars."* The Celtic Connection.

Butler, C. (2004). *"A Night to Remember at ISSC 30th Anniversary Bash."* The Celtic Connection.

Butler, C. (2004). *"Volunteers are the Mainstay of the Calgary Irish Club."* The Celtic Connection.

Butler, C. (2004). *"Chris Whelehan: 'The Irish Brought Hockey to Canada through Hurling'."* The Celtic Connection.

Butler, C. (2004). *"Toronto's New Windsor House Still Going Strong—41 Years Later."* The Celtic Connection.

Butler, C. (2002). *"Farewell to Danny Burns: 'A Great Gael, a Great Musician and Humanitarian.'"* The Celtic Connection.

Butler, C. (2002). *"Taking Cultural Events to a New Level—Mick Hurley."* The Celtic Connection.

Butler, C. (2001). *"Come Rain, Hail or Snow, Montreal Marches for St. Patrick's Day."* The Celtic Connection.

Butler, C. (2001). *"James Fitzpatrick: A True Gaelic Football Hero."* The Celtic Connection.

Butler, C. (2000). *"I think Gaelic Football is the best sport in the world!"* The Celtic Connection.

Butler, C. (2000). *"Gaelic Football: Great Craic, Plus a Workout."* The Celtic Connection.

Butler, C. (2000). *"More People Needed to Help with Organization."* The Celtic Connection.

Butler, C. (2000). *"Christy Whelehan: Playing Gaelic Football with Edmonton Team for 25 years."* The Celtic Connection.

Butler, C. (2000). *"Bailey's Cup Tournament Displays Athletic Talent."* The Celtic Connection.

Butler, C. (1998). *"Bailey's Weekend a Huge Success."* The Celtic Connection.

Butler. C. (1997). *"Football Season Round Up."* The Celtic Connection.

Butler, C. (1996). *"Technology Unites Gaelic Football and Hurling Fans."* The Celtic Connection.

Butler, C. (1995). *"Edmonton Celebrates St. Pat's in Fine Style."* The Celtic Connection.

Butler, C. (1995). *"Meeting Cultural Challenges Through Unified Community Efforts— St. Albert Irish Society."* The Celtic Connection.

Butler, C. (1994). *"Four Great Teams Share a Common Thread of Pride."* The Celtic Connection.

Butler, C. (1994). *"Calgary's Pioneer History Enhanced by the Irish."* The Celtic Connection.

Butler, C. (1994). *"Vancouver Defend Their Title for the Bailey's Cup."* The Celtic Connection.

Byrne, S. (1992). *"What? Irish Ice Hockey Players from around World in Banff?"* The Celtic Connection.

Canavan, S. (2006). *"News from the Toronto GAA."* The Toronto Irish News.

Canavan, S. (2005). *"All we want for Christmas is two referees…2005 in Review."* The Toronto Irish News.

Canavan, S. (2005). *"Canada Profile."* Ladies' Gaelic International Tournament Programme.

Canavan, S. (2005). *"What Lies Ahead for the GAA in 2005?"* The Toronto Irish News.

Canavan, S. (2004). *"News from the Toronto GAA."* The Toronto Irish News.

Canning, M. (2004). *"Irish Cultural Centre is celebrating its 10th anniversary."* The Guardian.

Cawley, J. (1991). *"A Tribute to the Late Frank Murphy."* 30th Anniversary Journal of Clan Na nGael.

Chappell, B. (2005). *"The Glorious Thirteenth—An Irish-Aussie Match."* The Celtic Connection.

Chappell, B. (2004). *"A Wonderful Day of Football between the Aussies and Irish!"* The Celtic Connection.

Chappell, B. (2003). *"Irish Raise the Bar Over Aussies."* The Celtic Connection.

Chessell, B. (1992). *"Gaelic Football: North vs. South."* The Celtic Connection.

Condron, F. (2007). *"History of the Irish Canadians, 1980 -1993."* Club History.

Connally, P. (2007). *"Irish Canadian."* Club History.

Costello, S. (1991). *"Down Memory Lane."* 30th Anniversary Journal of Clan Na nGael.

Cummins, J., P., R. (2007). *"The Irish Canadians."* Club History.

Curtis, R. (1990). *"Toronto Double Header."* The Star.

Deane, R. (2007). *"Here they are...the 2007 Ledcor GAA All-Stars of Western Canada."* The Celtic Connection.

Deane, R. (2007). *"Chieftains Men and Harp Ladies Rule West."* The Celtic Connection.

Deane, R. (2007). *"Seattle: Gaelic Games a Massive Success."* The Celtic Connection.

Deane, R. (2007). *"Vancouver Harps Double Up in Edmonton."* The Celtic Connection.

Deane, R. (2007). *"Seattle Gaels Welcomed at Vancouver Gaelic Games Day."* The Celtic Connection.

Deane, R. (2007). *"Harps: First Gaels to Enter Aussie Territory."* The Celtic Connection.

Deane, R. (2006). *"Edmonton Ladies Deliver—Aussies Stun Irish."* The Celtic Connection.

Deane, R. (2006). *"Hurling, Legends and Leprechauns."* The Celtic Connection.

Deane, R. (2006). *"2006 Western Canadian Championship in Calgary August 5 and 6, 2006."* The Celtic Connection.

Deane, R. (2006). *"Alberta Men Unite For Powerscreen Tournament."* The Celtic Connection.

Deane, R. (2005). *"The West Lays Down the Challenge: 'Big Brother Must Come West.'"* The Celtic Connection.

Deane, R. (2005). *"Getting Started: Practicing, Playing and Attending Tournaments."* The Celtic Connection.

Deane, R. (2005). *"Getting Started: Who wants to Play and Where to Find Them?"* The Celtic Connection.

Deane, R. (2004). *"Getting Started: The Most Likely Locations to Find Football Friendly Country."* The Celtic Connection.

Deane, R. (2004). *"Getting Started With Your Own Gaelic Football Team."* The Celtic Connection.

Deane. R. (2004). *"White Rock Hosts First Football Festival."* The Celtic Connection.

Deane, R. (2004). *"A Roaring Start to the Season for the Western Canada Division."* The Celtic Connection.

Deane, R. (2004). *"Finding the Irish in Fort McMurray."* The Celtic Connection.

Deane, R. (2004). *"Alberta: Go Chieftains Go."* The Celtic Connection.

Deane, R. (2004). *"Gaelic Football Returns to Fort McMurray."* The Celtic Connection.

Deane, R. (2004). *"Alberta GAA Report."* The Celtic Connection.

Deane, R. (2004). *"White Rock Host First Football Festival."* The Celtic Connection.

Deane, R. (2003). *"All Set for a Great Summer of Gaelic Games in Western Canada."* The Celtic Connection.

Deane, R. (2003). *"Calgary Chieftains Recognize their Finest."* The Celtic Connection.

Deane, R. (2003). *"Compromise Rules Series in Calgary."* The Celtic Connection.

Deane, R. (2003). *"Ciaran McGrath Treatment Fund Quiz Night."* The Celtic Connection.

Deane, R. (2003). *"Calgary Gaelic Football Sevens Tournament 2003."* The Celtic Connection.

Dempsey, M. (2000). *"Students try football with a Gaelic Twist."* The Ottawa Citizen.

Devoy, D. (2008). *"Tony Griffin – On 'Yer Bike, For A Good Cause."* The Toronto Irish News.

Devoy, D. (2005). *"Irish Community Gets Own Burial Site."* The Toronto Irish News.

Doyle, A. (1994). *"The Force of the North West League?"* The Celtic Connection.

Egan, C. (1991). *"Edmonton Wins the Bailey's Cup."* The Celtic Connection.

Egan, C. (1993). *"A Proud Calgary Player to Teach Young Players."* The Celtic Connection.

Fay, M. (1999). *"St. Vincent's Hurling & Gaelic Athletic Club 40 years."* Souvenir Brochure.

Finnerty, A. (1998). *"Football, Irish Style, in Montreal."* Essay.

Fitzgerald, J. (1995). *"A Passionate Sport Played For Honour."* The Celtic Connection.

Flynn, B. (2003). *"All on Board the Bus."* The Celtic Connection.

Flynn, B. (2002). *"Calgary GAA Tournament an Outstanding Success."* The Celtic Connection.

Flynn, B. (2001). *"Gaelic Football Shines in Pacific Northwest."* The Celtic Connection.

Flynn, B. (1997). *"Twenty Five Years and Beyond for Sporting Club."* The Celtic Connection.

Flynn, B. (1996). *"Sweet Victory for Vancouver at John Hendry Park."* The Celtic Connection.

Foran, S. (1990). *"Our History."* Irish-Canadian G.F.C. 10th Anniversary Brochure.

Gibbons, J. (1991). *"Clan Na nGael—Triocha bliain ag fas."* 30th Anniversary Journal of Clan Na nGael.

Gibbons, J. (1985). *"Clan Na nGael celebrates 25 years."* Gaelic World Vol. 6.

Gormley, E. (2005). *"GAA Survives in any Climate."* Squareball.

Hancock, G. (2007). *"Letter to Tony Griffin from the ISSC."* The Celtic Connection.

Hansen, K. (1999). *"Edmonton Tournament a Great Success."* The Celtic Connection.

Hansen, K. (1998). *"First Annual Wolfe Tones Tournament in Edmonton."* The Celtic Connection.

Hansen, K. (1998). *"Wolfe Tones Sets New Goals."* The Celtic Connection.

Harvey, J. (2005). *"Kicking it aul' school."* Ed Magazine.

Harvey, J. (2004). *"Gaelic Football in Alberta's Capital."* The Celtic Connection.

Harvey, J. (2004). *"Edmonton Wolfe Tones meet Montreal."* The Celtic Connection.

Harvey, J. (2004). *"Edmonton: Gaelic Football in Alberta's Capital."* The Celtic Connection.

Hayes, S. (1998). *"Great Performances at Bailey's Cup Tournament."* The Celtic Connection.

Hayes, S. (1998). *"The Sense of Fair Play is Back!"* The Celtic Connection.

Horgan, J. (1999). *"The Women of St. Vincent's."* St. Vincent's 40th Souvenir Brochure.

Hryciuk, D. (2005). *"Games the Irish Play."* The Fitness Edge—Your Health.

Humphries, T. (2005). *"International Outlets and Foreign Fields."* The GAA Museum Programme.

Humphries, T. (2001). *"The Great, The Good, The GAA."* The Toronto Irish News.

Ivany, S. (2005). *"A League of their own."* The Etobicoke Guardian.

Joyce, G. (2002). *"The pride of Ireland comes to Ottawa."* The Ottawa Citizen.

Juzenas, F. (2005). *"Gaelic Football stars off to Irish Tournament."* Metroland-Brampton.

Keane, J. (2001). *"Seattle Gaels at the North American GAA Finals in San Francisco."* The Celtic Connection.

Keane, J. (1998). *"International Gaelic Games Tournament."* The Celtic Connection.

Keane, M. (2002). *"Gaelic Football World Cup 2002—September 16th –20th."* The Toronto Irish News.

Keane, M. (2001). *"Gaelic Athletic Association News."* The Toronto Irish News.

Keeler, D. (1990). *"A Gaelic Time."* The Burnaby & New Westminster News.

Kelly, E. (2007). *"Over 100 Teams Participated at 2007 Youth Championships."* The Celtic Connection.

Kelly, E. (2002). *"International Gaelic Football Tournament."* Lynn Publications.

Kennedy, J. (1991). *"Northwest Gaelic Finals."* The Celtic Connection.

Kimberley, T. (2006). *"Begorra! Gaelic Football, right here in Cowtown!"* The Calgary Herald.

Kittelberg, L. (2005). *"Weekend's Celtic Fest includes some heavy sport demos."* The Westender.

Lagan, A. (2006). *"Calgary Chieftains Gaelic Football Tournament 2006 hosts the Western Canadian Championships."* Calgary Irish Cultural Society Newsletter.

Landers, B. (1998). *"Toronto Irish News: Diversification Key to Success."* The Celtic Connection.

Landers, B. (1994). *"New Editor Joins Toronto Irish News – Eamonn O'Loughlin."* The Celtic Connection.

Landers, B. (1994). *"Brampton Irish Seeking New Centre."* The Celtic Connection.

Lannin, M. (2006). *"Ottawa at the Crossroads."* Essay.

Logan, R. (1991). *"In 1961…"* 30th Anniversary Journal of Clan Na nGael.

Magus, M. (2006). *"Score from both sides of the goal?"* Canucks Magazine.

Maloney, J. (2003). *"Irish game wins converts."* The Voice.

Markey, J. (1996). *"Boston prepares for the American Board Finals."* The Irish Echo.

McCafferty, S. (1990). *"The Gaelic Games in Ontario."* Radio Erin Sports.

McCambridge, P. (2006). *"PEPS hosts first QC Gaelic Football game in over 100 years."* Quebec Chronicle Telegraph.

McCay, M. (1995). *"A Final Tribute to an Old Rebel."* The Celtic Connection.

McCay, M. (1994). *"A Celebration of Faith and Culture."* The Celtic Connection.

McGee, T. (1991). *"All systems go at the Skydome."*

McFadden, K. (1995) *"Galway Star Shoots Into Vancouver."* The Celtic Connection.

McKenna, A. (2005). *"Rams volleyball star turns Gaelic."* The Ryersonian Online.

McMahon, E. (2000). *"Calgary Cup."* The Celtic Connection.

McMahon, E. (1999). *"Victory and Defeat at the Calgary Cup."* The Celtic Connection.

McMahon, E. (1999). *"Women's Participation a Welcome Addition."* The Celtic Connection.

Milne, B. (1997). *"Setting the Record Straight."* The Celtic Connection.

Miller, C. (2004). *"Irish Rovers."* The Vancouver Courier.

Molloy, K. (1991). *"Seeking a Home, Fed Carries on Actively."* The Celtic Connection.

Molloy. K. (1991). *"Warm Camaraderie in Long, Wet Winter."* The Celtic Connection.

Molloy, K. (1992). *"Sports Groups Go into High Gear."* The Celtic Connection.

Molloy, K. (1992). *"Vancouver Wins in a Brilliant Save."* The Celtic Connection.

Molloy, K. (1993). *"Gala Social and Sports Events."* The Celtic Connection.

Moore, A. (2002). *"Minors Achieve Major Results in World Championship."* The Toronto Irish News.

Moore, A. (2002). *"Toronto GAA Ladies gear up for Olympics and World Cup."* The Toronto Irish News.

Mullan, E. (2002). *"Danny Burns: He Gave us Grace."* The Celtic Connection.

O'Ceallachain, S. (1990). *"Toronto Adds A New Dimension—Mulvihil."*

O'Donnell, G. (2000). *"Many claims for football's origin."* The Neighbours.

O'Flynn, J. (2008). *"2008 GAA Canadian County Board Convention."* The Celtic Connection.

O'Flynn, J. (2007). *"A Night to Remember: Two Old Friends Honoured with Western Div. GAA Cups."* The Celtic Connection.

O'Flynn, J. (2007). *"Twentieth Anniversary of the Founding of the Canadian GAA County Board."* The Celtic Connection.

O'Flynn, J. (2006). *"Author Seeks More History of GAA in Canada."* The Celtic Connection.

O'Flynn, J. (2006). *"Canada's Gaelic Games History Project."* The Celtic Connection.

O'Flynn, J. (2006). *"A Great Weekend of Gaelic Games at First Western Divisional Tournament."* The Celtic Connection.

O'Flynn, J. (2005). *"Despite Chilly Toronto Weather GAA Gathering was Warm."* The Celtic Connection.

O'Flynn, J. (2005). *"Hurling Once again in Vancouver."* The Celtic Connection.

O'Flynn, J. (2005). *"Schkelping and other Gaelic pastimes."* World Football Pages.

O'Flynn, J. (2005). *"GAA Referees and Coaches Clinic in San Francisco."* The Celtic Connection.

O'Flynn, J. (2005). *"An Outstanding GAA Weekend at Local Tournament."* The Celtic Connection.

O'Flynn, J. (2005). *"Support a Winning Team: the Women of Team Canada."* The Celtic Connection.

O'Flynn, J. (2005). *"Edmonton: An Exhilarating Display of Championship Football."* The Celtic Connection.

O'Flynn, J. (2005). *"Continental Youth Championships: A GAA report from San Francisco."* The Celtic Connection.

O'Flynn, J. (2005). *"New 2005 Executive Elected for ISSC."* The Celtic Connection.

O'Flynn, J. (2005). *"The Irish still play Europe's oldest field game."* The BC Catholic.

O'Flynn, J. (2004). *"ISSC prepares to celebrate 30th Anniversary of the Club."* The Celtic Connection.

O'Flynn, J. (2004). *"GAA News Update- Vancouver."* The Celtic Connection.

O'Flynn, J. (2004). *"Excellent GAA Coaches Clinics Held by NACB."* The Celtic Connection.

O'Flynn, J. (2004). *"Sad Farewell to Dunne Brothers."* The Celtic Connection.

O'Flynn, J. (2004). *"GAA Delegates Discuss Twinning Canada and Ulster."* The Celtic Connection.

O'Flynn, J. (2003). *"Football a Winner in Edmonton."* The Celtic Connection.

O'Flynn, J. (2003). *"Vancouver and Calgary Clubs Seek GAA Affiliation."* The Celtic Connection.

O'Flynn, J. (2003). *"GAA Western Division Working on New By-Laws."* The Celtic Connection.

O'Flynn, J. (2002). *"An Epic Victory of 'Limerick over Kerry' Proportions."* The Celtic Connection.

O'Flynn, J. (2002). *"JJ Hyland Memorial Gaelic Football Tournament."* The Celtic Connection.

O'Flynn, J. (2001). *"O'Malley Spirit Alive and Well at Seattle Football Tournament."* The Celtic Connection.

O'Flynn, J. (2001). *"More Structure for Pacific Northwest GAA under Discussion."* The Celtic Connection.

O'Flynn, J. (2001). *"Irish/Aussie Tournament."* The Celtic Connection.

O'Flynn. J. (1992). *"Vancouver Sporting and Social Club."* The Celtic Connection.

O'Gallagher, M. (1988). *"The Irish in Quebec."* The Untold Story: The Irish in Canada.

O'Hara, K. (1994). *"Montreal Irish Meeting at Hurley's."* The Celtic Connection.

O'Leary, B. (1991). *"Being Just a Bit Crazy Helps."* The Celtic Connection.

O'Loghlin, E. (2008). *"Editorial."* The Toronto Irish News.

O'Neill, E. (1997). *"Vancouver Harps Win the Bailey's Cup."* The Celtic Connection.

O'Shea. J. (1999). *"Gaelic Games in Quebec."* Montreal Centennial Programme.

O'Shea. J, Leyne. D, Loftus. P. (1984). *"Gaelic Athletic Association (1884-1984) 35th Anniversary of Montreal Shamrock Hurling and Football Club."* Programme Journal.

O'Sullivan, T. (2004). *"Vancouver Ladies Gaelic Football."* The Celtic Connection.

O'Sullivan, T. (1998). *"Making Plans for St. Pat's."* The Celtic Connection.

O'Sullivan, T. (1998). *"ISSC Wraps Up a Great Season."* The Celtic Connection.

O'Sullivan, T. (1995). *"A Dedicated Team on Board."* The Celtic Connection.

O'Sullivan, T. (1997). *"Ladies' Team Takes the Spotlight."* The Celtic Connection.

O'Sullivan, T. (1997). *"Seattle Gaelic Football Team are Champions."* The Celtic Connection.

O'Sullivan, T. (1995). *"Northwestern League Kicks Off Gaelic Football Season."* The Celtic Connection.

O'Sullivan, T. (1995). *"A Dedicated Team on Board."* The Celtic Connection.

O'Sullivan, T. (1995). *"Seattle's Golden Era."* The Celtic Connection.

O'Sullivan, T. (1995). *"Some Outstanding Players —Shining Examples of Sport."* The Celtic Connection.

O'Sullivan, T. (1994). *"Out With the Old In With the New."* The Celtic Connection.

O'Sullivan, T. (1994). *"Seattle Winners of NW Championship."* The Celtic Connection.

O'Sullivan, T. (1994). *"Seattle Finds Rhythm and Stuns Vancouver."* The Celtic Connection.

O'Sullivan, T. (1994). *"A Multitude of Events for Vancouver Sporting Fans."* The Celtic Connection.

O'Sullivan, T. (1994). *"The New ISSC Board—New Faces Going Places."* The Celtic Connection.

O'Sullivan, T. (1994). *"History-Making Sporting Ambassador—Hugh Duggan."* The Celtic Connection.

O'Sullivan, T. (1993). *"Gaelic Football Training."* The Celtic Connection.

O'Sullivan, T. (1993). *"Northwest Gaelic Football League 1993."* The Celtic Connection.

O'Sullivan, T. (1993). *"Vancouver Defeats Seattle in a Thrilling Game."* The Celtic Connection.

O'Sullivan, T. (1993). *"Vancouver Meets a Strong Challenge From Portland."* The Celtic Connection.

O'Sullivan, T. (1993). *"An Inspirational Team Player—Christy Whelehan."* The Celtic Connection.

O'Sullivan, T. (1993). *"A Fond Farewell to the Season's Northwest Gaelic Football League."* The Celtic Connection.

O'Sullivan, T. (1993). *"Annual Bailey's Cup Creates Excitement for Irish Culture."* The Celtic Connection.

Peters, U. (2003). *"An Edmontonian's View of Seattle Tournament."* The Celtic Connection.

Petersen, S. (2005). *"Gaelic Football climbing the sporting ranks."* The Edmonton Journal.

Reidy, L. (2006). *"Bill Flanagan: The Quintessential GAA Man."* The Irish Herald.

Rochfort, J. (1992). *"Aer Lingus Team Visits Vancouver."* The Celtic Connection.

Ryan, K. (2008). *"News from the Toronto GAA."* The Toronto Irish News.

Scott, P. (2005). *"Welcome to Ottawa."* An essay for Comaltas Ceoltóiri Eireann.

Shriane, M. (1995). *"Honouring Dedicated Community Leader."* The Celtic Connection.
Smith, R. (2007). *"The Irish Canadians."* Club History.

Speiran, J. (1994). *"Star Gaelic Football Player Retires After Knee Injury—Tom O'Sullivan."* The Celtic Connection.

Speiran, J. (1993). *"Seattle Steal the Show as Vancouver Miss the Boat."* The Celtic Connection.

Sutherland, A. (2006). *"Countdown to green day."* The Montreal Gazette.

Tobin, J. (1991). *"Team of 1988."* 30th Anniversary Journal of Clan Na nGael.

Vigneault, M (2005). *"French-Canadian Traditions."*

Walchuk, M. (2005). *"Gaelic Football newcomer plays for team Canada."* Metroland-Halton Division.

Walsh, P. (2004). *"Those were the best of times!"* The Celtic Connection.

Zdeb, C. (2004). *"Gerry's Tips."* The Edmonton Journal.

Sources

(1960). *Los Angeles GAA International Game Programme.* Toronto v. Los Angeles.

(1963). *Sons of Ireland Society of Winnipeg St. Patrick's Day Programme.* Manitoba, Canada.

(1963). *Souvenir Programme Eleventh Anniversary Toronto Gaelic Athletic Association Field Day and International Gaelic Football and Hurling*

(1967). *Gaelic Games Expo 67 Centennial Souvenir Programme—*Montreal Shamrock Hurling and Football Club.

(1968). *Ancient Gaelic Sport Launched in Hamilton.* Centennial Publication.

(1976). *The New York Irish History of the New York GAA 1914–1976.* Dublin, Gaelic Press Ltd.

(1986). *Clan Na nGael 25th Anniversary Banquet Programme*

(1987). *Presidential Dinner Dance Toronto GAA.* Souvenir Programme.

(1989). *Gaelic Athletic Association of Toronto Newsletter # 1*

(1990). *Fianna Facts #5.* Coalisland GAA

(1990). *"Power Behind Big Tour."*

(1990). *St. Michael's Hurling & Football Club 25th Anniversary Programme, 1965-1990.*

(1990). *St. Patrick's Day Irish Games Official Programme.* Toronto, Sun Ventures Inc.

(1990). *Toronto Select v Coalisland Fianna Souvenir Programme.* Toronto GAA.

(1991). *Coalisland Fianna v Toronto Selection Programme.* Coalisland GAA.

(1991). *Toronto GAA Presentation Banquet Programme*

(1991). *Toronto Football Selection versus St. Patrick's Palmerstown Programme*

(1992). *Canada v Ireland Ladies Tour Programme*

(1993). *Tour of Canada Marino Ladies G.F.C. Programme*

(1994). *AIB/GAA USA & Canada Tour Souvenir Programme*

(1994). *Dublin Masters Canadian Tour Souvenir Programme*

(1994). *Irish Holidays International Football Competition Tournament Programme*

(1994). *Ottawa Gaels Press Release*

(1995). *Toronto Irish News*

(1998). *Irish Holidays International Gaelic Football Festival Programme*

(1999). *Montreal GAA 50th Anniversary Centennial Programme, 1949-1999.*

(1999). *40th Anniversary St. Vincent's Toronto Gaelic Football Club.* Souvenir Brochure.

(2000). *Gaelic Football World Cup 2000 Programme*

(2001). *Hamilton Robert Emmets 35th Anniversary Programme 1966–2001*

(2001). *Under 14 Boys Feile Peile Na Nog Ottawa Programme*

(2003). *Strategy for High Performance Gaelic Football in Ulster.* Sports Institute, Northern Ireland.

(2005). *Club Manual.* Gaelic Athletic Association, Dublin.

(2005). *Team Canada.* Ladies International Tournament Programme.

(2006). *Directory of the Ladies Gaelic Football Association.*

(2006). *Minutes of the Annual Congress 2005.* Gaelic Athletic Association, Dublin.

(2006). *Programme of the Annual Congress.* Gaelic Athletic Association, Dublin.

(2007). *Ceili Irish Music & Dance Camp.* Programme of Scoil Rince De Danaan.

(2007). *Continental Youth Championships.* Programme of Gaelic Park, Chicago.

(2007). *An Bhratach in Airde sa Bhreatain.* The GAA in Britain Planning Group.

References

(2007). *"Calgary Chieftains Celebrate 30th Anniversary."* The Celtic Connection.

(2007). *"Tony Griffin Plays Gaelic Football in Quebec City."* The Celtic Connection.

(2007). *"An Epic Journey Across Canada Now Complete But Not Forgotten."* The Celtic Connection.

(2006). *"Ceili Irish Music and Dance Camp: A Great Week of Irish Cultural Immersion."* The Celtic Connection.

(2006). *"Gaelic Football returns to QC."* The Quebec Chronicle Telegraph.

(2006). *"GAA Football Tournament Hosted by Vancouver ISSC."* The Celtic Connection.

(2006). *"Gaelic Football clinics."* Metroland-Brampton.

(2006). *"Calgary Chieftains Victorious in Edmonton."* The Celtic Connection.

(2006). *"High School's Best: Part One."* The Ottawa Citizen.

(2006). *"Canadian GAA Board Elected for 2006 Season."* The Celtic Connection.

(2006). *"Rounders."* Scoilsport.

(2006). *"Gaelic Football in Vancouver: Why Don't You Try It?"* The Celtic Connection.

(2006). *"Croke Park Areas Re-named."* Eadrainn Fein.

(2006). *"Development Officer Appointed by GAA."* The Celtic Connection.

(2006). *"GAA Development Continues Overseas."* Eadrainn Fein.

(2006). *"Toronto Irish Person of the Year Award Proclaimed by Mayor of the City."* The Celtic Connection.

(2006). *"Another Banner Year for the Calgary Chieftains."* The Celtic Connection.

(2005). *"Ceili Irish Music and Dance Camp."* The Celtic Connection.

(2005). *"Irish Sport Connection."* The Canadian Immigrant Magazine.

(2005). *"Gaelic Football stars off to Irish Tournament."* Irish News.

(2005). *"Irish brand of football will smile at Mohawk Sports Park Sunday."* The Hamilton Spectator.

(2005). *"The Celts are coming to town."* World Football Pages.

(2005). *"The Mighty Irish."* The Peace Arch News.

(2004). *"Special ISSC 30th Anniversary Supplement."* The Celtic Connection.

(2004). *"In Fond Memory of Kevin McFadden."* The Celtic Connection.

(2004). *"Edmonton Wolfe Tones Looking Forward to New Season."* The Celtic Connection.

(2004). *"St. Pat's and Gaelic Games."* The Celtic Connection.

(2004). *"Vancouver and Calgary Clubs Seek GAA Affiliation."* The Celtic Connection.

(2004). *"14 good ways to spend your holiday weekend."* The Vancouver Province.

(2004). *"Personal Trainer: Gerry Muldoon."* The Edmonton Journal.

(2004). *"Irish community celebrates, remembers its dead."* The BC Catholic.

(2003). *"Workshop Presents Overview of Gaelic Football and Hurling."* The Celtic Connection.

(2003). *"Mick Hurley: 'Nothing Compares With All Ireland Finals'."* The Celtic Connection.

(2003). *"GAA Congress."* The Celtic Connection.

(2003). *"Calgary and Vancouver Receive GAA Accreditation."* The Celtic Connection.

(2000). *"Gaelic Games Feature Competitive Enthusiasm."* The BC Catholic.

(2000). *"Irish Sport Making In-Roads In Ottawa Schools."* Tournament Report.

(2000). *"Former Irish Footballer Honoured in Dundalk."* The Celtic Connection.

(2000). *"Passing the Torch to a New Generation."* The Celtic Connection.

(2000). *"Captain of the Vancouver Women's Gaelic Football Team."* The Celtic Connection.

(1999). *"Celebrating 50 years of Gaelic Football."* The Celtic Connection.

(1999). *"Football Champ Heading Back to Europe."* The Celtic Connection.

(1999). *"Edmonton Irish Celebrate Fortieth Anniversary of Club."* The Celtic Connection.

(1999). *"Date Set for Bailey's Cup."* The Celtic Connection.

(1999). *"Farewell to an Old Friend."* The Celtic Connection.

(1999). *"New Executive for Edmonton."* The Celtic Connection.

(1995). *"Fourth Annual Bailey's Cup."* The Celtic Connection.

(1993). *"Tom Butler Talking About Tom O'Sullivan."* The Celtic Connection.

(1990). *"Four Irish teams for Toronto."* The Irish Independent.

(1990). *"Canadian date for Patrick's Weekend."* The Irish Press.

(1990). *"Tipperary and All-Stars to play in Skydome."* The Irish Times.

(1990). *"Canadian Board of the GAA Welcomes Gaelic Games."* Souvenir Programme.

(1990). *"Gaelic Football."* The Edmonton Blarney.

(1990). *"All Ireland Gaelic Games."* The BC Catholic.

(1988). *"Seattle tops Vancouver in Gaelic Football."* The Irish Echo.

(1984). *"Our Irish Heritage."* Living Heritage.

(1975). *"Gaelic Football Sunday."* The Citizen, Ottawa.

(1975-1998). Minutes of meetings, correspondence and newsletters from the Ottawa Gaels archives.

(1974-1990). Minutes of meetings, correspondence and newsletters from the Vancouver Irish Sporting and Social Club archives.

(1962). *"...saw Dilboy Classic."* The Irish Herald.

(1952). *"Gaelic Capers."* The Globe and Mail.

(1950). *"Shamrock Hurling Team of Montreal."* The Connacht Tribune.

(1950). *"Irish Exiles In Canada Form GAA Clubs."* The Irish Press.

WEBSITES

Canada

www.archives.ca www.calgaryics.org www.reddeergaa.ca

www.canada.gaa.ie www.celtic-connection.com/sports.html

www.collectionscanada.ca/ireland www.FPinfomart.ca

www.handball.ca www.heritage.nf.ca/society/irish_newfoundland.html

www.irishhamilton.ca www.irishassociation.ca

www.irishclub.ca www.irishstudies.ca

www.toronto.gaa.ie www.vancourier.com/issues03/033103/sports.html

www.topatrick.com www.westerncanada.gaa.nr

www.stmikesgfc.ca www.isscvancouver.com

www.edmontongaa.com www.calgarygaelicfootball.com

www.st-vincents-toronto-gaa.com www.ottawagaels.ca

www.durhamgfc.com www.michaelcusackladies.homestead.com

www.bramptongfc.ca www.gaelicfootballforkids.com

www.stjohnsarchdiocese.nf.ca www.stpatstoronto.bravehost.com

United States of America

www.nagaa.org www.ny-gaa.org www.cyc.gaa.ie www.nyladiesgaa.com

Ireland

www.hoganstand.com www.unison.ie/irish_independent/stories

www.gaa.ie www.emigrant.ie www.ladiesgaelic.ie www.rounders.ie

www.anfearrua.com www.ulster.gaa.ie

Printed in the United States
By Bookmasters